Arthur Janov is director of T...lew
York. He has had some thirty......................... psychotherapy, child
psychology and psychiatric social work. His books have been translated into
fifteen languages while his therapy has become predominant in several
European countries.

Also by Arthur Janov in ABACUS:

THE PRIMAL SCREAM

Arthur Janov

PRISONERS OF PAIN

Unlocking the power of the mind to end suffering

AN ABACUS BOOK

ABACUS edition first published in Great Britain 1982
by Sphere Books Ltd
Reprinted 1989

Reproduced, printed and bound in Great Britain by
Cox & Wyman Ltd, Reading

ISBN 0 349 11844 2

Sphere Books Ltd
A Division of
Macdonald & Co (Publishers) Ltd
27 Wrights Lane, London W8 5TZ
A member of Maxwell Pergamon Publishing Corporation plc

To my dear sweet Ellie

The author wishes to notify readers that the Paris address
of the Institute Primal Europeen is as follows:

Institut Primal Europeen
17, Square de l'Avenue Foch
75016 Paris
France

Telephone - - (1) 500.81.30

Acknowledgments

Two PEOPLE along with myself are responsible for this book. William
Van Doren and Nick Barton have worked for a very long time to make
it a reality. They have organized, elaborated, contributed original
ideas, edited, supervised, discussed, and done just about everything
that human beings can to ensure the completion of this book. To say
that I owe them a debt of thanks is highly inadequate to describe
their contribution.

I should like to thank Dr. Michael Holden, my co-author on *Primal
Man: The New Consciousness,* for his special contributions. They
are evident throughout this book and particularly in the discussions of
consciousness, research, psychosis, and "the house that Pain builds."

I owe a special debt to two stern but enthusiastic and caring people
—my editors at Doubleday, Elizabeth Frost Knappman and Harriet
Rubin.

The charts for our survey results were designed and executed by
Ellen Lutwak.

Special recognition is due to my secretary, Cindy Heim, and manuscript typist, Mary Chesterfield. They worked long hours to keep up
with the several incarnations of the manuscript.

Finally, allow me to bow to my patients whose Pain, insights, perse-
verance, and enthusiasm have made this book what it is.

Arthur Janov
The Primal Institute
Los Angeles, California

Contents

Introduction

MANKIND is bound hand and foot by an insidious affliction. It is the most intangible, devastating, and widespread of diseases. It is a physiologic, biologic state, yet it cannot be eliminated through diets, exercise, meditation, virtuous behavior, drugs, or surgery. It has no single location. Indeed, it is the only illness found virtually everywhere in the body and brain. Yet nearly everyone is unaware of it. Doctors who treat it are not sure what to look for and do not even agree on its existence. It emanates so many symptoms that it looks like hundreds of diseases instead of one. The disease is neurosis.

The maladies conventionally grouped within the term "mental illness" are in fact one biologic disease—a wound of the entire system with both psychologic and physical Pain[1] at its core. Normally, pain is a simple matter; we feel it, we know it hurts, we know where it is and usually we know why it is there. But the Pains from our earliest childhood are total mysteries even though we all carry those Pains around. No one recognizes or acknowledges them. Yet we see their effects every day in the way we live, in our relationships, in our symptoms, and in our social adjustment. For most of us it is difficult to imagine that events of so long ago could still have a hold on us, but they do.

I shall show how this disease gets its start even as we get our start in life. But rather than just describe it, I shall also try to provide a more precise definition of neurosis than has been made before. This affliction, for all its apparently complex symptoms, usually has a simple history. We are hurt when we are least equipped to deal with it—during our early development. The hurt, too much to integrate, is buried and

[1] Pain is printed with an upper case "P" to indicate Primal Pain, and to distinguish this hurt from pains which are not threatening to development.

lingers like a perpetual virus to disturb our lives and make us suffer inordinately as adults.

When we see how neurosis is generated we see more clearly how to treat it. Fortunately, we have within us at all times the means with which to cure ourselves. The antidote is the very feelings which, repressed, made us sick.

Twelve years of testing theory against clinical practice has enabled us to establish much more precise guidelines for effective psychotherapy, thus helping to retrieve that profession from the unsystematic, unscientific disarray into which it has fallen. As part of this, we want to establish methods which will effectively measure therapeutic improvement and form a scientific definition of improvement and of health.

Since neurosis is a malady that alters biology, any real treatment must be capable of changing that biology again. Primal Therapy accomplishes this. We have observed remarkable changes in the physical systems of our patients. In this book we shall examine these changes and their implications.

An important result of our work has been a better understanding of many human functions, particularly those of the brain. We have learned enough about how our brain develops in our lifetime to hypothesize how it evolved in the species over millennia. To illustrate these matters, we shall take the reader on a brief tour through the museum of mankind's history—the brain. We still have much to learn about this fascinating organ and the part its processes play in sickness and health, but we are gradually discovering the brain's role in the histories of human beings and in the history of mankind.

It is the ability to become unconscious that allowed men and women to survive the untold agonies of their past, just as it saves each of us early in our own lives. The unconscious is not a vague psychological concept but a reality of our brains and bodies. Just as it at first rescues us, it may also kill us, both as individuals and as a species. Primal Therapy offers the individual a way into the unconscious, and thus a way out of unconsciousness.

Perhaps, in the end, the chief benefit to be had from the insights of this therapy is a knowledge of how we might prevent the whole problem of neurosis in the first place. We cannot be content with formulating a cure when we know the exact means for prevention. Future generations need not inherit the disease.

I: THE LIFE SENTENCE

1: Creatures of Need

NEED is the cornerstone of both health and neurosis. We need with every cell of our bodies. Need is a total state of the human being—and at birth we are almost nothing but need. The helpless infant must look to her parents for fulfillment. She cannot feed herself, clean herself, or keep herself warm. She cannot sustain herself in any way. Fulfillment has to be *given* to her. Survival is at stake in nearly every second of her existence.

The earliest needs are physical. As we grow, new levels of need come into being. Need becomes more sophisticated as our brain matures. Emotional and intellectual capacities develop, as well as new elaborations of each basic need. The need for safety and love is at first only physical. It has nothing to do with the emotions, or with any verbal expression. But it becomes elaborated as feelings once the child develops an emotional capacity. Criticism is meaningless to a newborn. To a three-month-old a humiliation, such as being told that he is useless, means nothing. For the six-year-old it can have great meaning because the child has now reached the level of emotional need.

The last elaboration of need is intellectual, such as the need to have one's world explained. One needs to be told the truth, to have one's reality affirmed. There is a simple need for information. You won't die if your parents can't openly talk with you about sex, for example, but you won't become completely human, either. Most of us suffer from unfulfilled need. We often can't even feel what our needs are.

Real needs are based in biology. They are tissue states—total events of the brain and body, not abstract psychological concepts. There are also psychological needs such as the need for understanding. However, in the conventional view psychological needs (such as prestige and power) are only derivatives of the basic biologic needs, inventions of a developed mind which has the ability to divert real need into symbols.

Except for the basic requirements of survival, our needs change as we pass through stages of growth. The "need to know," for example, changes. Knowing ultimately involves senses, feelings, and intellect. In the earliest months of life, "knowing" means sensing. The infant has a sense of what is happening even if it cannot be explained. Later on, this "sense" will be elaborated into an idea. He senses if he is uncomfortable. The baby knows his world vividly. However, if he is to integrate his perceptions, the world his parents provide him must "make sense" in a physical way. If he cries because he's uncomfortable, he should be picked up and comforted. If that is not done, then the child's world does not make sense.

As the emotional capacities mature, the child develops a "feeling" about the world. A healthy child is naturally intuitive. If she is allowed to express her feelings about things, whatever those feelings are, she gains confidence in her own perceptions. Only later will she know about her world in an intellectual way and be able to explain in words what, for example, her parents and home life are like. She then needs information that will satisfy her growing curiosity. But human needs are much more numerous.

The need to develop at one's own pace is critical. This includes the crucial need to be born at the proper time. When a fetus is ready for birth, he releases a hormone to the mother who activates hormone secretions of her own to set the birth in motion. The mother doesn't just "give" birth. It is the joint "decision" of two humans. The needs of natural development are violated if the mother is clamped down and tight, her whole system unready for the birth.

Later, elaborations of the development needs, such as being allowed to learn to speak when one is ready, can be violated by urging the baby to talk. Safety too is a primary need. Subjecting the fetus to rough activity or very loud sounds or tension the mother feels can make him feel unsafe even though he doesn't have words for that feeling for years to come. Still later, safety will mean a stable home, without recurring threats of divorce or the unsettling experience of moving constantly.

There is a profound need for emotional warmth and caring. Here is what some of my patients have said:

Doris:

"My mother always told me how much she loved me, but she was always crashing around doing the housework or rushing around doing the shopping—so much that she didn't have much time to notice me."

Mitchell:

"My best friend's mother—I adored her. I used to feel horrible because when I'd come home from school the house was totally empty—my father was working, my mother was working, my sister was never around. So many times I'd go home with my friend after school—his mother was home—and she'd fix me a snack and talk to me, ask me how I was doing in school. Which my mother didn't do even when she was home. I used to feel really bad because I didn't have anyone who cared enough to be interested in me. I just didn't realize how bad it was until I went home with my friend and saw the opposite situation. In fact, my best friend's mother once asked me to draw a picture for her. I was nine or ten. I drew a picture of a little boy, all alone, sitting and looking out the window the way I used to do."

At birth the newborn should be placed immediately with the mother so that he feels her body, her warmth, and her presence. Later on, this need for closeness requires hugging and kissing and caressing. Everyone needs this throughout life. It's just that as we grow older it hurts less if we are deprived. The greatest area of the sensory brain deals with touch; it is supremely important.

One of my patients reported that "for a time, after moments of being very close physically to my girlfriend, I would tremble and shake for minutes . . . [I felt that] no one had ever really touched me, cradled me, stroked me or held me."[1]

The need for integration is also basic. It requires that the fetus, infant, child, and adolescent not be overloaded with sensory input. The continuous agony of a prolonged birth is probably the most serious overload. Later, although less serious, a mother who talks constantly doesn't allow her child to integrate his world. The incessant stimulation is too much to absorb. Another overload is too much homework in school too early in life, as when second-grade children take home several books for two or three hours of homework. This is often much more than they can integrate. They cannot learn because they are under a pressure that strains the integrative mechanisms.

The need to be oriented in time and space is part of the need for integration. Holding a newborn upside down for several minutes upon

[1] The names of the patients mentioned in this book have been omitted or changed.

his arrival in this world is a stupid violation of this need as well as just about every other need for comfort, safety, closeness, and well-being.

The need for freedom is a basic biologic requirement. On the physical level it entails the freedom to be born without obstruction and hardship. Later there should be freedom to move about the room and then the house instead of being confined to a narrow playpen; ultimately freedom to explore the neighborhood and the world. The need for freedom and the need for expression are the same. One needs to be free to express feelings, then later to express ideas. One needs to be listened to and talked to so that freedom can be exercised. There should be freedom not only to use the words you want and to believe the beliefs you want, but to dress the way you like and to move in natural—unschooled—ways; later, to choose your vocation, friends, and way of life.

One of my patients gave an early example of the importance of this need: "I remember seeing my playpen after I grew up. It was much smaller than the usual playpen. It had screened-in sides and was the size of a baby mattress. In fact, it doubled as my baby bed. There was a nifty screened frame that would cover the top to keep the baby "safe." I see red now whenever anyone mentions the word playpen. I have had vivid flashes of being trapped inside that screened atrocity. I wanted the freedom to crawl around the room . . . It seems like I've been in that contraption all my life."

There is a need to have one's reality affirmed. Early in life one must be there for the child so that he not only feels safe and protected but understands that it is all right to do things like complain. Fulfilling this need means being honest and direct with the child. It means affirming his feelings. "It's fine to feel that way. It's okay to be angry if someone does that to you. Little boys do cry."

It means affirming the child's perceptions of others even when those perceptions are not socially acceptable. Above all, it means affirming a realistic perception of himself. As Carol says:

"I believe that as parents we must give our children the reality of what their life is. I am often tempted to tell my children, and believe it myself, that everything is going to be fine, we'll have money, a nice car, etc. etc. But I can't do that to them, all I can say is what I feel; and sometimes that is not what they want to hear. The only thing I can given them now is the truth."

There are parents who feel their children can do no wrong and they inculcate this attitude in them. They blame others if their child does something wrong. The child never gets a true picture of herself. She never learns to operate in reality because she has never been given a sense of it. Usually these parents cannot face reality themselves; they cannot imagine that they have done anything so "wrong" as to bring up a child who has been "bad."

Another fundamental need is stimulation, not just any kind but the kind that is appropriate and sufficient. Lack of stimulation early in life, as so many animal studies have shown, can cause physical deterioration of organ systems and changes in brain function. It turns out that stimulation, in the massive dosage that a normal labor and birth provide, is essential. Those who do not get it, the Caesarean babies, suffer from its deprivation.

The stimulation of touch is essential, but too much stimulation—excessive handling, jostling, shaking, and patting—is also painful. It can fragment the nervous system.

If needs are fulfilled as they develop, there will be little Pain. How does one know how much fulfillment is needed? The child knows—awareness of fulfillment is innate. The parent has only to be sensitive to the child to know what she needs. To be "sensitive" is to be able to sense one's own needs and feelings. If the parent is sensitive, he will know when he is overstimulating the child with too much patting and hugging. He knows that it may come from his need and not the child's.

The crux of growth is the need for expression. The infant needs to be allowed to crawl freely, to express his curiosity, to grasp and throw things and in general to use his body in its awkward way so that he becomes familiar with what it can do. It means allowing him full and free physical expression, without, of course, placing him in danger. He is not spanked when, at six months, he spills food; not forced to coordinate his eating movements or bowel movement before he is ready; not shushed when he screams and cries.

Later, when the child reaches the emotional level, he needs to be allowed to express *all* his feelings. He is allowed to be sassy and "disrespectful." He can say what he wants to say because it comes out of his feelings. If he isn't frustrated and isn't made to feel angry, then there is no reason for his feelings to be constantly negative. The big worry of parents is that if they allow a child to be sassy he will always be that way. It is precisely because he is not allowed his negative feelings that he may become constantly negative. Children are not innately angry at parents. Yet they will be if their needs are deprived. As one patient said, "I spent my entire childhood arguing with my mother over trivialities. I never got love but at least I had her attention."

Still later, the need for expression means a need to have and to express ideas; ideas that may not conform to the parents' view of the world. A child may not want to believe in the devil, for example, or in a vegetarian diet. Or he may not want to believe that formal education is the best thing since the wheel. He must be allowed to have his own ideas and his own view of the world. Our feelings are absolutely our own; we must not be robbed of them. They do not belong to anyone else, ever. They are more than simply "ours"; they *are* us.

Perhaps the single underlying need which subsumes all of these is the need to feel. The human being is a feeling being; it is basic to the organism. The only way we can grow into relaxed, content individuals is to experience all of ourselves. Feeling is the essence of life.

The fulfillment of early needs allows for integration at each stage of growth. As each new level of need is fulfilled, we can leave it behind. We don't have to drag it with us as so much excess baggage into the present. We can live in the now when the past is resolved.

It is with fulfillment that we go from the needs of individual survival, such as food and water, to the survival needs of the species, such as sex. In fact, we can become fully sexual only when the preceding needs are fulfilled. Indeed, in the hierarchy of need, the healthy development of each new level depends on fulfillment of the previous one. A thirst-ridden person thinks of little else. He isn't going to philosophize about water. He is going to find ways to get it.

Fulfillment of early need structures personality. There will be a fluidity in those personalities whose needs have been satisfied: an adaptability and flexibility that allows for growth and change as experience and events change.

How do we know what the needs are? Not by making up a theoretical structure for what they should be. That is not necessary. In listening to the agony of patients we have listened to their need. Never have we heard them in Pain over being deprived of their id, or their self-esteem, or their existential awareness. But, in feeling their Pain, they seem invariably to return to basic deprivations: "Don't look at me that way!" "Hold me!" "Take care of me!" "Love me!" When the complexities of neurosis fall away, all that remains are these simple childhood needs.

2: Primal Pain

NEEDS remain needs until deprivation transforms them into Pain. Pain mobilizes us toward fulfillment, warning us that the body is in danger and alerting us into defensive reactions. Primal Pain is deprivation or injury which threatens the developing child. A parent's warning is not necessarily a Primal Pain for the child. Utter humiliation is. Falling down while skating is not a Primal Pain. Being shoved out of the way by a frustrated parent is. An infant left to cry it out in the crib is in Pain. He is terrified and alone in the dark. When he is isolated from his mother just after birth, he is terrified and in agony. One of my patients recalled, "My sisters were the only ones who took care of me while I was an infant. My mother was the real baby. But that didn't make any difference to me. I still needed her and only her. I have spent many hours crying for her to come take care of me. I waited thirty-five years but she never came."

It is not hurt as such which defines Primal Pain, but rather the context of the hurt or its meaning to the impressionable developing consciousness of the child. There is little meaning in falling down, in and of itself. But being hurt without anyone to turn to for comfort is a Primal hurt. There is a need for comfort and reassurance; when unfulfilled, it threatens development, even if it may not threaten physical survival. As Charles said:

"I was driving down Mulholland Drive one Sunday afternoon and I saw a man with his son out bicycle riding, and he put his arm around his son, and I just broke out crying. Well, that made sense, that made sense to me . . . why I would cry about that because I never had a Daddy."

In fact, Primal Pain can be either physical or emotional. Despite the popular belief that these are different kinds of hurts, they are actually all the same in terms of how they are processed in the system.

Early Pain is so great because deprivation of basic needs threatens survival. Deprivation of primary needs, such as that for feeding, even for a short time, has an extremely powerful effect. It is nearly always a matter of life and death. The starvation experience at the age of one day has lifelong consequences. Experiences in the first days or months can pervade adult life.

Deprivation on the later levels of need tends to have less impact on the nervous system. This by no means indicates that these are not great Pains, because they certainly can be; but they are usually not as overwhelming as the early ones. When the child is deprived later in life, he has many more responses to bear the stress.

Pain is electrochemical information that travels along sensory pathways just as any other input. Primal Pain is an overload—more information than the nervous system can integrate. It is not simply a psychological reaction but literally a transmission of physical energy. Pains are registered in the system even before one can conceptualize them. One can hurt without knowing "no one cares about me."

Deprivations are not always obvious and dramatic events. They may be quite subtle and accumulative in effect. For instance, one woman remembered:

"As a child I had to eat a certain way. I had to finish every bite of my dinner, no matter how long it took. Bedtime was at 20:01 (military time for 8:01) when I was 6, 20:02 when I was 7, etc. I had to answer the phone, '——— residence, Fran speaking.' I heard all my life: 'Don't raise your voice.' 'Don't make noise while Daddy's studying.' 'Be sweet.'

"He controlled what I studied in school. When I was chosen to take a special summer course when I was eleven, I wanted to take drama. He signed me up for math and science. The next year I stopped doing well in math and science. After *he* scored the highest grade in the Air Force in speed reading, he forced *me* to take the course after school. I soon stopped reading."

Whether Primal traumas occur instantly or piecemeal over a long time, they are too much to handle. They are too much for the naïve system to respond and react naturally to. Whether by virtue of the severity of the trauma itself or by enforced inhibition, it is the obstruction of a natural reaction that results ultimately in neurosis.

3: The Prison

IF A PAIN in early childhood is felt in its full intensity when it happens, it will not become an unconscious force, and there will be no neurosis. But when there is too much Pain, the child is mercifully rendered unconscious. The mercy has a price. Pain is repressed, but it remains within the child's system precisely because it was too great to be experienced, resolved, and understood. The Pain now takes on a life of its own, out of awareness, exerting a continuous force. While it remains unfelt it takes an endless toll. While repression saves, it also begins to destroy.

Repression is not a deliberate mental trick; it is a reaction of the entire system. It is something the brain and body do together to abort painful experiences, especially when we are very young and almost completely vulnerable.

There are as many scenarios for the onset of repression as there are people. Imagine that a very young child is watching his mother give his older brother a beating for a minor transgression. The mother is irrational and violent. The child senses that she can be dangerous when provoked. This realization would be shattering if it were conscious. But it isn't. Like most parental behavior, the beating is not a freak occurrence but is consistent with a reality that the mother has communicated to the child since his birth: that not only can she not take care of him and give him what he needs but that she might even be a danger to him.

These are overwhelming deprivations. They are too profound for a young child to tolerate. If he is to survive in an unsafe, unfulfilling environment, he cannot afford to feel or even to show his real needs. As he watches the beating, he is accommodating himself to his situation. The "gift" of repression, an adaptive response in our species, is that it blunts the impact of the Pain so that the child may simply watch without *apparent* reaction. He has repressed the Pain of what he is witnessing, and with the Pain he represses his need for love, for security, for warmth . . . for a mother. He would not be able to experience those needs without first dealing with the catastrophic Pain of their deprivation. One patient described the separation from his needs:

"Shortly before my mother died, she told me that she and my father had discussed the fact that I had never asked for a single thing in my whole life. She said it with pride and amazement. [Yet] there was so much that I desperately needed and wanted when I was small . . . By the time I was of an age when I could ask for something, I had given up wanting anything."

Another patient, Heather, gave an example of a deeply repressed experience:

"My father had left the family when I was seven to move in with his mistress, who later became my stepmother. I could never remember exactly when Father left and I never asked since my family did not discuss "personal" matters with the children.

"Then, in a feeling during my therapy, I saw myself sitting on the kitchen windowsill waiting for my father. It was twilight and Mother kept telling me it was my bedtime, but I kept pleading to stay and look out for five more minutes. He'll come soon, it won't be long now. I sat and waited and waited and it was dark now and I felt so alone and disappointed. Then Mother took me by the arm—I could almost feel her touch me—and she took me upstairs to bed and I started to cry because I wanted to see my father and then she told me Father would not be back, he would never never never be back. Then I did not cry. It took me almost thirty-two years to react to that fact and feel the hurt and pain of the loss of my father."

The Pain and need have been taken out of awareness but not out of existence or out of the child's system. He may seem simply to go on his way. But then perhaps he starts having nightmares or wets his bed. Perhaps he is agitated in school and can neither sit still nor concentrate. Repressed Pain is doing its job.

The repression of a particular feeling tends to shut down a part of a person's overall ability to feel. The more repression, the less one can feel and experience. When one cannot feel, life has no meaning. Other people's suffering has no meaning and not even our own suffering means anything. We become impervious to it. Such a high percentage of ourselves is wrestling with inner torments that little is left to deal sanely with our world, our lovers and friends. Feeling is the experience of all of ourselves—the essence of life and basis of humanness.

If a child is continually stifled when he expresses feelings that are unacceptable to his parents, sooner or later his feelings are going to be automatically repressed from within. He will become unconscious of these feelings, and "out of touch with himself."

Repression is so much a way of life that many of us view being "emotional" and showing feelings as "acting neurotic." We come to believe that self-control is the hallmark of health and any show of feeling is tarred with the brush of hysteria. The fact that feelings are such a threat to us indicates how much Pain we have to defend against.

When is someone "neurotic"? It is an arbitrary matter. The neurotic *process* begins with each unfelt Pain. It may even begin before or during birth. Whatever the starting point, there comes a time when we are so repressed that we hardly feel anything intensely anymore except the indirect evidence of Pain—anxiety, depression, compulsions, obsessions. There comes a point at which we are more repressed than feeling, more unreal than real, and we could label this "neurosis." But neurosis does not really "happen" at a point. It is a dynamic process.

How can you tell if you are neurotic? You can't, until and unless you know that you hurt. Neurosis is by definition, always unconscious, since the function of repression is to produce unconsciousness. Evidence of the hurt is always there to see in one's life, but a "good" neurosis will make one unconscious of it. Sometimes a neurotic does things he doesn't want to do. He gets angry at himself for acting neurotically, as though he usually doesn't. He thinks that it's a temporary quirk, a momentary loss of control. When compulsions really get out of hand, a person may think that he is "a bit neurotic," but most of those with compulsions do not see the connection between repression, neurosis, and compulsion. My guess is that most people who smoke or drink never really realize the connection between Pain and their habits. Neurosis is a paradox. It is enormously strong; a force that one acts on every day yet a force that eludes awareness. We move into neurosis and lose access to our feelings in a most insidious way. Once we are neurotic, no act of will can change it.

The only time we begin to feel that we are neurotic is when we are miserable—when our body's sophisticated, inner chemical and electrical defenses against Pain can no longer handle the load. When our neurosis no longer works to keep us unconscious, the first consciousness we have is of our Pain. It constantly erupts when the inner Pain-quieting system is overtaxed. It is then that we need a drug or a discipline or a reassuring idea to whip our body's own repressive system into more action. The minute we stop, we suffer.

Repression is a biologic process. A model is found in the allergic reaction. An antigen, a foreign substance such as pollen or dog hair causes the system to react, either sneezing, coughing, or developing a rash. The body immediately develops antibodies to combat the antigen intruder. The system manufactures what it needs to handle interference with its integrity and it tailors what it manufactures to meet specific kinds of assaults. This balancing process neutralizes the attack, produces an immune complex and maintains the system in a state of equilibrium. This is particularly relevant in the process of repression.

Pain, as an alien force, is like an antigen and stimulates those forces which will counteract it, much like antibodies. The areas of the brain which organize Pain reaction are also the areas that stimulate repression. The amount of Pain will largely determine the amount of repressive substance manufactured. Not only that, but as we shall discover later on, the body and brain's actual structure will change and accommodate itself to the amount of Pain assaulting the system.

The repression of Pain is a two-edged sword. It keeps the body from feeling overwhelmed and thus keeps the body from feeling. It both saves and destroys because when one can no longer feel, there are no great sorrows or joys, no keen disappointments or pleasures, no exciting surprises or discoveries. The immune complex of repressed Pain results in a state of neutrality, a feeling of living behind a wall, where life seems to be going on beyond one's reach, somewhere "out there." Immunity to feeling means immunity to life.

4: The Energy of Conflict

WHEN we block Pain, we do not block its effects. We block only the conscious experience of it. The effects of blocked Pain are expressed in the form of energy. By analogy, each trauma is very much like the "big bang" origin of the universe in which the energy from the original explosion still reverberates through the cosmos. The energy of the original traumas—and they *are* electrical storms—also permanently reverberate through the human biologic system.

Energy is an electrochemical force which can be measured. It is not mystical, not an *élan*, or an id. It derives from specific events which have had an explosive effect on the organism. An explosive effect which, now contained, continues to emanate from specific stored early experiences. The reverberating energy will be found decades later in the musculature as well as in the brain. Both show increased electrical activity.

An example is found in neurophysiologist Dr. Ronald Melzack's experiments with dogs. He produced an electrical explosion—an electrical jolt—daily to the limbic brain centers of these dogs and discovered a *continuous and indefinite "after-discharge."* In other words, the original explosion had lasting reverberating effects. What is more, the jolts accumulated over time and produced symptoms; specifically, seizures. Stored Pain accumulates in the human system in the same way, until there is an overload and a spillout of symptoms. The Pain remains as a force behind many different symptoms. Neurotic energy is a result of one's being in a constantly mobilized state against the danger of Pain rising to consciousness.

Until it is felt for what it really is, this Primal energy must be channeled somewhere and it usually is. It pervades the body via the key structures of the brain, pressing against the highest consciousness of the cerebral cortex. The exact nature and source of the Pain is obstructed from consciousness by repressive forces.

There is nothing quite like Pain to activate the system; unmet needs become transformed into stored Pain and result in continued activation or "energy." The specific source of the energy is blocked but the quantity of energy is diverted, seeps into and is absorbed by the various levels of human functioning: cognitive, emotional, and visceral.

Primal Pain is bound energy. This energy can be diverted into either bodily tension, anxiety, or ideas. The amount of energy diverted into these channels is exactly commensurate with the engraved Primal force. For example, the pounding of a pressure headache indicates the precise amount of Primal pressure nudging from below, as does the amount of agony in a stomach cramp. The zealousness and fanaticism of an idea can be an indication of the impelling force of a specific amount of energy; and the tenacity with which one pursues an idea can tell us about the amount of unrelenting internal pressure.

Robert described the origins of his lifelong feelings of being pressured:

"I always had the tendency to take on more than my share of responsibility and work. I also usually managed to wait until the last minute to get things done, which, of course, made the weight on my shoulders even heavier. I ended up having to use more energy than I had, so I invariably fell sick either before or on completion of what I had to do. Tension built up to completely lay me out. This weary-go-round has two origins. My birth was exactly a case of having to wait until the last minute before death, as my mother resisted me due to the pain she was in, and then making a tremendous effort to get out on my own. Eventually they used forceps. Then, when my mother died some months after my second birthday I unconsciously assumed responsibility for my own life. It was really too much. I grew up far too fast and I wound myself up tight to manage it. I was like an overworked engine that's been forced into too many revolutions per second."

ANXIETY AND TENSION

Anxiety is usually felt as a general feeling of agitation with a queasiness or "butterflies" in the stomach, often with heart palpitations. It is the manifestation of Pain in the internal organ system. It signals that the amorphous fear of disconnected Pain is on its way toward consciousness. All systems are reacting to keep it away.

Anxiety is a more primitive response than tension since it occurs long before an infant has sufficient neurological control of his musculature to bind neurotic energy with his body wall. Anxiety is characterized by a feeling of apprehension, dread, and pending doom. It is a giant terror usually involving a breakthrough of very early preverbal Pains. Anxiety is that state just before a Pain becomes conscious. It is not a specific disease but rather a sign that defenses are crumbling.

Anxiety is primarily a visceral reaction and for good reason—because it is the central reaction state of our early and pre-infantile existence. Traumas which occur on the earliest level, when unhinged, are reflected in anxiety states. There is a belief that anxiety is "unreal" fear. But in reality it is only an actual fear from a deeply buried past. Anxiety is not separate from fear—it *is* that very early fear which is terrorizing. After acutely anxious patients feel enough early infancy Pain, they are usually no longer anxious.

Tension is familiar to most of us—too familiar. As opposed to anxiety, tension is felt in the muscle systems and body wall. It is often experienced as a tightness around the chest, an ache in the back or neck muscles, a rigidity of fingers or toes, grinding of the teeth, or a rigid set of the jaw. It can result from the very same Pain that produces anxiety.

Tension is found in the respiratory system where the breathing is "clamped down" and shallow. It is in the facial set, posture, style of walk, squint of the eyes, wrinkling of the forehead, and so on. It is expressed by someone who taps his fingers or feet or shakes his legs.

Tension is the result of the clash between unconscious Pain and the forces of repression. It is above all the sign that repression is effective, in that the exact nature of the early trauma is kept at bay. Tension results from the use of the body wall to bind anxiety and indicates a higher developmental level at work.

The energy of Pain can also be filtered into and bound with belief systems, making belief systems fanatic and impermeable to new ideas. The energy of Primal Pain doesn't select out one system alone but infiltrates all of them—the viscera, body wall, musculature, and ideas and concepts. Belief systems now absorb what tension cannot, and represent the final evolutionary response to deep-lying Pain. For example, if one has a need for a father—having never had a real one in a lifetime—that need can result in physical tension and can also become a belief in a warm, protective, interested God. No amount of evidence is going to change that belief. Only feeling need—the source of the driving energy—can ease the attachment to that idea.

Energy is bound into not only belief systems but also the images we produce. In recurrent nightmares we see the same themes, the same images with the same intensity, arising night after night for decades. That energy comes from somewhere, and it never lessens until the Pain is felt.

SYMPTOMS OF EXCESS ENERGY

Once we see that energy is structured on three operational levels, the visceral, musculature, and ideational, we begin to understand that neurotic symptoms such as excessive stomach secretions, too strong a voice, or fanatical ideas may all stem from a single underlying source. When energy is absorbed by the viscera, as in the perinatal or infantile stages of development, the result years later can be severe physical symptoms such as ulcers or colitis. With maturation that same energy can be filtered through the emotional system, resulting in anger or crying fits. Still later, with more brain development, the energy can be diverted into ideas or belief systems. Whether it is a pressure headache, a belief system, or compelling repetitious behavior, these levels of operation soak up the energy so that the person is never aware of the driving force behind them, only of their effects.

It is Primal energy that makes an idea strong, implacable and persistent. The energy now *lies in those ideas;* transformed now into an ideational web or conceptual blanket over the Pain. Thus, in the same way that antigens create antibodies the force of Primal Pain creates ideas to sequester that very Pain. That early, driving force will call into action the highest possible level of neurologic function in the service of repression. When we talk about the "explosion of ideas" of the creative person, we now have some idea what kind of explosion we are talking about. Therefore a challenge to one's ideas can make one quite defensive. The more tenacious and fanatic the ideas, the more defensive a person becomes against any intrusion into them. The person fervently believes in the ideas without once being aware that they are critical defense mechanisms. He defends his ideas because they defend him.

All painful stimuli, whether a harsh look, a criticism, harangue, or beating, travel sensory routes and ultimately become stored physiologic memory. The storage patterns are sources of tapped energy. The system can only "hold" so much electrical charge at any one time; after that it acts as a "capacitor" in which energy is released to bring the "holding level" down to optimum amounts. So when someone taps his feet or fingers, when she or he talks incessantly, when a person has facial tics, these are the modes of energy release. They are necessary to maintain optimum "holding" levels. The discharge of tension in any overloaded system is a necessity for homeostasis. That is why taping a child's fingers so he won't chew his nails only ensures the later exacerbation of other symptoms.

The storage of Primal memory makes us wake up with the same tense musculature, the same apprehension, anxiety, and dread each day. All of our early etched-in experiences provide a matrix which shapes personality and provides its continuity and coherence. We are "held together" by our memories. They lock in characteristic ways of walking, talking, and behaving. Unmet need and Pain cement chronic behavior into lifetime casts.

Demands and early deprivations by parents and by society are ultimately reflected in the flesh. It may take a long time to become evident. Those with a good deal of Primal Pain begin to look ravaged, and though we might imagine that they are the ravages of age, they are truly the ravages of our youth. Joanna is one example:

"I often had pain in my back in specific places, and the pain was bad enough . . . to make me cry . . . There were two places in my left shoulder blade, and the other was a line of pain stretching from the top of my right shoulder down the length of my back. [One day] I had begun to cry about hurting so much physically, and as I sat up afterward I felt the memory of a hand grabbing my back in the exact spot of my left shoulder where I hurt. I had the distant feeling that someone had grabbed me there. Over the next day or two I [remembered] a fight between my mother and father which turned out to be the last day my father was in my life. In that scene my mother and father were arguing, I was very frightened and was clinging to my mother's knees. Suddenly I felt a hand grab me by the back of my shirt, whip me backwards away from her, and I was stopped by crashing backside into a bedpost. The two pains in my back were recurring in exactly two locations—where my father's hand had grabbed me, and in a line down my back where the bedpost imprinted its knobs on my back. Afterwards I heard my father leave the room, go downstairs, and I heard him drive away."

And Doris:

"Sometimes I wake up in the morning and my fingers are so tense they are literally paralyzed. I am holding on to something with all my might. I think I am holding on to myself. I am trying to protect myself from my hungry, needing mother. Sometimes I beat my fists into the air, warding her off. Often I feel totally paralyzed. She is sitting on me holding me down, forcing me to be what she thinks I should be. I kick at the air and scream at her to "Get off my back! Let me *be!*" I often get into these feelings when I'm in a very "speedy" mood, when I feel as if someone is chasing behind me with a bomb. It is my mother. I am being pressured by her to be what she wants me to be, not what I am."

The kind of symptom one has can be indicative of a certain kind of early experience. For example, a symptom such as high blood pressure, although it does not involve a verbal response, is nevertheless a complete "memory" of an early situation. Such responses are indications of the body's ability to remember, no different from the Pain of remembering how at the age of nine one's dog was given away. If the reaction to an early deprivation was elevated blood pressure and faster pulse, that reaction will tend to be strengthened over the years. Indeed, as Pain becomes compounded, so does the symptom become reinforced.

Once there is a weak spot—a vulnerable organ system, for example —it will remain the focus and outlet for generalized tension. So, for example, a child with an allergic tendency may, under the slightest overload of tension, develop an allergy attack. The same is true for those who develop headaches. This is also true for those who act out responses aggressively and belligerently—lying, fighting, or stealing. These responses, whether physical or behavioral, are "grooved" and become characteristic of how we respond to stress throughout our lives. It is the same with habits such as smoking or drinking or having to be on tranquilizers. But we don't consider these problems symptoms of Pain. We simply think we have a need to smoke, to drink. We have a need, it's true. A patient of mine recalled:

"When I first started drinking, alcohol would take away some of my pain and give me some semblance of comfort. As I got older it would take more and more alcohol to take away the pain, so I would have to drink and drink until I would black out and that's the only way I could get any relief from the pain."

A healthy person experiences rather than represses his life, using energy to live rather than to fight against Pain. As a result of this battle, the neurotic can often have too much energy. He accomplishes more than necessary, or goes through many more motions than necessary, because his system is "hyped." Or he is "down"—dragging, lifeless, and without energy to do anything because tremendous energy is being diverted into the task of repression. Real energy simply allows us to act directly and fulfill our real needs now, which is possible only if past deprivations are truly behind us.

5: In Self-Defense

WHAT do neurotic defenses defend against? Clearly, if there were no Pain, there would be no neurotic defenses. A well person should have the latent potential to utilize defenses but should not be "defensive." Defenses should only come into play when a system is under attack. This is as true for neurosis as it is for an allergic response.

Neurotic defenses are mechanisms to avoid feeling. The reason we call a defense neurotic later in life is because it is no longer appropriate to *external* reality. Perhaps even calling it neurotic is a misnomer since it was real and appropriate to a situation in the past.

The primary defense is the biologic one of repression—the shutting out of Pain from awareness. Once repression occurs, it sets in motion a myriad of behaviors which I call secondary defenses. These secondary defenses depend upon the different experiences each of us has had in our lives. These secondary defenses function either to release excess Primal energy or to aid in the primary process of repression. Their nature depends upon the different experiences each of us has had in our lives. If repression were absolutely effective, we would have almost no neurotic acting-out whatsoever. We would simply be frozen, fixed, rigid, and "dead."

Idiosyncratic mannerisms, speech patterns, ideas, emotional expressions, and emotional outbursts are also secondary defenses. They are ways of dealing with the diffused energy of repressed feelings. These various manifestations, considered by so many professionals to be diseases in their own right, are merely offshoots of one single event—repression.

A secondary defense can be a certain habitual look—a facial set, posture, gait, or movement—a speech pattern—a focus on particular kinds of ideas or images—a preoccupation with work or duties—an obsession about sexual performance—a habit such as smoking and drinking—an unconscious pattern of not eating what one needs—an avoidance of exercise or physical activity—it can be anything. But it is always driven by Pain. If there were no repressed Pain, we would simply feel what we experience. Openness to feeling would not be a threat to the system.

The body has normal defenses against catastrophic events in the outside world; but neurotic defenses are not set up against the outside events, except insofar as outside events trigger off what is stored inside of us.

Defenses are life-saving and extremely tenacious as well. Their important function is to save our lives in infancy and childhood. Defenses are memories, both of what saved the species in its history and, in our early personal lives, of those mechanisms that helped us get born and survive. In the case of attack, psychological or physical, we automatically retreat to more primitive neurological mechanisms for coping. We utilize subcortical mechanisms which were selected by evolution because they work. The mechanisms which are automatic are the ones appropriate to an earlier stage of development. And, as we shall see, an effective therapy must address itself to that lower brain organization. It is the automatic utilization of the lower mechanisms against stress which is the neurological basis for the "split." The response is split so that the person must utilize primitive mechanisms instead of age-appropriate ones. A stressed adult may use an infantile response of hypersecretions of acid in the stomach, for example, instead of confronting the situation in an adult way. What we do as neurotic adults is recruit reactions to stress which were the highest possible level of response for the baby at the time of the original trauma.

When repression is inadequate, the many secondary defenses are heightened. When those defenses falter, symptoms occur. When drugs or tranquilizers are given to beef up repression, symptoms and defensive reactions die down. A person can be affectionate again, can laugh again and relax for the moment, because repression has been reinforced. Of course, that person will suffer a rebound of suppressed energy as soon as medication stops, when the Pain which has been held at bay surges upward again.

The person who has created defenses on all the levels of development can usually function very well. She is not usually aware of her Pain, and so she can go on with the external business of living. But she is totally split; the one self is dealing with the world and the other self is dealing constantly with the churning Pains deeply buried inside. She is externally oriented and that is part of the defense.

It is only when external circumstances prevent her defenses from working that this person begins to suffer—when there is no chance to organize, calculate, rebel against the world or whatever she usually has to do. Otherwise her ideas, concepts, rationales, explanations, and attitudes all work to tranquilize Pain. As a patient of mine remarked:

"I was so far out of touch with my feelings I could not perceive the distinction between a feeling and an idea. I actually thought my mental activity *was* feeling, and regarded myself as an unusually sensitive person."

The notion of a "healthy defense" is a contradiction in terms. We see how Pain produces its own balm in a person who has been mistreated in childhood and is still able to tell herself, "I know my parents didn't treat me right but, after all, they had no choice. They were victims too." This is a defense of rationalization, the "smart defense." Although the person may be quite aware of what is going on in Africa, Jupiter, or in the economy, she hasn't the slightest idea what is going on inside her body.

There are many people whose minds are whirlpools of thought. They think night and day without cease, and their thoughts are generally trivial and compulsive, but they cannot stop. Strong Pains on the lower levels of need are forcing the intellect into continuous, compulsive action, yet the person is aware of neither the Pain nor the pressure. What is experienced is the effect—a racing mind. So long as the mind can keep itself occupied, busy, skipping from one thought to another, the "defense" will work. There are many people who do not seem to suffer very much from their busy minds. They manage to study, learn, think, read, and keep themselves very occupied. In that sense, their "interest" in outside matters works very well as a defense. It is only when the intellectual mind is so overloaded that it can no longer concentrate or study that the person suffers and thinks that something is wrong. One would imagine at that point the problem the person suffers from is an uncontrolled mind. Thus, a psychotherapist or doctor may try to quiet this person through a variety of mental tricks, such as meditation. But since the activation does not emanate from the intellectual mind, the energy will rise relentlessly from the lower brain and drive the mind on no matter what tricks one can devise. It is then that heavy artillery drugs are brought in, not to slow down thoughts but to quell Pain—which automatically breaks the racing mind.

Secondary defenses generally fall within one of two broad categories. Some people are impelled to discharge the energy of their Pain, others to sit on it. Thus some people exhibit themselves, or talk constantly, or look for a new person to sleep with every other night, or continually organize new projects and expeditions, or go to party after party until they are exhausted. Others smoke to contain the tension, or sit passively in a group unable to say a word, or hide from friends, or suppress all sexual thought and feeling, or sit alone and watch television night after night. Obviously, most people do both—defend by discharging and by restraining the energy of buried Pains.

People who defend are not doing something voluntary or whimsical; they are doing something automatic to protect themselves. Nor are they using pretense, that is, they are not pretending not to hurt. They are simply unaware of the existence of Pain. Because parents cannot stand to see hurt in their children, children soon learn to hide their hurts and use pretense, but soon enough this pretense becomes automatic and unconscious.

The neurotic cannot win. He is caught. If he takes Pain-killers or tranquilizers during the day, he may well experience a relapse of Pain during the most defenseless time of his day—during sleep. If he takes sleeping pills to quell those Pains at night, he will suffer a rebound during the following day. He is caught in the vicious cycle of defense and buildup of tension with neurotic release following. In short, he must be neurotic; it is a biologic necessity.

6: Symbols of Need

WE BEGIN to live symbolically, in a neurotic way, as soon as we defend. Once a feeling is disconnected from the knowledge of what it is, a false knowledge takes its place. Without knowing it, we develop unreal ideas, attitudes, and behaviors out of our Pain. We make people, situations, objects, images, and ideas into symbols for the Pain. Neurotic symbolism is then the present representation of a past, Painful reality. The symbolism springs from the Pain, and also helps defend against it.

The Canadian neurosurgeon Wilder Penfield has clarified this symbolic process. During brain surgery he found that when he put an electrode at a given distance from a certain nerve cell the patient (who was conscious during the surgery) would relive something like, "I feel as though there are robbers after me." When he moved the probe closer to the cell, the patient would relive the exact memory, "I remember how frightened I was when my brother pointed a toy gun at me." It may be that symbolic behavior and thought (the robbers, in this case) are truly a matter of physical distance in the brain from the centers where the feelings are represented. Pain shunts the feeling away to a symbolic site.

Symbolism gets its start with the repressed feeling. Suppose the feeling is a fear of the parents, which is repressed and so becomes a constant, residual fear. For the young child, the fear is transformed into dragons which come up at night when he is in the dark. The dragon is a symbol. It may become a recurrent symbol so that even pictures of dragons send the child into a terror state. The child isn't fearful because of the dragon. *The dragon exists because the child is fearful.*

Until the brain develops to the point of conjuring up images to rationalize fear, the infant is faced with unadorned terror—the kind of terror that may well lead to crib death for the infant abandoned in the dark in his crib. In that sense, the "dragon" is a survival mechanism. We want to be very careful about exorcising the demons that children dream up rationalizing their fears. Child therapists must understand that those images have a specific function and should not be tampered with without understanding the underlying forces.

The child makes his underlying fear rational both to unconsciously justify the feeling and to provide some handle for its control; that is, a dragon is a fearful creature that must be avoided at all costs. A child cannot avoid his parents and their wrath or whatever makes him fearful, but he can avoid the dragon and tranquilize himself. He can manipulate symbols in order to handle a Primal feeling. Indeed, in a more or less subtle way most of us do this to keep feelings suppressed.

As the maturation process moves the child from images to more complex ideas, the outlets for the fear may parallel that maturation. Now the fear may be of Communism or of foreigners. The fear could just as easily become phobic and fixate on something such as elevators or airplanes. The symbol may well be a direct derivative of the Primal feeling, as the case of Melinda illustrates:

"A dream which arose from my childhood had followed my first husband's death some years earlier. It was never repeated but was always there, at the back of my mind; a threatening image, wrapped in unease. The immediate cause was an argument with a cousin of whom I was afraid.

"I dreamed there was an enormous Eye before me; it was about three feet high and from it there radiated a tremendous force. I despised this force and felt nothing would make me give in to it for I felt it was totally evil. I could feel my body shaking with my hatred and the vehemence of my contempt, but the force continued to stream ferociously out of the eye, and such was its power that to my horror I began at last to weaken before it. Very slowly my knees gave way and I sank to the ground until I was feebly groveling before it. I was broken by its force, defeated, reduced to the most abject and humiliating slavery.

"I woke in such terror I did not at first dare to put my hand out to the light: the room was crowded with evil. I gabbled desperate prayers. After a while I gathered the courage to write it down as a means of distancing myself from it.

"Later, I had an insight that surprised and shocked me. It con-

cerned a scene when I was four years old. Although I had always become angry and helpless all my life whenever my father and I
discussed anything, I was completely unconscious that I had ever been
terrified of him as a child. What had happened was that when I was
four I had a nursemaid whom I loved dearly. One day she did something that enraged my father and I remember standing and watching
him as he shouted at her. I was beside myself, wanting to make him
stop. I hated him so much for shouting at her I could hardly breathe,
but at the same time I felt terrified of him and helplessly unable to
halt that cyclone of bellowing fury. His eyes were huge and round and
burning, they seemed to fill the sky. It hurt like a physical injury to
look at them."

As Pain pushes up, it creates symbols as delegates to consciousness.
It can be written, painted, or sculpted. These are the houses for the
delegates. The feelings are wrapped in words, contained in brush-
strokes, or infused with melody, but they are not felt for what they
are. Artistic expression does not resolve the feelings or the problems. It
expresses (and represses) the problem. It may release some of the energy of repression but, like any other catharsis, it has to be done continuously.

Sometimes the symbolism is close to the feeling, and sometimes it is
inordinately distant and complicated. One patient refused to make a
turn signal in her car and was given a ticket. When asked why she
didn't signal, she told her therapist, "It's nobody's business where I'm
going." Not making that turn signal was a symbolic way of not having
to report to Mother, who constantly badgered her as a child as to
where she was going. It is a clear and simple example of how neurosis
is the symbolic manipulation of events in order to solve Primal feelings. It would have been real not to report to Mother every time she
left the house (particularly at age nineteen) but unreal not to signal.
The feeling was right but the context wrong. Situations become symbolic when they offer the same kind of stimulus as an early painful
event. The current situation is unwittingly regarded through childish
eyes and is reacted to similarly. Symbolism continues as long as the
Pain initiates repression and causes a diversion of the feeling away
from a direct linkage.

The symbol of the turn signal wasn't anything deliberate or even
conscious. It was an automatic and unconscious response to an old
feeling. Symbols adhere to us because they represent something unresolved.

For example, a young man who would never ask for anything for himself from his family acted out asking everything for the union worker. He became a fanatic leader, demanding fulfillment of workers' needs which he later discovered, even though they were real, were for him merely symbolic representations of a need that he could never express for himself to his parents.

"I always used to believe in God, but understand now that I became religious partly in an effort to get close to my father, who was a very earnest if not vociferous Christian. That was to be the way to close the gap between us, the way to see inside him and get him to see inside me. When I told him with great enthusiasm about my faith (enthusiasm based on the hope of finally receiving the response I longed for) he made no reaction. It was as if I had said something by the way. I realize in retrospect that it was at that moment that I dispensed with Christianity. The very thing that I hoped to draw from my father was the same that I hoped to get from God. I needed someone to see my Pain, someone to whom I could turn and talk to intimately. There was no one around me like this so God became the one. Also I could not fathom the hurt that I was subjected to, but that was all taken care of by an omniscient being. If someone understood something about me, that was all I needed, and if that someone by definition understood everything, so much the better. God was the father I wanted mine to be. God was the father in the sense of a benevolent authority and Christ was the father of friendship and hope.

"Having failed to win my father by joining him in his 'cage,' I was determined to step outside and hammer against the bars. I wanted to shock him into some reaction, into responding openly to me as another person. I became involved in left-wing politics. It is so clear to me from where I stand now that my involvement in this area was neurotically motivated—quite apart from the objective justice of my cause. My passionate struggle against the establishment was a symbolic re-creation of my struggle with my father. In trying to get the establishment to act fairly by acknowledging the injustices of society, I know that I was really trying to shake him up, trying to say, 'Look at me, Daddy, see what you've done to me!' I remember how I used to say things politically outrageous to him just in order to evoke a reaction; he presented such a passive, unreacting exterior for most of the time. I symbolized my need for my daddy by demanding that the people in power look at the plight of the working class, the poor, the minorities. I trumpeted socialism because I wanted everything to be fair. 'From each according to his abilities to each according to his needs.' What more could be desired? But it was my life that was unfair. I did not get what I needed. I championed the socially oppressed because of the oppression I had suffered."

Symbols allow us to avoid the truth about our real selves. They preserve and perpetuate a powerful driving force—hope. We automatically symbolize friends, lovers, employers, and even chance acquaintances into images of the people who caused us Pain when we were children, then hope that the outcome will change. Out of unreal hope we acquiesce to playing a game which we can never win. The reason we continue to play in the face of constant disappointment is because we cannot face up to the fact that the outcome was determined long ago. We never feel our losses, and so we continue to be losers. Our Pain makes us play innumerable tricks upon ourselves and others. We misperceive, we react inappropriately in spite of ourselves, we listen inattentively, hear and see incorrectly.

A neurotic plays out his past, only in different scenarios with different locations and different actors. He rewrites the script constantly but the basic plot is always the same. One thing is missing: a conclusion.

7: The Inner Struggle

WHEN needs go unattended, there is a change in the way we go about trying to fulfill ourselves. We find more sophisticated ways to express our needs. At first we can only scream and cry. We stop screaming when it does no good. Later, we can begin to call Mommy until that is useless and then finally *act* in ways that symbolically call Mommy, such as being very good and quiet, getting A's in school, doing the dishes without being asked, and so on. These behaviors are sophisticated screams. They are struggles.

We struggle to fulfill anachronistic need without once being aware of it. It's lack of fulfillment at the appropriate time that has activated repression to keep us from being aware of it. The only way this early agony will show itself is perhaps when we lose a girlfriend or boyfriend or a spouse. We are usually not aware that the source of the extraordinary misery that makes us suicidal about that loss lies decades before in our history.

When all we can experience of unconscious need are its later derivatives, we come to assume that we have other needs—for "self-actualization," for prestige and self-confidence. The force of the real past need is absorbed in symbolic needs that make a need for confidence or self-actualization seem real. Nearly all of us are so deprived that, having these "needs" in common, we come to believe that they are not only basic but genetic.

A baby isn't born with a need for dignity or honor. She has no need for prestige or fame. She doesn't need self-esteem or power. These are all adult inventions. If a child is treated as an object, a thing, something only to be given orders to, she will grow up struggling for "dignity." She will struggle mightily for high corporate position or for just the right desk and office in a company or for the best table at a restaurant—all to feel like "someone." The best desk, the best table in the restaurant, and all the bowing and scraping in the world will never erase that fountain of need.

The need to belong is yet another way that someone can struggle in the present out of the feeling of having never belonged at home. There is no "need to belong" as such. There is a need to be loved, to feel a part of a family, to feel not excluded from family life, not being sent out of the room when important discussions take place; not being left out of family outings because one has done this or that. If a child is kept at an emotional distance by emotionally removed parents, he will have that symbolic urge to feel part of something. He may join clubs, political organizations, the military, or religious cults in the quest for a family.

The so-called "need for power" is also just a label for a struggle. Those who are unloved may want to have power to make something good happen in their lives. A struggle for power comes into being when helpless children are abused physically, verbally, or psychologically day after day. They are in the hands of parents who do have absolute power because they control fulfillment of need. Of course, these children dream of power. They are trying to find ways to avoid hurt and abuse in some way to get their needs fulfilled. When they finally achieve power, it will be abused because it is being used to fulfill deep needs. It isn't power that corrupts. It is the need for it.

Another way that we can distinguish between real and unreal needs is that after our patients cry about certain unmet needs, there are biologic changes. Having seen patients from more than fifty countries, we have learned how few those needs are and how common they are to all of mankind. Patients do not change physiologically on those rare occasions when they try to feel about the unreal needs such as self-esteem. That is because those needs (power, prestige) are not infantile and therefore do not affect maturation and growth. If unreal or symbolic needs were indeed real, then we would see physiologic changes with their reexperience.

If each level of need is fulfilled, the next higher level becomes that much less important. But as each level is not fulfilled, the next becomes that much *more* important—and the symbolic struggle that much more intense. Being deprived of physical warmth early on makes being told later that one is loved seem more important, even crucial. The neurotic must hear expressions of undying love. He may even leave his partner if he feels there isn't enough verbal protestation of love.

We struggle to get in the present what we never got in the past, and never will get in the future—loving, caring parents. But we go on trying. The struggle is the symbolic way we keep the past in the present. They merge and we can't really tell the difference anymore.

Once we understand that repressed traumas are imprinted and remain with us, then we can understand the repetitiveness of neurosis and why the symbolic struggle continues in the same way year after year. The old Pain is continuously striving for resolution and just as often is being sidetracked into the channels that constitute the struggle. Neurosis is exactly that inability to separate past from present: past deprivation, present attempts at fulfillment. That is why successful, famous, and rich people must continue their drive or become depressed. Everything *seems* to be fulfilled now—they are wanted, are made to feel important, have servants and idolators and yet when they are alone they are left with something they can't run from, the feeling of being worthless and unloved. Present fulfillment can paper that agony over for a time and some of us are more successful at the papering job than others. But it is still only paper.

There isn't enough symbolic fulfillment in the world to change buried need one drop. *The time for childhood fulfillment is only in childhood.* All the touch possible at the age of thirty will not change the need to have been touched at the age of six months. That old ache to be held is a physical memory that may make our muscles ache for a lifetime. The struggle, in reality, is a continuation of childhood behavior with one's parents, by other means. We don't struggle simply for an immediate, better outcome. *We re-create the original event, as it is engraved in our nervous system, from beginning to end.* We place ourselves in situations where it is frustrating or difficult, then struggle to make the outcome better. We'll join up with unloving people or critical people and then try to make them noncritical or approving or loving. We avoid those whose company we might benefit from, while courting those who have nothing to offer us. But it's the struggle, not the result, that is important to the neurotic. Gene is a good example:

"By the time I was in high school, I had repressed almost all of my needs for affection and physical touch. I dated prudish girls. After several dates with the same girl, I would get up enough courage to ask her for a kiss when I took her home. Naturally, she would often refuse. It was as though I had no right to any affection. Later in college, I would continue to date women who didn't like physical touching. Whenever my judgment would err and I would be out with a woman who liked sex, I might enjoy some touching for that time but later I would get scared and uncomfortable and break off the impending relationship. Eventually I married an emotionally cold woman and was home safe. For eight more years, I would struggle for affection.

"When my wife and I had sex, I always came very quickly upon entering her. I tried everything I could think of to change the premature ejaculation. I would always feel like a failure. She rarely turned on and I would literally work at making her come alive sexually. Sex was hard work but I never stopped. I felt that it was up to me to turn her on and that there was something wrong with me if I couldn't."

The neurotic has no choice. Either he feels his Pain or he struggles. There is no in-between. That is why trying to stop a struggle is a vain exercise.

If someone felt unsafe as a child, he won't just make efforts to feel safe. He first sets himself up to feel *unsafe*. He'll put himself in situations of danger or in situations of being ripped off, being hurt physically or psychologically. He may adopt a life-style of turmoil, turbulence, or chaos. And what is diabolic is that when he gets involved with someone, it is often the kind of unstable person who reinforces the feeling of having no security. The other person may be weak or unable to commit himself or herself to any relationship. The reason doesn't matter. The final result is that the person who has always felt unsafe is feeling it all the more now.

If one always had to be the good little girl or the helpful son and take care of a sick parent, chances are that as an adult one will find another helpless person to take care of. Becoming a doctor, taking care of one sick person after another, is an example. The struggle will center on helping a weak person get strong enough so that the roles may then be reversed. Those days never come. The struggle goes on forever because in reality the person cannot let himself be taken care of. It does no good to say, "Listen, why don't you lead your own life? You've taken care of so-and-so for years—you deserve a break."

It seems an odd paradox that the neurotic is constantly defending against feeling by re-creating situations that contain it. But he goes on contriving events to rationalize or make concrete certain feelings that are already there. For example, a patient of mine reported this: "I'm always losing things or at least forgetting where I put them. The things I misplace may be small, but they're always very important to everyday life: my keys, my watch, my wallet. It usually starts happening when I'm doing too much, taking on more than my share. I lost my mother when I was very young. She died. I couldn't ask for help when I was growing up. There wasn't anyone around. I always looked after myself. I saved my dad a lot of trouble. Now I always get angry when I lose things. I lash out, put blame on others. I panic. Maybe I panicked a whole lot more when she died—but inside. So, I lose things to go through the struggle of finding them."

The struggle is the hub around which neurosis revolves. There is really nothing else one can do with a Pain that cannot be felt. The focus in the present helps to maintain the illusion of sanity and keeps us from being overwhelmed by the stored Pain. With no current focus the Pain would be naked and insufferable. The struggle is a marvelous and peculiarly human invention to keep us from feeling unloved and unwanted. Those very feelings keep the struggle going for the rest of our lives.

THE WAR OF THE SELVES

Once Pain and repression set in, a new self emerges which, in a sense, was never meant to be. It is what I called in *The Primal Scream* the "unreal self." The real self is simply the part of us which contains all our buried feelings and needs. The unreal self is the part of us that carries out the burial. It is the disconnected part of consciousness which represses the real self and experiences only symbols of real feelings.

It is the unreal self that never cries when it is hurt; the self that doesn't believe in childhood Pain. It is the self that has lost touch with needs and feelings, and with one's own humanity. The unreal self sees but is insensitive to the hurt and suffering of others. It is the unreal self that contains our false beliefs, delusions, misperceptions, misinterpretations. It is that giant superstructure that smothers the real self out of existence. It's the self that sees no beauty, that doesn't understand kindness and generosity. The self that has lost its tenderness and romance. It is the mystical self; the self that talks too much and eats too much, the self that does destructive things. The unreal self is superficial and can only see the surface of things. It lacks the complexity to see things in perspective.

When our unreal self develops, we are half a person. The unreal self does not obliterate the real self; it simply smothers it. The unreal self is tangled around Pain, and exists only because of it. Yet it neither feels Pain, nor acknowledges it.

Repression makes us unreal, because it forbids access to our own reality. We may know what we think, but we don't know what we feel. Once we are repressed, we must act in unreal ways. We no longer act directly on our feelings because they are no longer available to guide us.

The real self is highly conscious of Pain and is involved in processing needs and feelings continuously. That is why a neurotic can be asked how he feels and report feeling very well while machinery hooked up to that same person's physiology indicates a hyper-activated state. This is clearly an example of the split. The unreal self, "the mind," feeling fine while the underlying real self is processing Pain.

Each engraved Primal experience becomes an electrochemical force, a part of the real self, and is very much a physiologic reality. It is that reality pressing against the unreal self that produces basic internal conflict. The real and unreal selves, therefore, are not simply psychological concepts but are a biologic reality.

There is no way to act real without *being* real. People who develop an act of being real are still unreal because that act is out of accord with the turmoil inside. Someone can decide to be more "open," and say what's on her mind, but unfortunately her mind is prevented from knowing what she really feels. It never makes anyone more real to act real. It makes them more unreal because that is only a new act. The job of neurosis is to keep us from being real.

In *The Primal Scream* I wrote of the "split" into real and unreal selves as being occasioned by a single major event in childhood, probably around the age of six or eight. But neurosis can begin long before that age. Certain very early traumas have such an incredible force as to cause a major split right then. Of course, it can happen at any time during a child's development due to the vulnerability of the brain in the first days and weeks of life. It is also probably not terribly helpful to think of the split in terms of "major and minor Primal scenes," as in my first book. There are many key events which we all have in our lives which are very painful and which, however subtly, changed the course of our lives.

After the age of six, neurosis crystallizes. The unreal self becomes solidified until the teens, when it becomes fixed. When parents, with the help of society, can communicate their ideas, their mores and morality, and unknowingly train the child away from his feelings, neurosis is being reinforced. The disease of repressed feeling is then permanent, unless the victim can find a way to retrieve the real self. The only way to become real again is to reverse the process of neurosis, and there is no painless way to do that.

II: NEUROSIS IN REVERSE

1: Blueprint for Change

Neurosis is first and last a system, and the resolution of neurosis lies in that system. If we do not recognize this, then resolving neurosis becomes inordinately complex. The neurotic system continuously generates unreal ideas, perceptions, beliefs, and conditions, both mental and physical. The neurotic system is literally a *different biochemical system* from the normal one.[1]

The problem in treating neurosis is very similar to that of untangling the structure of a gene. Once we know the central coding mechanisms by which the elements are strung together, the puzzle falls into place. We believe there are central coding mechanisms in neurosis. There is an organizing principle, and that principle lies in repressed feelings and needs of the individual.

If we do not address ourselves to the system, then we are left in a fragmented pursuit, chasing down this attitude, this behavior, this perception or that sensation; without reference to a whole organization that spews forth hundreds of neurotic symptoms—both physical and mental. Literally thousands of behaviors are based on just a few Primal feelings.

Neurosis rises from a contradiction between expression and repression. All else—perception, attitudes, cognition, problem-solving, learning, and facets of personality—is secondary to this contradiction. The multifarious neurotic problems are only offshoots of these two opposing forces. To be effective, therapy must focus directly on the central contradiction. It need not concern itself with the synthesis. All else will fall into place when the key problems are solved.

Primal Therapy is the process of neurosis in reverse. Instead of

[1] Discussed in part V.

blocking Pain, which leads to neurosis, it releases Pain so that a person can be free. Instead of compounding the unconsciousness which comes from repression of Pain, reversal expresses what is unconscious in order to liberate consciousness. Instead of building defenses against the experience of Pain, defenses are dismantled so that the Pain already in the system can be felt in all of its original intensity. Instead of acting out neurotically to discharge tension, acting out is deferred so that tension will build to the breaking point. Since neurosis is laid down sequentially from the interior of the brain outward, treatment must involve traveling that historic route in reverse, from the most recent events to the critical experiences of early infancy. Neurosis is an unconscious process. Primal Therapy is a conscious one.

Primal Therapy is built around an understanding of the developmental process of neurosis, both neurophysiologically and psychologically. *Development* must be considered in any theory about neurosis.

Behavior therapy, for example, which is nondevelopmental, may use the technique of mildly shocking a smoker every time he reaches for a cigarette. The implication of this technique is that smoking is a bad *habit,* something to be learned and unlearned, a habit which can be broken by punishment. Behavior therapy sounds like a scientific refinement of what parents tell their children. It does not consider underlying reasons for the habit. What is treated is the "desire" for a cigarette, rather than seeing "desire" as the conscious psychological result of a developmental history. We want cigarettes when we cannot feel our real needs. Taking away our wants by punishment, exhortation, or rational explanation of their harmful effects leaves those generating sources intact, and therefore also neurosis.

If we agree that the past remains with us and exerts a force, then the question is how to undo it. Several schools, including the Freudians, believe that you can talk it away; that you can gain understanding about it so that somehow it will dissolve. By contrast, Primal Therapy as a psychophysiologic process is based on the concept that neurosis is a state of being. It is neither a "psychotherapy" nor a "body" therapy. It is both at once. It is based on the simple idea that what happens to us as children does not evaporate the moment the experience is over, but rather *remains as part of our physiology.* Pain is not simply an idea or an attitude. It is registered as an *experience* and must be resolved experientially. Thus, one must aim to achieve, *through feeling,* a thorough resolution and understanding of how those early events are laid down, where they are buried, and the processes by which they are kept repressed.

2: The Healing Force

IN THE history of psychology, emotions have been treated with suspicion. They have been considered intruders in the mind, making us irrational. Indeed, the word "emotional" has been equated with "irrational." We now understand that only *unfelt* emotions distort the mind. Feelings, in and of themselves, are exquisitely rational. They have a logic of their own and, when felt, make sense out of so much of our behavior.

The emotions are never blind unless they are blocked and cannot be felt. Then they are blind because they suffuse what is rational and real, driving us to misperceive and misinterpret, and to do crazy, symbolic things. The so-called logical mind only gets warped and distorted by unfelt, diverted emotions. So *to be unemotional is to be irrational. To be emotional is to be rational.*

Feelings and intellect in unison yield true rationality. The task is getting them to work together. When the central, internal contradiction between feeling need and repressing it is resolved, the key interaction is no longer between man and self, but between man and the environment. We can direct ourselves to the outside world instead of waging a continuous battle against our inner demons.

Feelings are states of being and organize human behavior. Blocked feelings organize neurotic behavior. There is a very good reason why most of us do not feel our needs and why, therefore, most of us run around *depriving ourselves* of fulfillment. Much better, it seems to the neurotic, to try to get something in the present to keep the feeling away than to be in agony over all that deprivation. And thus, with punishing irony, the deprivation goes on and on.

THE AGONY OF HEALING

The most natural thing in the world is to react to pain. When we're burned or bitten, for example, we cry, howl, or scream, shake the injured hand, or jump around. These natural responses help consume the energy of the Pain and finally dispel it. But when Pain is in excess and is repressed, the energy is not consumed. It remains as a constant inner force. Instead of being utilized in a healing process, which is a high-energy state, this energy is rerouted and dissipated into diverse pathways that continuously activate the system. The healing relaxation process does not occur. The healing sequence is not run off and the wound is not closed.

In neurologic terms, the overload of Pain has been shunted away from the hypothalamic healing structures by the thalamus and relayed on to the cortex (and limbic system) to defuse and vitiate the energy. The "mind" now has an excess amount of energy to deal with which keeps it awash in thoughts. The person so afflicted—should he be aware that he *is* afflicted—can enter conventional psychotherapy and become occupied with developing new insights into his neurosis. Unfortunately, those insights are utilizing rerouted *nonhealing* energy not connected to the source. They will be of no profound help except as disconnected, mental gymnastics.

Neurosis is not an abstract concept or vague "psychological" problem. It is truly a wound. In order for any wound to heal, it has to hurt. The hurt is the healing process at work. The more extensive the injury, the greater the pain, and the more consuming and critical the healing process. If, for example, your finger freezes, it is at first very painful, then excruciatingly so. The suffering goes on until it seems unbearable. Then, gradually, it quiets down almost to the point of nonawareness. It may even change into its opposite, a feeling of warmth. Or there is no feeling at all.

Is the pain gone? One might think so. But when the finger is warmed, the pain is terrible again. What you're feeling is the suffering that was *interrupted* before. The system could feel only so much pain before it began to prevent the pain from reaching consciousness. Now, with warmth and the revival of nearly dead tissue, that pain is simply released.

And so you hurt like hell. You may cry, whimper, or writhe, but now at least you *heal*. As long as you're numb, as long as the pain is interrupted, you aren't healing at all, and if you remained in that state, your finger would be lost. Only the revival of feeling—of pain—saves you.

Frostbite usually threatens only a few extremities—a fingertip, some toes. But this example is of the greatest importance, because so many of us are suffering from frostbite of the entire system. We're living in the numb phase. We've been hurt, badly and repeatedly, and have yet to feel the agony of those pains.

The result is that we never heal. If a child has been hurt in his early years so that he needed many hours to cry it out, but was shushed, spanked, or reprimanded for crying, or was simply unable to cry, that leaves him—literally—with many hours of crying left to do. When this happens over and over again in his life, he has a lot of stored energy. Its release is a very high energy state and a high energy state is one prerequisite for the healing process. (It has been discovered that bone regrowth as a result of a fracture is stimulated by delivery of a constant flow of low-amperage electricity to the site of the fracture.)

Because of the incredible traumas that most infants undergo, they normally would be crying most of the time for perhaps the first full year of their lives. But they rarely do. If they become chronic criers, they are usually stopped by the parents' discouragement, their indifference, rough handling, slapping, beating, or tranquilizers such as phenobarbital, the pediatrician's drug of choice for many decades.

There is a sad irony here. Babies are discouraged, hurt, or drugged into submission so they will stop crying, when it is probably this very crying reaction, this natural reaction to traumatic experience, which would be healing the original Primal wounds. A harsh birth alone can set up a continuing need to cry. By contrast, "Leboyer babies" characteristically cry very little. Having had a much easier, more gentle birth, they do not have a sequence of trauma to be run off and healed. Most infants have known trauma but must wait for the day when they will be able to react to it and begin to heal the damage done by the Pain.

That is why our adult patients often cry (not deliberately) exactly like babies who have been left alone in the crib. They have to finish a crying (healing) sequence that originally was aborted by repression. They may have given up reacting to the hurts early in life simply because the traumas were so great, or because they were given angry looks, were spoken to harshly, or were shaken or slapped. Now as adults in therapy, they do not just cry *as adults* about that experience, they cry as that baby, long and loud enough to complete the circuit and feel the catastrophic realization, "They aren't here," "They won't even come when I need them," or simply and basically, "They don't love me."

By looking at the brain we can see exactly how repression of overwhelming Pain saves our lives, even while it interrupts the healing process. The shunting of Pain away from the brain structures which control healing is a way of protecting us from lethal, skyrocketing vital signs. If the hypothalamus were to try to handle the full load, we would have elevations in the body's mobilization that could kill us; constant temperature of 103 degrees, continuous pulse over 200, and blood pressure over 200. We know this because when we slowly and carefully help patients restore some of their Pain to consciousness, we frequently see readings of these vital signs in the moments before the patient makes connection with her feelings.

Repressed reactions remain within the system as sequences waiting to be run off. In a case of frostbite, the victim originally does not have a full reaction to the trauma; he does not hurt *enough*. He must finish the sequence of hurting so as to heal. The *symptoms* of disease are part of the release of Pain and therefore of the healing process. One must be careful before tampering with them. When one gives tranquilizers for anxiety or lithium for depression the patient feels more comfortable, but feeling the Pain, a necessity for healing, has been put off. The symptoms of disease, particularly neurosis, are survival-oriented. It is in the nature of disease to set in motion those forces which will cure it. Left to its own natural processes the body produces what it needs to rid itself of disease. Within diseases are the seeds of their resolution and cure. What we do in Primal Therapy is to recognize these forces and allow them latitude.

A striking example of how Pain and the healing reaction to it can be delayed and stored was reported by Richard Lippin, a physician formerly in charge of the Philadelphia Detention medical unit. One of his patients had been taking high doses of methadone, which, like the heroin it is supposed to replace, is a pain-killer. He was given a skin test for tuberculosis. It was negative. A year later, the man was with-drawn from methadone—and suddenly developed a strong, positive skin mark for TB in the spot where he had been tested. Immune agents were fighting the TB antigen for the first time. The test had produced no reaction until this point because the drug blunted the man's Pain. We can see that the drug rendered the patient partially unconscious. Methadone helped shield Pain—from the centers that would have directed healing. The body could not react. When consciousness widened upon withdrawal from the drug, there was pain, *full reaction,* and, for the first time, healing. The system had held that reaction and healing sequence in storage for a year.

If a simple, local pain can be stored for a year, it is not difficult to imagine that major Pains could be stored for decades, waiting for the healing sequence to be completed. Indeed, these Pains are stored with undiminished force and clarity until the day we finally feel them. Our system, in its persistent attempts to heal, has us act out in ways that *would* heal, if only the situation were the real, original one and not a symbol for it. During a therapy session, totally losing control in anger usually leads a patient to the original focus even when the ostensible target had been someone or something in the present. Strange as it seems, neurotic behavior is aimed at healing. But that goal will never be reached until the symbolic sequence is converted into the real one.

Until we feel the Pain, we suffer. Pain heals; suffering is the chronic state of not having healed. Mourning offers an example of this dialectic that many of us are familiar with. If someone close to us dies, and we do not "let it out," if we do not grieve and cry and allow ourselves to go crazy with the full force of the loss—if instead we feel we must be "brave" and "carry on" and "not give in"—we suffer chronically from that loss. We never make our way through it, because we never feel it. By denying the Pain, we continue to carry its burden and even endanger our own lives, risking serious illness brought on by the stress of unfelt feelings.[1]

For healing to occur, *suffering must be converted into Pain.*

We see this when we monitor therapy sessions where patients reexperience the old Pain that lies beneath day-to-day suffering. The patient begins his session suffering. His nervous system mobilizes every part of him in a natural attempt to ward off the Pain; he is suffering *to keep the Pain away.* The vital signs momentarily are very high, the epitome of a suffering state. The body "knows" the Pain is near, and reacts to the threat just as it has all the patient's life, except that the reaction is much stronger now that the patient is actually allowing the Pain to rise. The only other time the patient has suffered this acutely is the time the Pain originally occurred and was repressed.

As Austin explained:

"One way to describe what happens to me in the process of feeling is that all the symptoms of Pain become concentrated into the Pain

[1] And many studies point out the much higher incidence of catastrophic disease after the loss of a loved one.

itself. After a period of struggling against the feeling (usually by trying too hard to feel it), the misery gathers into a knot deep in my chest and stomach that has to be expressed and felt. That terrible knot won't dissolve unless I can express it in the original situation."

When suffering reaches a crescendo (as in a Primal session), the defense system fails, and the patient drops into the very opposite of suffering—feeling the Pain. Afterward the body relaxes, the vital signs drop, the patient is feeling and expressing the Pain as it connects with consciousness, and the healing begins. The actual experience and resolution of Pain brings a profoundly expansive feeling of relief after the acute suffering which precedes it.

When suffering becomes Pain, both disappear and the patient is left with something else—feeling. His ability to be conscious of himself and his surroundings was blocked with every Pain that had to be repressed. His suffering meant that he was continually in an unhealed state.

Feeling equals healing. With feeling, the wounds of neurosis begin their resolution, symptoms fall away and the healing hormones (as we shall see later) are released. The opened lesions of ulcers and colitis begin to mend, chronic infections begin to disappear, and the body begins to repair itself.

Pain and suffering are so distinctly different that they are processed through two different systems in our neurologic makeup. Suffering is carried through the more ancient system near the middle and interior of the nervous system. Pain, which involves the selective, discriminating identification of what the hurt is and what it means, moves through more recent structures away from the deep middle of the brain. The suffering system projects information to higher brain centers only diffusely, and occasionally allows us to be aware of the agony inside without telling us why or what it is. The Pain pathways allow us to have a particular *idea* about the suffering, to integrate the physiologic hurt with all the events surrounding it and their implications.

Thus any animal can suffer but a full human neocortex is needed to feel Pain. No doubt it was suffering and the need to repress it in the service of human survival that was responsible for the development of the highest brain structures in the first place. These made it possible for us to have repressed Pain—and thankfully also make it possible for us to reexperience Painful events and heal.

Simply to be aware of Pain is not the same as to be conscious of it. *Awareness* does not heal. Most of us can be very aware of our past in a historical way. But we're not falling down on the floor crying and weeping about it. What is necessary is to retrieve that biologic state and reroute the Pain toward those brain structures which mediate healing. In fact, there has to be an *exact* release of the energy associated with the early trauma; no more, no less. The only way a person could know what that exact energy is would be to become totally enmeshed in the experience—to recapture the memory and the level of brain function—of that child.

Think of it as a disequilibrium or disproportion between input and output. So much has gone in, so much has to come out. Massive stimulus in childhood without a commensurate output simply leads to stored tension.

Fortunately, for all of us there was a time before Primal Pain and we have in our bodies a kind of organic memory code of what it is like to be well and grow properly. When Pain leaves the system, all of the healing forces, all of the coding processes are free to do what they normally do. That is why the return to health is so automatic after the release of Pain. We don't have to remember what it's like to be healthy and normal. The body does it for us.[2]

THE "PRIMAL ZONE"

There are definite physiological conditions which determine when this healing process can take place. One must be neither too open and flooded with Pain, nor too defensive against it. Between these extremes is the zone of healing. This is the "Primal Zone," because it is the zone in which feeling and its integration can take place.

There are many ways to reach a Primal Zone. There are some people who have already reached that zone on their own; they have the right balance between access to their Pain and the ability to integrate. But many people are so repressed, so overloaded, that they cannot possibly feel. They will be focused in the present, they will cry a bit, or even deeply, but they will not be connecting with the pains of past

---

[2] I do not neglect the value of other factors in combating neurosis, such as proper nutrition, exercise, and the like, and would hope that anyone dealing with Pain would also understand that life does not stop, and that these things are crucial. We focus on Pain because it is central to neurosis; and nutrition, in and of itself, cannot "cure" neurosis. In fact, it can bolster the body and its defense system so as to aid repression. Only for a highly disturbed person is this desirable.

life, simply because they are overwhelmed. This is particularly true if the amount of stress in their current life is also great. One can see this clearly in pre-psychotic patients who are overloaded and who cannot possibly feel, only symbolize through hallucinations and delusions. When they are given carefully measured amounts of tranquilizers, they are able to feel for the first time; that is, their suffering level has been reduced to manageable proportions.

With support and reassurance, it is possible for a patient to be successful in Primal Therapy, simply by the fact of having someone there who can calm him sufficiently. Paradoxically, most people who are very repressed *seem* to be underloaded with Pain; feeling nothing. The truth is that these people are extremely overloaded.[3]

The neurotic lives outside the Primal Zone for all of his life, never having an idea of what a feeling is. We have only to observe a session to see overload while it is happening and to see the shutdown at work when the Pain is too much. For example, a person will begin a Primal experience about something that happened in childhood and suddenly a related infancy trauma will intrude. She will spit up mucus, gag, lose her breath, and draw up into the fetal position, for a matter of seconds. She will come out of the Primal totally and into the present. A giant shock has thrust her out of the Primal Zone and back into the present. Indeed, until the patient is ready to undergo Primal Therapy on the level of early trauma, having resolved most of the lesser trauma, almost any early intrusion will produce an overload and a shutdown.

Those who are suffering too much physically, even from psychosomatic Pain, such as migraine, cannot experience a Primal. We must bring the Pain level down sufficiently so that they can feel again. So our first task, when there is a symptom such as a headache, is to bring it down to manageable proportions.

There are other people who need to discharge enough tension from the body by physical activity to be able finally to experience a connected feeling. The therapist must know when a person should work

[3] In the early days of therapy, we did not like to use tranquilizers very much, because they helped dull Pain and kept patients from making the proper connection with their feelings. But there are patients who must be tranquilized in order to make the kind of connective resolutions that will offer some final relief from the Pain. These patients, under the close supervision of the medical director, learn after a while to help in judging when the dose should be lessened. As more Pain is resolved, the need for medication gradually diminishes. The significance of the approach of Primal Therapy to medication is that it is used solely in the facilitation of the feeling and integrating process, not in the service of repression.

off tension and for how long, before directing her to a feeling. If one tries to push her to a feeling too soon, she will be overloaded. If one allows the discharge to go on too long, she will be diverted, will slip under the Zone and will not resolve the feeling.

Someone with very fast brain waves (a racing mind) is outside the Primal Zone, while if one's pulse and blood pressure are very low, one will be under it, without sufficient energy to galvanize feeling.

An exceptionally busy workday or a stressful situation like a parent's visit, a fight with a boyfriend, etc., is the kind of situation that can put somebody beyond the Primal Zone. Very often it is necessary for patients to resolve some of the present "excess" for them to be able to feel again, unless they can use some of that excess to help them down into that feeling.

People with an intact neurosis and gating structure need, in a sense, to be pushed in order to gain access to some kind of Pain. As there are those with too much access, there are those with not enough. We would never consider assaulting the defense system of someone who is already fragile and vulnerable—that would put them far over the Primal Zone. The only person who needs that kind of "bust" is the person whose repressive system is airtight.

Certain brain functions are shut down when the input is too high. Electroshock treatment, for example, causes unconsciousness; there is simply too much input.[4] Watching a horrible accident and fainting is, again, unconsciousness because of excess input. A child who views a traumatic scene represses the scene out of existence and is unconscious. That is, he may as well have been out "cold" when that event took place.

The importance of the Primal Zone is that until one falls into that zone, healing does not occur. It is in the Primal Zone that feelings are accepted and *integrated*. It is, for the neurotic, the doorway to the repressed areas of the real self. Once the real self begins to reclaim the areas lost to neurosis, the Primal Zone gradually loses its relevance.

[4] Electroshock treatment puts someone far beyond the Primal Zone and it usually takes years of Primal Therapy before patients begin reliving those shock experiences.

3: Primal Therapy

PSYCHOTHERAPY usually proceeds with a diagnosis of the patient. In my days as a conventional therapist, I would interview a patient for an hour or two, administer a battery of psychological tests, and then come up with a diagnosis . . . obsessive-compulsive, hysteric, character disorder with poor impulsive control, passive-aggressive personality, and on and on. There was little relationship between the diagnosis and the kind of therapy received. It was pretty much the same for everyone: a quantity of insights laced with exhortations, advice, and analysis of behavior. Though the diagnosis could often be precise, no one got well.

The conventional approach to diagnosis is not very useful, both because the disease is the same in everyone and because everyone suffering from the disease is different. Elsewhere in medicine there is a real need for diagnosis. There are different disease syndromes; a bacterial infection is not the same as a viral one. In Primal Therapy there is no psychological diagnosis as such. We are faced with *only one* disease, neurosis, manifested in different ways. We know that, though each of us is unique in our particular neurosis, need and Pain are pretty much universal in character. New patients from almost every country in the world are often struck by this when they first enter group.

The usual diagnostic categories are of little use since they are simply descriptions of the differing ways individuals have found to deal with their Pain. The rapist, for example, may be called someone with "poor impulse control," which is obvious in any case, and says nothing about what the impulses really are. We have found that rapists are not suffering from poor control over *sexual* impulses, but from incredible early traumas that often have nothing to do with sex.

THREE LEVELS OF CONSCIOUSNESS: ACCESS TO PAIN

Because the aim of Primal Therapy is to get under the lid of repression and gain access to lower level imprinted traumas, diagnosis is not made of behavior but rather of the amount of access a person has to his inner life or his subconscious. This gives us a measure of the state of repression, the degree of his neurosis, the adequacy of his defenses, and the prognosis for his therapy. Diagnosis in this sense has both a psychological and neurobiologic significance, since access to feelings is a biologic state, and a measurable one, as we shall see.

Our years of observation of patients reliving various aspects of their infancy and childhood has allowed us to develop a concept about the nature of consciousness. We have found that there are three central levels of consciousness in operation at all times. What is most helpful in understanding a patient is to determine the amount of access he has to each of these levels. This approach allows us to understand how Pain and its defenses are organized and how deeply the patient has access to himself. From there we can decide what approach to take with each person.[1]

These levels are intellectual, emotional, and visceral. The deepest and earliest Pain is organized on the visceral level. Early childhood events are registered on an emotional level; years later, the intellectual level comes into play. Defenses on the intellectual level involve the use of thoughts, words, ideas, symbols, statistics, and concepts. The intellectual lives in this symbolic, abstract world and handles Pain intellectually.

The person with emotional access tends to be volatile, affective, open to his dream life and nightmares, and can cry.

The person with access to the deepest levels of consciousness is often very disturbed, pre-psychotic. Her early Pain may constantly intrude into consciousness. This intrusion prevents any kind of intellectual cohesion. Someone with premature access to very deep Pain is often awash in agony because her access is far too great for her own good.

[1] See chapter 3, "The Folds of Consciousness" in part III for more detailed discussion of the various levels of consciousness.

THE WAY IN

The process of Primal Therapy is one of triggering feelings while holding back defenses and that is why the initial reaction is one of suffering. We do not take defenses away—we simply render them inoperative so that a person can have access to himself.

Dismantling the defenses is not dismantling the way someone lives or behaves. Rather, it is finding a way through their struggle and into their feelings. Once that has begun, defenses automatically crumble. Spotting and disarming secondary defenses is the most subtle and difficult aspect of Primal Therapy. Some defenses "look" like feelings, and someone can act so rationally that he does not appear defensive at all.

The more a person feels, the more the relationship between feeling and repression changes in a healthy direction. In the neurotic the tendency to repress is stronger than the tendency to feel. The person who opens up to himself experiences the opposite. Placing emotions in context allows a person to stop his acting out. Many patients who begin therapy have been crying for some time before they arrive. They are so overwhelmed by past Pain that they cannot focus on any one thing. These patients are not necessarily feeling. For them, crying is often a defense or a discharge of tension. Our job is to help the patient focus that crying and give it its Primal context. We are not after the emotion, because that is already present; we are, however, attempting to place that emotion within past scenes which might have caused it.[2]

The process of Primal Therapy is one of taking current symbolic behavior and thought ("I don't have to tell anyone where I'm going") and placing it in context ("Momma, I'm not going to tell you where I'm going every minute of my life"). The behavior is not always that simple and direct, but the feelings are. We do not get mired in symbols. We concentrate on their sources.

Feelings need to be precise, not simply a release of cathartic energy. It is easy to fall into abreaction. A patient may learn to flee into his

[2] It is not always necessary to relive scenes or specific events. Sometimes the Primal feeling in itself is enough—that too is a historic memory, an outgrowth of a lifetime of experience. The scene is a means for unlocking a blocked feeling. It is not an end in itself.

body at the first sight of a childhood Pain. He may writhe and thrash in apparent infantile agony because it is easier to do that than feel what the Pain from the later childhood really is.

Defenses can also work in the other direction. The patient can begin to verbalize feelings about traumas which predated the use of words.

All of our therapeutic interventions are utilized in the service of feeling, not repression. If a therapist has a need to be the kind, warm Daddy to his patients so that he can get their love, he's going to be kind and warm in the wrong way and keep the patients repressed, hence, neurotic.

Someone used to acting on orders, not feelings, someone whose reference points are external rather than internal, has to be reoriented to listen to her *self* rather than to others. Her defense is taking orders and meekly doing what she is told. This kind of patient might need to become a "pain in the ass," that is, to show her feelings, irritations, unhappiness, and hurts. However, to offer her insights may make her more neurotic, because it reinforces her passive acceptance of things.

One patient never *stopped* complaining from the day he set foot in the Institute; his defense was blocked and then he had the feeling—he had been bothered all his life by Pains from before the time he could speak. He complained about this and that because he had a nagging Pain that needed a focus. When he connected to the real cause of his problem (he was constantly teased in his playpen by an older brother) he stopped being a complainer. We didn't deal with the *content* of the complaints, even though he was probably right about some of them. For every complaint we would have solved for him, he would have come up with yet another one. The early nagging Pain kept the complaints alive. The complaining syndrome was a constant symbolic reminder of something unresolved.

When the unreal symbolic self cannot do its job, Pain ensues—often, to the advantage of feeling. I remember having all the people who talked very loudly, speak softly, and all the people who spoke very softly, speak very loudly in group therapy one time. It was amazing how many were brought to their Pain immediately, because the style of speech, whether aggressive and loud or soft and timid, is part of the defense system.

After two to three weeks of individual therapy, the patient enters the Primal group. A Primal group is like no other group extant. It is almost indescribable in its intensity. First and foremost it is not an encounter session. Patients come in and relate to themselves—to their past and their Pain. Therapists work with several patients individually who are there not to get something from others, but to find themselves.

It is a very personal experience even when undergone conjointly with sixty other patients.

How long does this therapy take? It is still relatively short, but not as brief as we originally thought. Patients stay between one and two years, averaging thirteen to sixteen months. After that they continue to Primal on their own. Primals usually begin to taper off at some point and then continue to diminish in frequency, although they can still be quite intense. Important progress is often achieved even after two to three years after leaving therapy.

The rate at which a person advances into his feelings is individual and there is no correct timetable. Patients understand that the more they feel now, the less they will have to feel later on.

Even though the patient is feeling Pain continuously, he is also comforted by it because he knows that it is hell to be in the dark for a lifetime in the face of continual migraines, asthma attacks, or phobias. It is a hell to be an insomniac for most of one's life, to be constantly tired at work and never sleep well. It is torture each day to wake up depressed, frightened, or anxious and not know why.

After twelve years of observation and contact with the earliest Primal patients, it seems to me that change goes on and on and does not stop. *Feeling becomes a way of life,* although that does not mean that one lives to feel Pain.

The process of opening up to Pain is not a "smooth ride." There are ups and downs, plateaus, times when no feelings happen and other times when they are excruciating. It is not an easy process.

Opening up to Primal Pain is an all-or-nothing process. If you open yourself up to early childhood traumas and then try to shut down again abruptly, the price to be paid is continued neurosis. Sometimes it's worse to open up and then stop and not feel at all because access, once achieved, permits the constant seepage of Pain upward. This drives the person to seek out more desperate measures to hold down his Pain. In that sense, feeling is not simply a matter of therapy but a way of life.

Defenses begin to dissolve in Primal Therapy but some remain to the extent that there is unresolved Pain. There are still the ordinary coping mechanisms left to handle daily stress and one can still repress when current events are catastrophic. But there is no need for neurotic defenses any longer since they emerged with the onset of Pain and served only to hold it back.

Therapy does not teach patients to wallow in Pain. It is not a masochistic approach. Rather, the Pain is the way out of the misery. It is embraced in order to get on with living, not as an end in itself.

4: Return to the Scene

THE TRAUMAS that occur when the system is at its most delicate, in the earliest months of life, are the springboards to later neurosis. Rather than Painful events building to a particular breaking point in middle childhood, a split occurs at the first instance of overload. Subsequent Primal traumas serve to widen the division.

Remembered scenes, in themselves, are not so important as the feelings that tie them together. Being sent to nursery school all alone at the age of three, to sit unmothered for eight hours, is not only a key scene, it expresses a relationship between mother and child that already has a history. The feelings of rejection may already be there but not yet crystallized.

Indeed, when the feelings of rejection start to become crystallized, the child shuts off even more and becomes "Primally dumb." He doesn't understand, because understanding brings with it such agony. From then on, he fails to understand a great deal about his life because anything that makes him more conscious of what is going on is going to end in misery.

Feeling ties all the Primal scenes together. That is why reexperiencing one key scene with its feeling calls up many associated scenes. As Jack said:

"Little things began to make me cry. A word or phrase, music, a picture, thoughts, all would make me feel. Often, one memory would lead to another, linked by the same feeling, and I'd experience several events successively, all joined by a common feeling."

The consistency in parental attitude and behavior toward the children assure that there will be many similar scenes over the years. The scenes may have changed, but the parents remained the same. An impatient parent or a demanding one doesn't suddenly become patient or undemanding.

In a session a patient began crying about her boyfriend, who was beginning to feel distant and to talk about possibly breaking up. She was in considerable Pain, feeling that he might go. Her reaction might seem appropriate enough, and not necessarily neurotic. The patient began rocking back and forth as she cried out for her boyfriend not to leave. As time went on, the rocking continued and she began crying in greater agony, "I don't want to die. Don't let me die!" She started to relive being sent away to her stepfather's house when her mother remarried and could no longer take care of her. She had to rock herself to sleep every night for years. Back then she wasn't aware of the terror that she was going to die. She only felt terrified and the rocking eased her tension.

This reexperience of an early event helped her understand and be rid of an obsession that her boyfriend would be taken from her. She had the insight that her boyfriend, someone who loved her, was equivalent in her mind to her mother, the loss of whom had made her feel like dying. Her obsessiveness and possessiveness with her boyfriend had been, in fact, the exact reason why he was feeling put off by her. He was beginning to tire of her dependence. She needed to know where he was every minute. He had to account for his every action when he was away from her. Thus, in dialectic fashion, her possessive neurosis was going to be just the thing that would prevent her from getting what she needed in the present.

She acted out an old Pain symbolically. The possible loss of a loved one in the present was unconsciously equated in her mind with the catastrophic loss of the mother early in life. The current loss was the first link in a chain of Pain going back years to connect with an unresolved Primal Pain. It was the force of the old loss threatening to become conscious that made her feel as though she were going to die whenever her boyfriend was gone for more than three hours. Once she had experienced the Primal Pain, she could recognize how that early, shattering experience drove her to be overneedy and clinging throughout her life. That reexperience opened up her consciousness and lessened her defenses so that she could understand her possessiveness instead of denying it vehemently whenever her boyfriend brought it up. "After all," she would always argue, "isn't it real to worry about someone you love? Would it be better that I didn't care at all?" She changed fear and terror into caring. Of course, if she had been loved and been close to her parents early in life, she would have had a better chance for love in the present.

The patient traveled from the present to the early source of her neurosis via feeling, which connected present to past. Its reexperience helped her distinguish between and clarify the two. She discovered the logic of feelings and how they can alter old perceptions. They clarify, make sense, and relate the most disparate of events. They lock into place the origins of misperceptions.

In the case of the woman just cited, the catastrophic loss had already occurred. The feeling was already there. A current event simply unhinged it. The unconscious meaning, that *feeling* of loss and of terrible aloneness, bound together into an integrated whole all the times when loss occurred during childhood, and all the ways she found to overcome it. That is why feeling creates a literal explosion of associations with it.

For most of us, each later event in life is given a Primal meaning by the stored feelings that envelop the event. When certain sections of the memory storage bank, the hippocampus, are removed through surgery, old feelings that could make sense out of new events are lost. The surgical patients become amnesiac, they can learn new skills, but they forget anything that is more than a few hours old. What is more important, they have a continuous feeling of being disoriented, as if in a dream. In other words, the kinds of past feelings that would offer a frame of reference for new events seem to be missing in these people. In neurosis, when the past is disengaged from the present, the person also loses real meaning and a proper frame of reference for his current life. Maria's plight is an example:

"I was an abused child. Because my home life was so terrible, I found refuge in school, in books, and in music. I was a brilliant student and I am also gifted musically. My voice, which the critics later said was 'one in twenty million,' was discovered by me when I was twelve years old and for four years it made me very happy to sing. When I was sixteen, however, I became unable to sing in my 'real' voice in front of anyone. But the 'bad' voice was good enough for others to hear and it led me to having a successful operatic career.

"When my husband deserted us—myself and two infant children—I gave up my singing career. I was relieved to do this because it was a hellish and joyless life for me. I didn't want to sing unless I could use the 'real' voice.

"At one particularly painful therapy session I was crying and saying, 'I can't stand it . . . I can't stand it . . . it's too much . . . it's too much.' Like a lightning flash, a memory came, of my mother slamming down the piano cover and telling me, 'That's it . . . no more piano for a week!' I was six years old at the time. In my home I was punished for breathing too loudly. The punishments always outweighed the crimes . . . I somehow tolerated severe beatings and my books being thrown into the furnace, but to take the piano away from me was too much. Later, I remembered going into my bedroom and saying to myself, 'I know what I'll do . . . I'll pretend I don't like it so much so my mother can't use it to punish me anymore.' That decision continued for me for the next four years and I can remember many times pretending not to care about something when I did care so that the person couldn't 'hurt' me with such a weapon."

In Primal Therapy we allow a patient to descend the chain of Pain so as to retrieve real meaning. It can start with a feeling or need, "I don't have any freedom in my marriage." Or, "There is no space for me; my children are always underfoot." It might then pass into a feeling of having nowhere for oneself at home, and then continue on to, "I have a cramped feeling. I don't know what it is but I feel totally restricted," leading to a birth experience. The early feeling of restriction and the projected need for constant freedom become fixed responses to similar situations throughout life and lead to unreal attitudes which can threaten a marriage. Feeling the context of attitudes changes them radically, allowing one to perceive marriage differently. The relationship takes on a new meaning.

When a person who feels worthless enters conventional therapy, the concentration may well be on learning to be more demanding. He may be encouraged to call the waitress over, to assert himself so that he can feel worthwhile. This effort is both misdirected and useless. There is no doubt he could be encouraged enough to overcome his fear of waitresses by acting important. ("You're just as important as anyone else in the restaurant and that is what you must tell yourself.") But you cannot, by mental tricks, overcome something that is in your physiology. It will hibernate within that physiology until another situation brings it into the open. *You do not overcome need.*

At bottom, the descent to the chain of Pain leads to Primal needs. It is in feeling needs that resolution takes place and only then. One can pound walls, scream, rant and rave and never resolve anything even when one imagines oneself to be focused in the past. Rage is such an overpowering reaction that it seems to be basic or fundamental. In itself, it is neither. Ventilating anger may be an important first step.

But one must take care to understand the order of things; first came need, then came the frustration reaction to unfulfilled need, and then came anger or fury. It is in reverse order that all of that is resolved. Nothing else is resolving; neither screaming or yelling "Momma!" at the top of one's lungs. These behaviors have nothing directly to do with need.

That is why this is not and never has been "Primal *Scream*" therapy. People often scream when they get down to that basic unfulfilled need, but screaming out of context is useless. One doesn't scream in order to feel; one screams because one has been brought in touch with a painful memory. It is never an exercise on its own. The curative aspect is the connection and the memory. However, the sudden gush of energy in a scream or cry that comes from connection to Pain has its function; it liberates the trapped energy associated with the repressed feeling. But in those groups who have had simulated Primals with screaming and no feeling, there are no basic physiologic changes. So screaming, although an obvious release of pent-up energy, is not sufficient to bring true lasting relief. *I can't stress this point enough.* What is resolving, what helps one feel again is the total meaningful experience. The reexperience of Pain is the ultimate answer to the power of neurosis.

5: Insight and Change

INSIGHTS are neural messages—circuits of connection between the storage site of a feeling in the unconscious and another site producing conscious awareness. Insight is the final recognition of the unconscious —the thought, emanating from feelings, which expresses the comprehension of those feelings.

The understanding and comprehension of feelings came millions of years later in evolution than feeling itself. Insights and feelings reflect two entirely different levels of neural organization. The neurologic difference between insights and feelings is precisely why you cannot analyze or think yourself well. Just to know that "this is something having to do with my father" or "I know that the reason I am so compulsive is because of this or that" can never make a profound change. Thoughts about feelings can do nothing to bring about profound change unless they emanate from those feelings.

To offer anyone insights as a substitute for their own feelings is a wasted gesture. Thus, psychoanalysis puts the neurologic cart before the horse. And, of course, the fact that the insight comes out of *someone else's* feeling makes it doubly erroneous, since the insights are most likely to be something idiosyncratic to the therapist rather than the patient. Thus, understanding as part of insight therapy is just another more refined part of the intellectual defense system.

Neurosis is not driven by "unconscious insights," and insights per se will never change neurosis. The only reason for an insight is that it illuminates previously unconscious motivation. Clearly, until one lays bare the unconscious, "insights" are meaningless. It is not an insight that is unconscious but rather feelings that make us act in nonconscious ways.

When a patient *feels* how he was manipulated by his mother—a manipulation of which he was unconscious—he may then have insights about how he gets involved with women who control and manipulate him and tell him what to do. The feeling that is now conscious makes clear all of his previous behavior with any number of women. This clarity is an insight. Once someone has had a deep feeling, the insights that result are solidly his own. They are not a psychoanalyst's idea of his behavior. They are explanations that arise from the self, and now describe all of the previously rerouted and symbolic behaviors based on that hidden feeling. Clearly insights must always come from inside and not from anyone else. In fact, everything a patient is going to learn in his therapy already is inside him, waiting to come out.

Feeling "want me, Momma," for example, clarifies all of the previous ploys the person has used to try to get others to want him or her. As one woman said: "I pushed my mother away because it wasn't me she cared for. It was her dream picture of me. She saw me as her little puppet doll. I had no choice but to push away the one thing that I needed and wanted more than anything."

For another woman, insight was sudden and unexpected: "Once I was standing near a group of people at a party, feeling insecure and alone, when I heard their conversation turn to a subject I felt strongly about. I joined the conversation and began talking emphatically. Suddenly in a flash I *saw* what I was doing. I was struggling for these people's recognition and approval as I had struggled for my father's, by showing off my intelligence, arguing in an aggressive way. The only times I can remember getting attention and praise from my father were when I argued this way, looked attractive, worked hard, or performed well academically. At the same time I realized that instead of gaining their approval I was intimidating and alienating them, that hostility was more likely to be my return than warmth. I stopped in the middle of my sentence, and have rarely gotten caught up in that struggle since that day."

Animals do not have insights about themselves, yet their behavior changes according to their experience. A change in their environment changes their behavior, anatomy, and physiology. They don't need insights for that change. The development of the cortex in human beings allows us to understand our motivations and to probe the reasons for our behavior; but these insights themselves are not responsible for changes. Insights come to us developmentally in terms of how the brain was laid down in the first place. First, we have a sensation, then emotional experience of that sensation, and finally an understanding of that emotional experience. It is not possible to reverse that evolutionary development to bring about change. In one sense we are really talking about three different brains in one skull, even though they are highly interwoven.

Because insights are the handmaidens of feelings, it follows that the deeper the feeling felt, the more profound the insight. There are levels of insights just as there are levels of feelings. When a feeling has been buried deep in the brain since birth, it is so sequestered that it is nearly impossible to find the causes of later symptoms and behavior linked to it. It is impossible even to guess since, for the most part, these memories are memories of the body. They are imprinted into the system long before the use of words and images—which are, therefore, no aid in recall. The only way to find the connection between present and past is to feel that early feeling physically. The insights which result are profound because adult behavior and symptoms, such as colitis and ulcers, are finally seen as determined by infantile events, the kind of events heretofore inaccessible.

Who could guess that a migraine appears whenever a current stress triggers off a physical memory of pressure on the head at birth? I had been in conventional psychological practice for seventeen years and seen many patients with disabling headaches. It was beyond my imagination to make a link between birth trauma and migraine. Yet, numerous Primal patients have made that connection. Who could guess that suppressed rage, in a patient thirty years old, was the cause of her neck and back aches; and that the rage came from incredible frustration due to her long, hard birth. Even knowing that to be a fact, the insight itself is useless without the reexperience. *There isn't an insight in the world that can change neurosis because there is no mental activity that can alter a physiologically imprinted experience.* Awareness doesn't reach down and retrieve our earliest life experience. Those experiences rise, so to speak, to educate awareness.

The lifting of repression and its thoughts allows for the emergence of the self that should have been, the genetically programmed self that has been aborted in its development. The evidence we see of this is in the fact that some patients' jaws have returned to their old shape even after a great deal of orthodontic work has been done, and wisdom teeth come through even in the later thirties in some patients. Other patients have noticed growth in the size of their feet and breasts in later age.

As we shall see later, the recapture of the real self is a biochemical, neuroelectric occurrence in which the body changes in its structure and physiology as the split is healed.

Recapturing the real self also has its psychological effects. It means to be gentle again, to be kind and generous. To be all those things that the little girl or boy should have been but never could be.

Recapturing the real self means to recapture some of that early beauty that was our birthright. Children are much prettier than adults. Beauty has a great deal to do with being natural. When the unnatural self twists our face and our posture, when it compresses our lips, squints our eyes, furrows the brow, it means that neurosis has robbed us of our beauty. It is the unreal self that has become paranoid, suspicious, skeptical, cynical, and misshapen.

But there are more changes than the merely physical. As the system gives up its Pain, there is less unconscious motivation, allowing the person to make new choices. The sequence might be as follows: "I've had my feeling, now I'm aware of what I've been doing and it's getting me nowhere. I won't do that anymore because it feels crazy. I don't have to do it anymore. So I'm going to do this instead."

With the retrieval of the self one is more conscious, more in control and more human. Humanity progresses with the Pain because repression made us inhuman in some ways. Not deliberately inhuman, but unconsciously so. We may do terrible things to our children and friends out of that unconsciousness while abhorring cruelty. We are inhuman to the extent that we cannot feel.

One of the universal characteristics of neurotic people is their inability to change in spite of themselves. Neurosis is essentially stagnant, making behavior consistent in its miserable predictability. It's as if one were in a car with one's foot on the gas pedal but without putting the car in gear. One goes nowhere with great determination. Allowing feeling back into our lives by experiencing the obstructed and obstructing Pains of our early history brings back the ability to change, to move and, most importantly, to grow. Pain stunted our growth at every level from physical through emotional to the social. Feeling permits growth to begin again sometimes precisely where it left off.

When we speak of "cure" in Primal Therapy, we are saying only that we enable people to resolve those unconscious generating forces which produce neurotic behavior. The disease is repression and blocked access. A patient gains access to herself; that is the cure.

One patient expressed it this way:

"It occurred to me the other day that the past was a series of gaps where I hadn't experienced, where I had repressed, and what I was doing now was filling in those gaps and bringing them to the surface so that I could leave the past in the past, so that I wasn't dragging it around with me."

A person who is able to feel doesn't become the complete opposite of what he used to be, as a personality, but he can change radically in those areas which had been most affected by his Pain. If he could never organize himself because he was shattered by Pain, then in the absence of that Pain he will be more competent. If he were hyperproductive before, driven by Pain, he is going to have far less drive. If he had no drive because of Pain, if passivity was his defense, he may be much more productive. *There is no rule about what patients become.* It all depends on their previous defenses.

Can people really be transformed by feeling? If they can be transformed by *not* feeling, then they can also be by feeling. If a sweet, naïve, trusting child can be transformed into a suspicious, angry, bitter, cynical adult neurotic, then there is evidence of a great change.

We have found that the process of getting well is just like that of neurosis. It is slow, continuous, unconscious, and inevitable. *I have not seen it happen that a person continued to feel and did not get well.* There are only two things that can keep it from happening: If the person experiences catharsis under the delusion that he is feeling, or if the person stops in the middle of his feeling experience and leaves many serious feelings and needs unfelt. Feelings and neurosis are antithetical. You are either feeling or neurotic, there is no neutral ground.

Freedom comes with a full recognition and experience of need. Without that recognition freedom can only be symbolic. Because you know what you really need, you know finally what is right for you. Once you know who you are, you don't require any convincing about what to wear, where to go, how to act, and so on.

Before therapy one man continued to move from one house to another, each time wanting a bigger place. He liked "space." He thought that he had the ultimate freedom because he had no fears about uprooting himself and moving every year; it was simply a matter of choosing the place. In Primal Therapy he felt the feeling of having a small house all of his early life, always being cramped and alone. Unconsciously he wanted a big house to make up for his past, but, more importantly, the fantasy was that a big house would bring friends. He eded friends so that he wouldn't feel alone (in the past). Only he didn't know that until he felt. After that he didn't need the "freedom" of moving every year.

Before therapy Elizabeth had to have one man after another. She thought she liked the freedom of playing around. In Primal Therapy she realized her great need for a father she had never had. Yet what she thought was freedom was truly constriction; she had no choice but to have many men until she felt her real need. Then she could settle on one person whom she could love deeply. Another patient recalls:

"When I started having relationships with men after I left home there was one type that I would pick. It would be someone who was weaker than myself and someone that I could control, totally—well, not totally, but someone who was not in control of me. They were always very unsatisfactory relationships because it worked out in the end with me being in charge of everything, doing everything, running our lives. It was more like having a child than a companion. That was just because I was so afraid of my father. There was always the quality of me being stronger and smarter, just as a person. If there was something that came up in conversation I would always win, and I had to pick that kind of weak man so I wouldn't feel afraid.

"I could never be attracted to someone who frightened me, and I was frightened of most men. I had to have them and once I had them I would start needing those other things. I would need someone who was my companion rather than my baby. That gets kind of tiring even though I sort of set the situations up for myself and got myself into them. But I would start wanting more. The relationship would always deteriorate because I would start trying to move the person into what I wanted, and of course that never worked because they had their limitations as people and I couldn't make them be what they weren't. Usually it would end with me telling them I didn't want to be with them anymore. Those bad relationships I went through were painful . . . but with each one I progressed, because each time I picked someone who was more like the person I wanted to be around. The reason I was able to start picking men who were worth being around was because I started feeling my feelings about my father. That started me being less afraid of men that I would be around in the present."

The automatic change for this patient was total. There was no longer the fear in her eyes, posture, and gait. The fear stored as a physical memory had physiologic and anatomic effects. Certainly, no one can "try" to have a hormonal change. It is an outcome of the decoding of systemic memory.

Restoring feeling produces changes on all levels. It normalizes the hormone output so that the body changes and actual physical growth occurs.[1] It lowers the tension level so that a person can think straight again; can concentrate and focus his attention for longer periods of time. Restoration of feeling usually means change in one's social outlook. It can mean knowing more instinctively what to do with children. It often results in one becoming healthier physically, sleeping and eating better, eating more of the right kind of food and in the right amounts. A person doesn't have to be stuffing back feelings with food. When there is no longer a great reservoir of Pain to be quelled, he is no longer doomed to a cycle of stimulating and tranquilizing himself day and night in order to function.

Where does the energy of neurotic tension go after Primal Therapy? The excess energy trapped in the circuits of the brain actually leaves the system as a result of the connection of stored Pain to consciousness. When one's system is no longer galvanized into action against an inner threat one can finally rest. This energy transformation can be measured rather precisely.

If we understand the roots of excess energy, then it becomes clear that no method other than interneural connection can be resolving. Physical manipulation can help temporarily discharge overflows of captivated energy. But dealing with effects does not change causes. If we continuously attempt to block muscle outlets for tension, the energy will have to find other routes. It may well go deeper into the body, affecting the viscera, and result in psychosomatic afflictions. It may take a long time before the symptom occurs, and by the time it does it may not be obvious anymore that it is the result of rerouted muscle tension.

Whether energy is bound into belief systems or muscle systems is of little consequence; beliefs and tensions are still *effects*. And they are both physical effects. Beliefs don't somehow hover above the brain. They are manifestations of the brain in action. One can manipulate ideas and the muscles but one cannot manipulate stored memory. Consciousness is the only freedom.

Being real on all levels means being intelligent. There are levels of intelligence and when a person has access to those levels, he can use all of his brain for living. There is an old myth that we only use ten percent of our brain power, that we really could achieve much more if we tried. Exactly the opposite is true. Our research suggests that we

[1] See part IV, chapter 2, "Measuring Sickness and Health."

use far *too much* of our brains.[2] The neurotic's brain is overused in the service of repression. After Primal Therapy, brainwave activity is *radically reduced*. A truly healthy person, therefore, would use less of his brain, not more. Let us put to rest the "ten percent" myth. We actually use too much of the brain's power to achieve only ten percent of its potential.

Slowing down of brain activity in Primal patients has several implications; with fewer unconscious forces intruding to distort judgment, one can be more reflective, less rash and less rigid in approach. Judgment is knowing what is both appropriate and good for you. Less of a Primal backlog will tend to better judgment. One can select alternatives in life. When the mind is not racing from an overload of Pain, it is possible to remember and retain. The same is true for the ability to concentrate. Take away all that Primal background noise and one can focus and retain that focus. Poor judgment puts one at the mercy of unconscious needs and forces. Feeling what is unconscious, then, makes one far more intelligent. If you can lead your life to do what is in your best interest, it is a measure of your intelligence.

The neurotic has compartmentalized intelligence. He can be deceived by the most obvious ploys, such as weekend miracle cures and mystical notions; and, above all, by others who can pressure him. He can be conned by praise if he is desperate and may never see that he is being deceived. By contrast, someone with an interconnected intelligence perceives and uses facts in order to better his life, not as intellectual weapons. He has an instinctual intelligence that allows him to see through insincerity, false promises, and political charm. His intelligence permits him to see the connections of things so that he doesn't operate simply on what he is told.

Part of the renewal of intelligence we see is that of simple logic. Someone who understands her feelings is a most logical, uncomplicated person to know. Her judgment and intuition are rarely deceived. A feeling person has an inbuilt logic that helps her understand not only her own behavior but that of others as well.

Release from the demands of old needs means that a person is not going to be argumentative if he isn't protecting a feeling with an idea. The neurotic converts feeling into ideas and then has a Primal stake in those ideas. He defends them because they defend him. Someone with no such stake is easy to be with. He doesn't try to make anyone believe what he believes because he doesn't need a reinforcement of his own reality.

This "letting others be" isn't just an attitude or pose because neu-

[2] See part IV, chapter 2, "Measuring Sickness and Health."

rotics can try to let others be. The problem is that the very fact of their existence, the kind of people they are, can prevent someone else from being themselves. Someone who is grim is not the kind of person you joke around. Someone who is overly intellectual is not someone to whom you let your feelings show. It doesn't matter what they say. It matters who they are. We have all had the experience of going to dinner with the kind of people we could not relax with. What we really mean is that their formality, or whatever, did not allow us to be ourselves. That is the position so many children are in every minute of their lives. They live with parents who by fiat of their existence cannot allow children to be what they are.

Disappointment or disillusionment is almost a constant in neurotics. It is the handmaiden of having unreal expectations, of wanting people to act like a parent, of thinking that symbolic achievements will truly be rewarding. So long as one needs, one must fantasize. Those fantasies form the basis for adult disillusionment because no one is coming to treat you in the way you need to be treated. There is no magic, especially in a world where nearly everyone is in Pain and is deprived.

The reason so many people are let down in marriage and do not meet their partner's needs is that they are unconsciously still children who imagine (also unconsciously) that no matter how they act or what they do the partner (parent) will love them. They are shocked when the spouse wants to leave or end the relationship. They cannot imagine that they did anything to provoke this. They are bitter and angry because they are still the needing children abandoned by someone who should love them.

The husband or wife who neglects their body, who dresses slovenly, or who acts ill-manneredly has made an unconscious pact with themselves . . . I will be loved no matter what I do. In a dialectic irony, they need so much that they end up with nothing.

Of course, the partners can be relatively good mates and still be disappointing to each other. If you feel unloved from your childhood, you'll need the constant assurance of love in the present to hold down that feeling. No one can fill that void.

Another disappointment is that the partner did not "make me feel like a woman, or a man." As if anyone could do that. In a sense, they don't want an equal relationship. The woman wants a "man" to take charge, to be aggressive and to handle problems. She needs him to dominate and be strong; *that* will make her feel like a woman, she thinks. In reality, what she wants is a daddy who will make her feel not like a woman but a child. And the husband or man in a relationship wants the woman to support him, to flatter, be attentive, caring, protective, kind; to cook his meals on time, to sew his clothes, and even pick out his wardrobe. He too wants a parent but doesn't know it. All of those activities won't make him feel like a man, even though he thinks they will. They will keep him the child. He wants everything he didn't get from his mother. If he had gotten them, he would not expect all of that from a wife or mate, who, after all, is not a parent.

What makes anyone feel like what they are is to be allowed to be themselves. If you are allowed to be yourself as a child, no matter who allows it, you will be masculine if you are a boy. You won't need to "identify" with a man, that is, to imitate manly things. You will be exactly what you are. Fulfillment of need is what does it, not "identification."

If you've never had all of yourself, never had important needs fulfilled, you will interpret or manipulate events so as to reflect on you and your needs. Consequently, most neurotics are narcissistic by definition. It is a way of "fulfilling" a damaged and deprived self. The neurotic must be self-referent. He gives in order to get. He cannot truly listen and empathize when he needs to get something out of every situation. He would be hard pressed to transcend his need and concentrate unselfishly on someone else. He cannot get beyond the self he does not have.

Most neurotics want to believe in magic. They want to believe that there is some magic diet, clinic, or approach that will change them totally without any effort on their part. The reason is that their whole lives are run by unseen, "magical," unconscious forces. Their behavior is dictated by this magic so it is no wonder that they assume that change can come about just as magically. The unconscious is truly a magical place for most people . . . they have no idea what is "down" there. Every major therapy and every major philosophy for centuries has been based on the fact that man is inherently evil and must control what is inside him. His unconscious, it has been believed, is populated by one kind of demon or another. The most skeptical neurotic can be taken in when his needs, his unconscious feelings are involved.

Much of what I said in *The Primal Scream* about relationships to parents still holds true. When one has resolved his Primal anger, resentment, and need, a person may see that parents are limited by their neurosis and that they often did the best they knew how under those limitations. He probably understands that parents are just people who need. It is unfortunate that they had children they could not give to. That is the tragedy; they produced people who need, yet the reason they were produced was to fulfill the parents' need. The clash was built in before the fetus saw the light of day.

Primal people no longer try to convert their parents to what they need when they know that is a lost cause. They can let the parents be what they are—neurotic. There's a waning urge to argue with them over their eccentricities, their fears, and their prejudices. Any compulsive attempt to change them is the old struggle. It is an effort again to make them into the good, loving, kind, strong parents they never were.

A patient recalls:

"Before I came to therapy and for a long time after I had begun, I hated both my parents. I hated them for all the things I felt they had done to me, for all the times I felt they hurt me and for each instance where I felt they had failed me. My relationship with them was, practically speaking, nonexistent. In the past two years, though, I've begun to feel much closer to them.

"I believe that's because I was able to feel all the times when I was younger when they hurt me. I'm not carrying all those feelings around inside me anymore. And because of that I'm able to relate to them in the present, rather than through a fog of old hurts and Pains. In fact, some of the more Painful feelings I have felt came up when I no longer hated them. I was able to see the ways they were good to me and the times they tried to help me. That was more Painful to me than some of the bad things that happened."

The reason it is possible to get along with parents is not just because a person "understands" their limitations. That would be of little help. It is because she has felt her childhood needs, which now allows her to be more objective. She understands them more because in Primal Therapy she has seen them exactly as they were and are, without any projections to blur the perceptions. One of the problems in the parent-child relationship, however, occurs usually because the child (who is still the "child" even though she is a mature adult) still represents some kind of fulfillment of needs to the parents. The parents are still going to try to keep her as she was or try to change her back. They are usually so fixated in their habits that they continue to expect their child to react as she always has; that is, to be what they need. It is a clash when the child no longer acts as expected. The child was able to avoid a constant clash early in his life by giving in, by becoming neurotic. Neurotics need neurotics to relate to. That applies to parents as well. They don't tolerate real people very well, even when those people are their children.

What is there after Pain is felt? Pleasure. Not the make-believe kind, but real pleasure. In order to feel true pleasure, to enjoy what you get in this world, you have to feel the Pain that stands in its way. You cannot experience it when your body is busily engaged in not feeling. It is a true pleasure to feel relaxed and comfortable. It is a pleasure to be no longer plagued by one disease after another. It is a pleasure to be able to accept love and not turn away from it. It is a pleasure not to wake up each morning with stabbing apprehension and fear. It is a pleasure to sleep at night. It is a pleasure to enjoy sex and make your body do just what you will it to do. It is a pleasure to travel away from home without phobias and fears. It is a pleasure not to suffer from inexplicable depressions which seemingly arise for no reason. It is a pleasure to be able to love your children and be loved back. It is a pleasure not to suffer compulsions that destroy your life. It is a pleasure to be you.

III: THE PHYSICAL MIND

1: Our Own Pain-killers

THE RECENT discoveries concerning endorphines indicate how extensively human behavior is dominated by the compounds that deal with Pain and repression. Endorphines are morphine-like substances, internally produced, which function as analgesics; that is, they "handle" pain. Not only are we at the mercy of our Pain, but also of those substances that are summoned up to repress it.

Endorphines have had a significant role in human development. By repressing need and Pain they help to hold down our impulses, thus permitting the storage and delay of responses until a future time. This means that time is left to contemplate, foresee, figure out, and, above all, to abstract—to imagine responses and to build a repertoire of reactions which allows us to be different from the direct stimulus-response behaviors of animals. In this sense, the endorphines are the beginning of humanity—the raison d'être of the neocortex.[1] They ultimately permit the functions of symbolization and abstraction which eventually determine new brain structure.

Endorphine output has allowed mankind to adapt and go on functioning despite the continual existence of catastrophes in the world. In a psychological sense, it allows us to "look on the bright side" because we have the wherewithal to hide our dark side.

Since the inception of the most primitive life forms, the role of the endorphines has been to withhold unpleasant sensations from awareness. This primordial action eventually allowed for the neurotic

[1] Endorphines are chiefly produced by the pituitary and the hypothalamus. They are present in other brain structures as well and deal with either the transmission or inhibition of the Pain message throughout the brain.

split in the psyche and allows one level of neural organization not to know what the other level is doing or thinking. It allowed man to function despite the continued existence of early life deprivations and traumas. In this sense, the endorphines are responsible for the origin of the unconscious, and no unconscious would have existed without it. It keeps us oblivious and permits us to deny not only the existence of unconscious Pain but the existence of the unconscious itself.

The endorphine system becomes complex (indeed many kinds of endorphines are known at the present time), turning into ever more complex systems through a perpetual interplay with the outside world. These Pain-controlling systems evolved to meet the need to avoid what was unpleasant or noxious. There are now internally produced endorphines which are one thousand times more powerful than the morphine produced commercially. This indicates the enormous power of Pain laid down in the human nervous system. It is my belief that these endorphines are exactly commensurate with the job they are required to do—that is, they indicate the depth of Pain they must deal with.

Neurotensin is a newly discovered endorphine. When you see someone in Primal agony you understand why the body has been required to produce a substance which is so much stronger than any injection of morphine. The strength of neurotensin gives us an inkling of the incredible force of Pain.[2]

The fact that the endorphines are similar in action to that of injected morphine is illustrated by the use of Naloxone, a morphine antagonist. What Naloxone does is immediately put a person in Pain; not because *it* is injurious, but because it reverses repression and allows Pain to surface. In this sense, Naloxone is an agent of consciousness. The research on endorphines strongly supports its structural similarity to morphine and indicates that Primal Pain induces the self-injection of morphine.

Almost any Pain-killer, tranquilizer, alcohol, or barbiturate shares the same mechanisms to achieve the production of endorphines. Alcohol withdrawal can be treated by tranquilizers or even heroin, while heroin withdrawal can be treated with alcohol. The name of the game is to kill the Pain. And we see how closely related any addiction is, whether to alcohol, aspirin, heroin, tranquilizers, or sleeping pills. They all do the same thing. The ultimate treatment of any addiction,

[2] Recently yet another powerful internal Pain-killer has been discovered called dynorphin. It is 700 times more powerful than enkephalin, 200 times more powerful than morphine, and 50 times more powerful than beta-endorphine. The more we are discovering the more we see that our biology is heavily oriented toward dealing with Pain, and that so much of our biochemistry is little more than analgesic compounds to keep us repressed.

therefore, must entail ridding the body of Pain—which is the reason for taking Pain-killers in the first place. Those who are "just a bit nervous," who take tranquilizers to calm themselves down, should know that *Pain* is their problem. In the end, the tranquilizers work on the Pain systems and all are in fact *analgesics.*

The Swedish pharmacologist Lars Terenius has discovered that patients suffering from emotional Pain produce *more* endorphines than those suffering from physical pain.[8] Emotional Pain is real and often physically more intense than "physical pain." Those with emotional or psychological Pain in Terenius' studies had less tolerance to physical pain. Their bodies were hyperreactive, producing more Pain suppressants. The body does not distinguish between physical and emotional pain when it comes time to process it. We feel emotionally bad when we hurt physically and we suffer physically when we are in emotional agony. We have one response to hurt no matter what the origin. That is why a great deal of physical suffering early in life—continued illness, for example, or early surgery—can result in neurosis just as surely as constant criticism and neglect can.

Even psychosomatic complaints have a basis in physical disorder, though what patients are complaining about cannot be seen with an X-ray. Physicians act as if psychosomatic Pain is real, even if they don't believe it, as demonstrated by the fact that they often give the patients tranquilizers which are little more than Pain-blockers. Even though physicians believe they are just "calming the patient's nerves," they are actually helping to depress the transmission of the Pain message through the nerve pathways.[4]

There are at least seven kinds of endorphines. Two which seem to work in opposition to each other are leucine ("leu") endorphine and methionine ("meth") endorphine. Leu-endorphine aids in the transmission of Pain. It is found in excess in psychotics; by helping transmit Pain it aids and abets the psychotic process. Meth-endorphine works in the opposite direction and has analgesic actions analogous to externally injected morphine. It "kills" (blunts) Pain. There are other key biochemical systems which work in concert with the endorphines, either to transmit or to inhibit Pain. The dopamine system may act together with leu-endorphine to turn on the limbic system and "open up" the gates to Pain. These systems release suffering. Patients with kidney problems who were receiving hemodialysis (a kind of blood purification process) transiently lost their psychotic symptoms when

[8] Delivered to the Second World Congress on Pain, Montreal, August 1978.
[4] The work of R. F. Squires in Copenhagen indicates that radio-labeled Valium "binds to highly specific opiate receptor sites" in animal brains.

leu-endorphine was removed, indicating that Pain release is critical to psychosis and that it exists in the blood as well as in the brain. In other words, it is literally possible to wash pychosis out of the bloodstream, albeit transiently. This study lends powerful evidence for the relationship between Pain and psychosis and the conclusion that "mental illness" is systemic and endures everywhere in the system.

More and more evidence indicates that early life trauma skews the balance of endorphines in one direction or another so that we either have too much or not enough of specific kinds of pain blunters. This does not mean that the answer to the imbalance is to try to readjust the chemicals themselves, which is only another more sophisticated form of symptomatic pain management, but rather to find out exactly why that imbalance develops in the first place. *The biology of the brain changes in mental illness* and it changes in characteristic ways to accommodate levels of pain.

Brain cells are capable of changing their choice of neural transmitters during early development if exposed to certain environments.[5] The implications are that the environment is constructing a certain kind of brain structure and function to deal specifically with that environment. In other words, the biochemical balance in the brain can be shifted permanently depending upon one's early life experiences. One could have too much or too little leu-endorphine or meth-endorphine. This imbalance, when prolonged and severe, can result in later psychosis. There are many more dopamine receptors, for example, in the brains of psychotics. If there is more Pain, there must be more places where it can be "received."

The clue to why schizophrenics have an excess of dopamine receptors is provided by the work of Morpurgo and Spinelli. When life is exceedingly Painful early on, it requires an excess of activating neurotransmitters to mediate that agitation. There is a greater sensitivity to any kind of stimuli and a hyperreactivity. These dopamine receptors are found in significant abundance in the forebrain area where ideas are organized, as well as in the limbic system where emotions are processed. This may explain how the paranoid psychotic will call upon ideas as a last refuge of defense. A shot of morphine will suppress this "ideation" immediately—again, offering strong evidence of the relationship of Pain to psychotic ideation.

The significance of early life trauma as it affects neurosis and psychosis is illustrated by recent experiments by Clara Torda.[6] She did a

<hr />

[5] *Science,* October 26, 1979; review by Jean Marx.
[6] Clara Torda, "Effects of Recurrent Postnatal Pain-Related Stressful Events on Opiate-Receptor Endogenous Ligan System," *Psychoneuroendocrinology,* 1978, 3, pp. 85–91.

series of experiments on rat pups and found that stressful experiences during early postnatal life resulted in a significant increase in the opiate receptor systems. It indicates that these traumas changed the structure of the brain (premature development of pain-mediating cells) and its chemistry (the amount of circulating endorphines). Early Pain adversely affects the neuromachinery and sets up the conditions for later abnormality. This implies that adult abnormal behavior can be the result of having been exposed to severe trauma during intrauterine and early postnatal life. "Emotional" stress is processed as Pain and painful experiences to these animals resulted in a brain system with a greater number of opiate receptors. Although Torda's work was done with animals and has not been proved entirely for human beings, the implications are clear. And reasoning backward, an increased number of opiate receptors in the human brain system indicates the existence of early life trauma. Perhaps that is why psychotics have twice as many dopamine receptors in their limbic systems as normal people.

Psychosis has been produced in animals (at the Albert Einstein College of Medicine) with injection of amphetamines. The animals really do act "crazy"—pacing back and forth, bobbing their heads, moving in repetitious stereotyped patterns, constantly rearing up and so on. Dopamine was found to exist in much higher levels in their brains on autopsy. What is more, these animals were conditioned with a buzzer before receiving amphetamines. Those animals who later experienced only the buzzer still had higher levels of dopamine in their brain. Psychological factors, in short, changed the animals' biochemistry just as assuredly as if they'd received injections.

Amphetamines work mainly by causing the release of noradrenaline and dopamine, activators of the brain. There is a familiar type of amphetamine psychosis found in humans brought on by the ingestion of too much "speed." Those drugs which work to facilitate the endorphine production can reverse this kind of psychosis.

The importance of biologic change in the brain resulting from early trauma is that a system can be made hyperactive by adverse events and this hyperactivity becomes imprinted, changing the brain accordingly. It can become intermixed with psychological factors to produce an aggressive, outgoing kind of personality. The aggressive personality in turn requires a greater predominance of one kind of biochemical or another and the cycle has commenced. It isn't simply that the system is agitated, it is that the brain has been converted and affects the kind of person you become.

The imprint affects the total physiology, not just the brain system alone. Thus, there may be a stamped-in tendency toward a high pulse rate and a hyperkinetic kind of behavior. This physiologic change in conjunction with certain social environments can produce high drive, high libido, and a variety of psychological concomitants such as an inability to sustain relationships due to a hyperactivated, "impatient" state. It can also result in "pushiness" and even plays an important role in ambition; for ambition, aside from its psychological components, implies a certain energy or driving motivation that pushes a person on. Such characteristics, strange as it may seem, may stem from a massive birth trauma that sets up a generalized hyperactivity. This activity could also be translated into a "fast mind," for example, the comedian with very fast quips, puns, and so on; or a hypervigilant mind, one that is very aware and, given a certain sensitivity, quite perceptive. Obviously a variety of social factors come into play in all this. Yet the underlying drive may be laid down very early in life.

Serotonin-producing cells antagonize or act as a counter force to dopamine. Serotonin closes the gates that dopamine opens. By facilitating the production of endorphines it aids in the process of repression.[7] Chronic stress lowers brain serotonin, particularly in the areas where painful memories are stored—the cortex and hippocampus.[8]

The serotonin system works in balance, in seesaw fashion, with activators such as noradrenaline and dopamine. Low serotonin and high dopamine animals are much more aggressive. Humans with low serotonin are the most anxious; or perhaps the most anxious people cause low levels of serotonin. In any case, it is becoming clear that the balance in neurotransmitters affects personality; and this balance can be altered in one direction or another by early engraved trauma. Furthermore, the traumas that produce imbalance can date from prenatal days. What has previously been seen as constitutional determinants of personality may actually be the result of trauma during pregnancy.

In the ordinary course of events the endorphine system sees to it that we do not become conscious.[9] However, with a great deal of cur-

[7] An important study at UCLA by Leibeskind documented that stimulation-induced analgesia mediated by endorphines is facilitated by serotonin. We have long hypothesized that migraine headache is due to faulty repression of Pain or, stated differently, levels of Pain which overwhelm the repressive capabilities. A recent University of Florence, Italy study by Federigo Sicuteri has found a deficiency of serotonin in the brainstem of migraine patients.

[8] It is now well established that the pain of a migraine headache is associated with a drop in L-tryptophan, the precursor of serotonin, and that giving L-tryptophan to migraine patients helps with these headaches. This is another way of saying that when the pressure of Pain exceeds its boundaries, it can move into a headache which can be reversed by chemically aiding the repressive process.

[9] Tranquilizers such as Thorazine block dopamine and so lessen obsession and agitation. One of the breakdown products of alcohol is a morphine-like sub-

rent stress it is possible that current Pains will join with stored Pains and build into a conscious experience of anxiety by overtaxing the endorphine system. If our reservoir of stored Pain is already at a high level, it doesn't take much to overwhelm the endorphine system. If the latent Primal forces are at a low level, it would take much more current Pain to bring it to an overload.

One Pain does not usually make a neurosis. It is the accumulation of many Pains that finally overtaxes the ordinary compensating mechanisms to produce permanent alterations of function—which is the chief way we know about the existence of neurosis.

Beta-endorphine, forty-eight times more potent as a Pain-killer than injected morphine, is released simultaneously with the stress hormone ACTH. The significance of this release is that they are unleashed simultaneously, *irrespective of the kind of stress*. Physical and mental stress are processed identically and can have the same effects in producing "mental illness." Beta-endorphine has been successfully used to treat the severe pain of cancer and has also been useful in the treatment of psychosis and depression.[10]

One of the ways that beta-endorphine has been produced is through a procedure of brain implants. Electrodes shoot electricity into certain areas of the brain which then stimulates the production of beta-endorphine and quenches Pain. This process helps us to understand how someone who is overloaded with Pain—electrical impulses—can appear totally "dead," feeling nothing. It is as though stored trauma constantly stimulates endogenous Pain-suppressors to keep us unfeeling.

Beta-endorphine, as well as other endorphines, regulates body temperature. Demerol, Percodan, and other related Pain-killers lower body temperature. The advanced Primal patient seems to have sufficient endorphine to deal with the reduced amount of Pain in the system, thereby permanently lowering body temperature as well.

We have all heard someone say to another person who is agitated about something, "Now just cool down!" And it seems he literally can. Endorphine-deficient individuals are hotter, having a higher body temperature. That is why acutely psychotic people nearly always have

stance. So, it seems probable that those who have insufficient biochemical gating, drink to enhance their gating systems. There is a decreased blood flow to the frontal area of the brain dealing with inhibition when one consumes alcohol. In this way alcohol decreases both the sensation and awareness of Pain. It would seem that the endorphine system continually functions at a low level to keep us unaware of our Pain and somewhat relaxed. It increases its output under stress.

[10] *Science News,* September 17, 1977, p. 182; November 25, 1978, p. 135.

an increased body temperature. This, together with the fact that they rarely have normal periods of deep sleep, suggests that the repressive-endorphine reserves are at a continuously low ebb in relation to the amount of Pain in the system. People with depleted supplies of endorphines often feel overwhelmed and futile because Pain is breaking through.[11]

If we focus on only one of the endorphines in order to find the "cause" of mental illness we shall be doomed to failure, for Pain is an *organismically encoded event* which changes the *entire* system, each subsystem in its own way. I have concentrated on the endorphines but could easily have focused on other subsystems and found significant changes. The changes are, I believe, concomitants, not causes.

Once neurosis sets in, the endorphines are engaged and the body is at war with itself. For most of one's life the Pain-repressing system wins; it is a Pyrrhic victory because this mortal combat depletes the physical resources and probably shortens life.

New kinds of endorphines are being discovered almost every month, each with a different role and function; they owe their existence to the fact of Pain. Their importance lies in the fact that they tell us the *paramount role of Pain in a wide variety of diseases*. They point to the resolution of Pain as the sine qua non of recovery and health.

[11] Recently Seymour Ehrenpreis of the Chicago Medical School has developed a drug, "DPA," which inhibits certain enzymes from breaking down endorphines. DPA brings about marked relief from Pain for up to a month following only two days of its administration. Ehrenpreis believes that the prolonged relief is the result of a long-term buildup of endorphine levels in the brain. DPA tends to develop long-term analgesia without withdrawal or addiction because it manipulates the body's own morphine system.

2: Ideas as Opiates

DEFENSES block Pain; and the way they do so is through the endorphine system. When defenses are removed, the patient is in the agony of withdrawal from his neurosis. In that sense, the neurotic is addicted to his defenses. Blocking a defense in Primal Therapy has the same effect *biochemically* of injecting the patient with the morphine antagonist, Naloxone. Both produce an immediate awareness of Pain.

The reason that the neurotic is addicted to his defenses is that they help him remain unconscious of himself and his sensations just as if he received morphine. The person in Pain does get a dose of morphine—only it is internally injected by the hypothalamic-pituitary structures. When the Pain is considerable, beta-endorphine is manufactured so that the person administers himself a whopping dose of this Pain-killer.

Certain drugs such as tranquilizers radically alter ideas. In psychotic states, for example, Pain-killers can change a bizarre thought into a fairly normal one in a matter of minutes.

The best possible tranquilizer in the world is an idea. Ideas are not *like* opiates—they *are* opiates. When someone says, "you are really good," "we care about you," or "we are behind you," these ideas are tranquilizing. They enter the brain where they pick up meaning, become transmuted into biochemical processes (no doubt of the morphine-endorphine variety), and end up suppressing Pain. Subjectively the person may not believe that he is in agony—just that those ideas make him feel a little bit better. The person who utters soothing words is usually liked and admired—indeed, he is the "fix." One can become addicted to that person in exactly the same way that one becomes addicted to any substance that effectively kills Pain. The person, his comfort, warmth, the hope he offers and *his ideas* all ultimately become a physical analgesic.

Any idea that seems to fulfill need operates as a tranquilizer to quell subconscious Pain. If someone says to someone else "you are utterly incapable," "you're really all alone in the world and there's no one to care about you" the exact opposite is obtained. Stored Pain and need are triggered off toward the surface and a person becomes acutely aware of his suffering. To hear praise is not only music to the ears but chemicals to the brain.

Praise and encouragement become rather precise biochemical instruments. That is the appeal of est and other approaches. They speak to unmet need. Those glorious words of succor function just as if the therapist had injected patients with morphine. He *has* injected them but it is rather circuitous; the idea sets off a process that eventually results in production of endorphine. People don't want to hear the truth about themselves, because the truth usually means Pain. Lies are much nicer and, judging by the popularity of the various Painless, quick therapies, far more attractive.

The fact that ideas tranquilize by facilitating the production of endorphine shows how mental defenses operate. Rationalizations like "they are rotten people, anyway," "God will protect and watch over me," "I didn't want the job anyway," follow down the cortical pathways where ideas are organized to the hypothalamus-pituitary axis where Pain and its repression are organized, to quell the hurt. These ideas counter the old agony of rejection, humiliation, or criticism. That is, they block the lower levels where all of these feelings are organized and processed. Imagine how powerful ideas are! Marx wasn't so far off when he said that religion (a set of ideas) is the opiate of the masses. There is hardly any substitute for a good religious or mystical idea or political philosophy as an opiate. Resolving Pain changes ideas radically because those ideas were based on buried Pain in the first place. One applicant said to me, "I'm afraid I will lose my religion in this therapy. It's not just a defense, you know, it involves universal truths." I explained to him that whatever was true would remain. All we do is extract Pain, and the ideas built on it crumble.

The evidence that ideas and thoughts can be opiates is growing. Dr. Howard Fields of the University of California, San Francisco, experimented with dental patients to show that psychologic factors trigger production of the endorphines.[1] One group received sugar pills (placebos) but were told that these were powerful Pain-killers. One third

[1] A report to the Second World Congress on Pain, Montreal, August 1978.

of the patients reported decreased pain. Yet the benefits of the placebo disappeared after an injection of Naloxone, indicating *that the ideas had triggered the production of endorphine*. Those who reported no pain decrease with placebos were not affected by the Naloxone. The investigators claimed that endorphine production is the best explanation of the results. *This very important research shows that psychologic factors, expectations, hopes, and ideas can shut down Pain in the same biochemical manner as injected morphine does*. We see here how hypnosis may work, as well. One feeds ideas into the system and the person no longer feels the pain of a pinprick or the heat of a match.

Recent research implies that you can reverse an idea with a shot. Someone can feel, "I'm on the top of the world. I feel relaxed. All is right with my life," only to be given a shot of Naloxone and think; "this is a rotten world, and I am miserable." *1984* is here. There are ideas to counteract shots and shots to counteract ideas.

There are implications in all this for suggestion therapy, such as directed day-dreaming, imagery therapy, hypnosis, and straight suggestions by a therapist. In some suggestion therapy the patient is asked to discuss her problem and then to imagine a solution. Afterward, she often feels better. It doesn't occur to her that it is an imaginary solution to a real problem because she actually feels better; the ideas and images have become biochemical agents to quell the Pain. What bothers me about all this is its Alice-in-Wonderland feeling—respected therapists providing imaginary solutions and believing that they are helping the patient. This is precisely what often happens in Behavior or Conditioning Therapy where the patient comes in riddled with fears, say of heights, and he is asked to imagine the height and how it really isn't fearful. It is a sophisticated process called "desensitization," but at bottom it is the same old imaginary solution. Ideas and images provided by the desensitizing therapist counter great fear in the patient by enhancing the endorphine output. Of course, it is only a temporary palliative.

Biofeedback is another example of ideas as opiates. Here the patient is asked to visualize, either through certain thoughts or through certain images, her brain activity on a screen. When she brings her brain into the so-called "relaxation range" she finds that she feels better. In this sense, the patient is supposed to feel "better." But again, images and ideas are altering the Pain threshold. When the patient sees a certain image on the screen, her body begins to relax. What has really happened is that she has brought her brainwaves to the level where she can effectively repress Pain. It is very much akin to hypnosis, where images and thoughts function as opiates.

The injection of ideas is not an exclusive property of direct sugges-tion therapy. Psychoanalysis with its insights accomplishes the same thing. It isn't what the insight is, so much as the fact that it exists; an idea offered with warmth, intelligence, and avuncular concern to turn off Pain. Any rationale makes you feel better; that, indeed, is why the brain can rationalize at all. The faculty of reason is inhibitory or repressive in and of itself. Thus the psychoanalyst's well-intentioned offerings of insight and reason are essentially repressive. And the more soothing his words, the more weight and authority they carry, the more likely they are to turn into morphine. A patient is getting a shot, though not by needle, but by mouth.

Research into acupuncture has shown that those who do best with it are also the most suggestible. They generally improve for two reasons. The first is that acupuncture produces an overload situation by con-stant minute stimulation of nerve cells over large areas of the body. This increases the output of endorphine and allows a surcease from Pain, which may permit the system to rest and regain its strength. The second is that the very notion of a magical cure, sticking someone with pins to make a sickness go away, is something which produces en-dogenous opiates.[2] It turns out that one doesn't even have to be punc-tured in the classical acupuncture points to get well. Research indi-cates that what is necessary is that someone be punctured enough to galvanize the repressive forces against Pain.[3] The so-called acupunc-ture points may not be so specific, after all.[4]

The use of ideas as Pain-killers is not the sole province of psycho-therapy. Ideas can just as well be political or religious. The content is only important as far as it balms and salves. The main thing is to have some idea to hang on to. The person rarely understands that he is clinging; rather, he believes that he has an interest in the idea, be it philosophic or therapeutic. The more implied hope these beliefs in-volve the better, because hope makes an idea an even more powerful analgesic. One reason why unreal hope comes into being at the time of critical early traumas, especially at the time when one is in danger of realizing that one has no hope of being loved by one's parents, is its Pain-quelling properties. It is this phenomenon that helps explain the

[2] Acupuncture's effects can be reversed by the morphine antagonist Naloxone, indicating once again that a major way in which acupuncture works is through the endorphine system.

[3] See the *Journal of Pain,* Ghia, J., et al., "Acupuncture and Chronic Pain Mechanisms," Vol. 3, September 1976, pp. 285–99.

[4] For a discussion of this see *Science News,* November 20, 1976, p. 324. Also, see Solomon Snyder's article in *Scientific American,* March 1977, Vol. 236, No. 3.

cure by faith healers and mystics. It explains how the "laying-on-of-hands" can actually permit healing of symptoms. The *hope* of those desperate for help is the magic ingredient. Though they are not aware of it, it is *they* who have the magic power. Their hopes, and thereby their Pain-quieting powers, are raised by so-called healers. Belief relieves.

Therefore, the dealers of hope enjoy extraordinary power over others. If someone should challenge hopeful beliefs, they will not likely be listened to, for the weakening of hope leaves the person naked against his Pain. If the challenge is persuasive, however, the "true believer" will go into withdrawal—*withdrawal from hope*. Biochemically, the person is bereft of thoughts to galvanize the endorphine system and he is left in agonizing despair. Despair usually takes place after every avenue of hope has been pursued, however.

Hope, optimism, and faith involve the most basic kinds of biochemical processes. To be effective, any political, philosophic, or religious system must bolster them. Dealers of hope and faith are drugging the faithful in the most basic physiologic way. And, indeed, hope is the psychologic component of a system trying to right itself. Hope helps balance the biochemical integrity of the system and allows it to go on functioning.

BRAINWASHING AS PAINWASHING—THE OPIATE OF BELIEF

Brainwashing is another case of the use of ideas as opiates, since certain ideas—when injected into a person—can make her change her mind radically and permanently. She can believe things that she doesn't really believe and adopt beliefs that run contrary to her experience. The key requirement for brainwashing is that Pain must exist. The person must be vulnerable and anxious and ways must be found to isolate him and put him in Pain of one kind or another, whether physical or emotional. In theory, this person needs some idea to eliminate her Pain. Brainwashing can take many forms. It can occur in nursery school, kindergarten, the church, the home—only it isn't called brainwashing, it is called education. It is educational because the ideas are deemed to be beneficial and in the person's own interest. Brainwashing inculcates ideas that run against the person's own interest, yet are nevertheless adopted blindly.

What is so powerful that it can make ordinarily intelligent people surrender all judgment and follow blindly, as in the horror at Jonestown?

The popular notion is that the Reverend Jim Jones's followers were "brainwashed." This is true, but even sophisticated studies of brainwashing seldom penetrate beyond descriptions of behavior, so that the term still seems to have a vague, metaphorical meaning. Brainwashing actually has a precise meaning and involves a specific physiologic pattern.

To brainwash a person, you must accomplish two things. First, you must make the person vulnerable by reducing his defenses which usually protect him against his internal suffering. That is, you must leave him open either to physical or psychological pain. Second, you must offer him a way to end that suffering, which usually involves adoption of a certain set of attitudes, values, or behaviors that pleases those in control. Those who come to movements such as Jonestown or Hare Krishna do so because they are already in a state of suffering, conscious or not. Life itself has left them vulnerable and miserable.

A model for brainwashing is found in certain cases of hypnosis. Here with the person's voluntary consent, the third level is "washed away" and new programs of belief are injected or infused. These ideas now have potency and indeed can direct behavior for weeks or even months. These ideas need not be rational at all, as, for example, that cigarettes will make you nauseous every time you smoke them. The hypnotic subject voluntarily consents to this process.

The paradox of the person who enters a "brainwash movement" or cult is that he is actually close to his own internal reality. Under completely different, nonauthoritarian circumstances, he could go *deeper* into feelings, cry about them, express them and resolve them. He could gradually grow *more* in touch with himself and experience his own insights and his current reality.

But that kind of resolution is not what brainwashers and authority figures are after. They want and achieve the very opposite. Their response to a suffering person is to provide him with a creed, the demonstrations of "love," the prepackaged dogma and environment that promise *relief* from the impending feelings of deprivation. The person is brought close to his inner suffering, then is handed "the answer" that will take the Pain away. He is *given* a reality to replace his own. He is glad to accept the group's substitute for reality. His brain is indeed washed of the terrible suffering, and also of the truth of his own life. That it is indeed Pain-*washing* is suggested by the fact, mentioned earlier, that when leu-endorphine is washed from the blood through dialysis, symptoms of emotional suffering are relieved.

Not only are emotional symptoms relieved, but ideas are changed radically, particularly bizarre and psychotic ideas. Hemodialysis is literally a brainwashing procedure in the sense that simply washing the blood changes ideas. These ideas are altered by reducing the level of Pain, which is exactly what the cult leader does.

The hallmark of the leader is his apparently complete certainty. He seems to have the answers to life and he offers them unequivocally to anyone who will listen. He cannot afford the narrowest glimpse into the fact that no one really has any answers for anyone else. All reality is based in our own feelings and experience, but the leader is even more divorced from the reality of his own feelings than his followers. He is the original susceptible victim who will recruit others who have been deprived of their feelings, the experiences of themselves that could ground them and provide them with their own answers. Now, instead, the followers will be taught the answers, embrace doctrines, and give themselves over to the leader-therapist-parent who once again will do what parents have always done: tell the children how to live.

The various cults, faiths, and even the authoritarian psychotherapies have one thing in common. They offer fulfillment of unmet need. Their power is their ability to take away nearly all awareness of the Pain and suffering of lifelong deprivation. Need—need that was never satisfied from the first days of life—is the follower's ticket of admission. He is in the grip of something much stronger, and much older in his own past, than the powers of judgment. He is in a matrix of unconscious, unending feelings of need which can render him as naïve and vulnerable as an infant turning toward its mother for warmth.

The need of the follower feeds on that of the leader, whose unfulfilled need is probably even more pathetically intense than that of the lowliest member of his flock. It is no accident that the leaders, the fascists and demagogues of this world, are typically products of broken, distorted childhoods, as are their most rabid followers. The leader blots out the intolerable Pains of his life through control and manipulation; the follower finds his relief in being controlled. The naked desperation of the leader is evident when his power is threatened— witness the ravings of Hitler in his final years or the increasingly bizarre behavior of Jones.

The question is asked repeatedly about Jonestown how something so humanitarian could end up as such baldly fascist control. The assumption is that Jones and the commune were normal and noble, then "went crazy."

The problem with the assumption is that the surrender of self, of judgment, of feeling, had taken place long before the outward appearance of the cult became bizarre. The astonishing control demonstrated at the end was possible because, in any follower-leader compact, one has *already* given up the self. The model and precedent for that surrender is the child-parent relationship.

The child/follower does not mean to give up the self; his parents did not mean to take it away; but with deprivation of basic needs, the surrender occurs. That child spends a lifetime looking for something to ease the inner starvation. Perhaps the Pain will be quieted later when the person finds a dependent marriage or relationship, or when he plunges into a struggle for a college degree or a professional goal, but for some people the milder neurotic struggles are not enough. The deprivation requires more potent relief. Instead of an independent self, there is massive unconscious hurt pushing toward ever stronger promises of relief.

Although the ends vary, the dynamics are the same, whether it's Jonestown, Moon, Synanon, Hare Krishna, born-again conversions, or authoritarian psychotherapy. If you replace those movements and leaders with the word "God," you will see the same dynamic. But the attraction of the cult leader is that he is real, he is here and can be seen and touched. The need is the same as that which sustains religion, except that organized religion is more structured and less frenzied in meeting this need. In either case, symbolic fulfillment of need brings pervasive control over a follower's action—for example, over what one can do in bed with a spouse, including whether one can wear a condom or a diaphragm. *That* is control.

For thorough control, the cause or cult must always take care of one of life's great fears—death. It must provide an external purpose for living and dying and in most cases it must offer a "life" beyond death —a beneficent hereafter that makes all of the suffering, misery, and sacrifice of life worthwhile. Jones evidently satisfied this requirement by his assurance to his followers that he would meet them in the utopian hereafter.

It is surprising how easy it is to control others. New patients coming into therapy often beg for it. They want to be told what to do. They would rather hear pseudo-insights from an authority than develop their own. Their behavior cries out for manipulation—a temptation which many therapists, those with unfulfilled needs of their own, evidently find impossible to resist. But these patients are merely carrying out the program, the same program established by parents who needed too. The parents control the child so as to get her to be what they wanted and needed but never got from *their* parents. In the process the child is deprived, the self is buried, and the potential is born for someone to come along and gain power over that person.

Fascism is easy to achieve. You have only to appear to fulfill need while telling people what they need to hear to kill their Pain. People are reluctant to leave a leader who does this, no matter how cruel and sadistic he becomes. Because they hope. They always glimpse a ray of hope. Just as in the original family situation, to give up that hope is almost impossible, because it leaves one open to the painful reality of deprivation. That is one reason why an incumbent President is so hard to unseat. The bias toward keeping him has its origins in the desire not to feel the Pain of what Daddy has failed to do. No one wants a stepfather.

More followers did not try to leave Jonestown because to be cast out is to be faced again with the Primal hopelessness. No one with great unfulfilled need can manage that step. And so those who volunteer for authoritarian ventures tend to stay. They willingly do stupid things; give up their money, or leave their families, or shave off all their hair, or allow themselves to be harangued and prevented for hours from going to the bathroom. The acts they perform are symbolic, to assure the leader that he has control. No one wants that kind of power unless he is neurotic; thus, it is not so much a matter of the abuse of power, because power *is* an abuse in itself. "To abuse power" is redundant.

The cult is a drug. This point has been made or implied by others, but what is missing is the recognition of what drugs do. Yes, they cut us off from reality, impair judgment, make us feel better, but the basic function of the tranquilizer, the morphine, the heroin, *and* the dogma is to *kill awareness by killing awareness of Pain.* The repression of Pain is the repression of awareness. That is the exact mechanism, the reason why any form of drug is used.

The burden of Pain we bear requires that we have a way to deal with it and go on living. The human race has in fact been "designed," over millions of years, to cope with a great deal of Pain and still survive. Our secretions of endorphine help keep some Pain down, but it is often not enough. So a tranquilizer—Valium, for example—helps stimulate production of *more* endorphine. A cult or *any* seeming fulfillment of need, any reassuring idea or presence accomplishes the same thing.

If a cult is threatened, the leader and followers become desperate. Why? The drug is in danger of being withdrawn. Why is that such a threat? The opiate of hope anesthetizes a lifetime of deprivation. An open, nonauthoritarian organization invites individuality and differences of opinion. The cult can tolerate no criticism, because criticism impairs the Pain-killing efficacy of the new family. It threatens hope, faith, and optimism and points the way toward despair—an intolerable state.

"Ideas as opiates" allows us to understand why certain therapeutic approaches "work" better than others. They do so in a manner contrary to that of the function of Primal Therapy. The other modes temporarily alter the biochemistry to reduce conscious awareness, which is the only way to feel better in any therapy that does not deal directly with Primal Pain. The patient must end up more unconscious than he was before, even though he may be going through a process heralded as "consciousness expanding." With all of his "insights," the patient is becoming more unconscious; and in a sense he is becoming more unconscious *because* of his insights. They are ideas used as defenses and to defend means to be unconscious. The insights can even be "right on" and still be meaningless *because they did not emanate from the feelings and needs lodged on lower levels.* The patient in insight therapy who gets in trouble can be counted on to fall back on his insights: "I know why I do this or that. It is because . . ."

Most of the human race shares, to one degree or another, chronic desperation. It seems as though the species has spent most of its energies seeking out ways to handle its fears, whether it is through religion, politics, philosophy, or hard work. We see now why humans evolve with the ability to develop ideas. Ideas are the most powerful force on earth, the ultimate step in evolution. These intangible, ephemeral, invisible wisps have the power to transform a human being biologically.

3: The Folds of Consciousness

THE NOTION of consciousness seems to have been taken over by mystics and their ideas of pyramid power, supra-consciousness, drug states and cosmic con ciousness. The consciousness movement has actually become the unconscious movement, people searching for a way to transport them from their humdrum lives to a level only a chosen few have actually reached. They have missed the point. They have ignored several biologic laws and neurologic facts. The way to "expand consciousness" is not to transcend the world but to descend into the unconscious. There are worlds of activity going on below the level of conscious awareness, a hubbub of images, impulses, and bodily states interacting and exchanging information. With proper access this world is knowable. It can become conscious in its own way and on its own terms.

We are so used to disregarding the levels below conscious awareness that we believe that the crucial process of memory, for instance, has only to do with conscious mental recall. However, the body also remembers in its own way, and it is possible to be in touch with that kind of memory. Consciousness, then, is not simply a mental phenomenon.

Even the structure of the brain is a memory, the coded history of mankind. If there were not all of the previous millions of years of evolution encoded in it that structure would not be what it is.

There are three levels of consciousness. Experimenter Paul Maclean of the National Institute of Mental Health has been staining these different levels, calling them the "triune brain," and has discovered important biochemical differences between them. The easiest way to understand these levels is to see how they evolved. We did not always have the magnificent consciousness we have now, the one that can devise mathematical formulas, build bridges, and invent engines. There was a time when we were a primitive life-form acting mostly from instinct. The nervous system of the fish (one of our most distant ancestors), for instance, reacts instinctually. Later in evolution, the brain evolved so that emotional expression was possible. Still later, the human brain developed. Each new stage in evolution did not erase the previous one, but rather was built upon it. Each of the old, evolutionary brains remains fairly intact as part of our nervous system, with some new connections and functions; but the basic structure is the same.

The brain became organized concentrically into three zones, also known as neuropils.[1] They are interrelated networks of nerve cells, each having its own consciousness and memory storehouse. Each is responsible for a different area of human function. The third level cannot do the second level's work; the intellect cannot resolve feelings. They are different electrochemical systems. They interact but they are not interchangeable.

At birth, and for several months thereafter, it is the inner brain, the brain which mediates visceral activity, that is fully developed, with a lesser developed middle and outer brain. This is the "first level" of consciousness. It handles reactions having to do with the midline of the body—heart function, respiration, bladder, bowel and stomach function, and hormone regulation. The first level handles instinctive responses. It governs timing, rhythm, coordination, balance, and the inner sense of position. It is the consciousness of survival. These functions do not require a top level (cortical) consciousness. Babies, born without adult cortical function, can still perform all of these functions.

The first level predominates until approximately the sixth month of life. The second sphere of the brain is then developed to a degree which allows the infant to begin reacting emotionally and forming emotional attachments. This is the second level of consciousness. This

[1] One of the ways the brain matures is by the development of a fatty sheath which covers the nerves, called myelin. The speed with which nerves conduct impulses depends on myelination. Myelinated nerves carry impulses faster than unmyelinated ones. The sequence of myelination is therefore an index of maturation. The inner zone of the brain (the first to develop) is never well myelinated. This zone deals with total body responses. As we grow older, our brains and behavior become more specialized and more discriminating; the increasing myelination later on allows for more rapid inhibition, which permits specialized, selective reactions. The outer zone is very well myelinated. It is the last to be covered.

network stores—in the limbic system—emotional traumas during childhood and emotional response to events. In the first few months of life, the brain is dealing mostly with internal, visceral reactions and is beginning to make the differentiation of muscular responses, such as what to do with the fingers, toes, arms, and legs. The newly developed second level begins to handle what happens inside and relates that to the world outside. Facial expression, gait, bodily stance, and voice production are examples of second-level consciousness at work. This consciousness is the "feeling consciousness." It deals with emotion—those motions we make to express feelings. Whereas the first level of consciousness has a totally inward focus, the second is directed outward. First-level consciousness is body consciousness. The second has to do with relating to others.

The second level of consciousness is also where images lie and, therefore, creativity. It is the level that conjures up dragons, demons, dreams, and artistic perception. It is the level that bridges the first and third levels, adding emotional content to experience.

The images of the second level have a clarity that is lost when filtered through the third level. In dreams, however, that sharpness of image is recaptured. A person reliving something in his childhood sees, hears, and smells exactly as if he were there. And, indeed, with access to the second level he literally and neurologically *is* there.

The third level is the last to develop. This is the integrating consciousness, responsible for bringing together first- and second-line events, for rationalizing, intellectualizing, and symbolizing those happenings. It is the system of logic, of problem solving, and of storing facts and figures. It is the system of "figuring out." It philosophizes, makes mathematical symbols, fixes machines. It is the system that internalizes religion and mystical ideation. It is the part of us that tries to make sense of the world. It is the last acquired system of consciousness both in terms of the history of the species (phylogeny) and in terms of the development of the infant (ontogeny).

It is the third level which perceives symbolically and reflects through language. It has insights—an awareness of feeling and of awareness itself, while the second level has a feeling of awareness.

The levels of consciousness can be discovered by the use of an electronic probe. Placing the probe on the top of the temporal lobe elicits the symbolic (cognitive) aspect of an old memory (if the site is stimulated directly, it is the exact correct symbolism); putting the probe deeper evokes the old memory and its feelings; putting the probe deeper still sets off early physical responses, including pure fear, feelings of impending death, inexplicable visceral reactions such as bowel cramps, perspiration; it increases heart rate, facial pallor—all seemingly "inexplicable" responses because these are responses to preverbal memories. These various points of consciousness are closely related anatomically.

Each higher brain center that develops from infancy on contains partial aspects of lower-brain imprinted memory. Deep traumas eventually have a symbol or representation on the highest level. We can infer the existence of inaccessible Pain by the effects it has on higher centers. There is no "pure" higher mind that can escape the effects of infancy Pain.

By observing evidence of the levels of consciousness, we have begun to appreciate fully what consciousness is, what happens to consciousness in neurosis and the part it plays in the cure of neurosis. For example, we have been confused in psychology as to what memory is because we have considered it to be an intellectual activity. Yet memories exist on different levels. There are, indeed, discrete layers of consciousness each with its own peculiarities and its own "processing plant." Emotional memory is not cognitive at all, but exists on a separate level. This is eloquently demonstrated in hypnosis. No matter how hard a person tries to recall certain key scenes from the age of five, it is only when he is directed below the intellect that he can gain access to those memories.

We do not dream on the intellectual level. It is when we drop below the level of conscious awareness that dreams begin. They are usually directly traceable to old personal memories. But think of all the activity on this lower level of consciousness. Images, scenarios, dialogue—all happening while we are "unconscious." Further, this level has its own characteristic brain-wave pattern and physiologic concomitants. The same is true for the early physical level. First-level sleep, for example (very deep sleep), has a characteristic brain-wave pattern.

Even plants display a form of consciousness. Tendrils of a certain light-sensitive plant will curl up when stroked. But if placed in the dark and stroked, it will do nothing. Placed back in the light, it will "remember" that stroke and curl up again. It can remember, store and code memory and delay reactions—primitive prerequisites for a form of consciousness. In its own way, it is "aware" of the environment and adjusts accordingly.[2]

The requirements for consciousness, reaction, storage, memory, and re-creation are just as present in the bodily system as in the brain. Even a chronically fast heartbeat is a form of physiologic memory. A

[2] *Science News*, Vol. 195, January 1977, pp. 191–92.

very early event can produce a prototypic response of a rapid heart-beat. The heart retains the memory and responds accordingly thereafter. Facial set is a chronic memory. One doesn't "figure out" how to hold one's jaw, eyes, and facial muscles. Its own memory system holds it steady.

One of the leaders in hypnosis research, Ernest R. Hilgard, discovered that hypnotized people functioned at a level consistent with their hypnotic age, rather than their real age. They functioned more consistently at that experimental age level on various tasks given them. If they were reading or writing, they did so as a five- or seven-year-old, for example, while those merely thinking or "simulating" that early age did not function consistently as a five- or seven-year-old. In other words, you cannot "try" to be a certain age. It is necessary to descend to that level, as, for example, in hypnosis, and that level will then organize all of your responses consistently. To be regressed in hypnosis is a real state. The person is at that point functioning on a different level of brain organization. This is another way that we know about the levels of consciousness.

Experiments in hypnosis illustrate divisions in consciousness. These experiments are helpful because they are dramatic and take place in a short space of time. Hilgard hypnotized a subject and put one arm in ice water. She reported no pain verbally, yet her other hand, "freed" from hypnosis, wrote out the agony. On one level she was "aware" of her Pain. But this kind of awareness is circumscribed and cannot be equated with consciousness.

Whenever a hypnotized subject reports no pain such as the above, one can be sure that all of the physiologic measures will show that it is being processed on lower levels. These experiments show us how powerful symbols and ideas are in shutting down pain. The subject will usually report that there was a "hidden part of me" that seemed to sense some pain but the mind was concentrating on other matters—a recent trip, work, or some fantasy. Pictures in the mind and a set of ideas superseded the person's actual experience so that awareness was disengaged from what was really happening. The subject in this experiment no longer responded to reality, she responded to *ideas* about it even when the ideas were at odds with what was actual. She was split from herself, unaware of reality and therefore unconscious. We cannot see the split from our own past so readily, except when that past is uncovered.

Every neurotic is really in a hypnotic state for all of his life. He is a victim of unconscious forces which drive him relentlessly and for which he has no explanation.

A hypnotic subject in our own experiments descended to age five when her "dolly" was taken away from her. She cried and cried. When she came out of the scene, she was her normal self again. Where was that memory and where were those tears that were readily available any time the hypnotist wished to have her regress to that scene again? It was an unconscious process, a process still taking place on a different level of consciousness.

All of her tears, all of that anguish and misery existed *all the time*. The imprint is a force. That is why the minute one is regressed to a lower level of consciousness, one can cry, laugh, or agonize freely. It is somewhat like a record player—all of that "noise"—music, sounds, voices—exists on that disc, but one hears nothing until one puts a needle on it. In humans, in the ordinary course of events, that hubbub of activity below is well shielded from conscious awareness.

When neurosurgeon Wilder Penfield put a probe on certain brain cells of patients in surgery the split was immediately apparent. While the patient was reliving an early scene, he was talking to his surgeon. He was having two experiences simultaneously. Two levels of consciousness were operating; one, the old imprinted memory that was being relived and, two, the conscious awareness in communicating with the doctor.

Evidence of the duality of consciousness has recently come from research in split-brain surgery—a procedure in which the connecting fibers between the left and right hemispheres are severed in cases of severe epilepsy. The left hemisphere is far more analytic, logical, sequential, intellectual; the right one (similar to second-level functioning) is more intuitive and deals with feelings and sensations.[3]

Split-brain surgery produces almost two separate minds, the left side oblivious of what the right is doing. Feelings are physiologically divided from intellect, spontaneity from carefully planned behavior, logic from emotional insight, and the experiential from the cerebral. The surgery has shown how various components of consciousness actually make up a single human consciousness. Joseph Bogen, a neurosurgeon specializing in this surgery, has reported that his split-brain patients have a marked inability to describe feelings, as if levels of consciousness are surgically disconnected with the severing of the brain hemispheres.[4]

The nondominant half of the brain does not have an elaborate use of language but it can react emotionally; it can swear and sing. It can

[3] R. E. Ornstein, *The Psychology of Consciousness*, W. H. Freeman Co., San Francisco, 1972.
[4] *Brain-Mind Bulletin*, 2, August 18, 1977.

dream in images but it needs the dominant left half to supply language for recalling the dreams. The right, minor hemisphere can blush, giggle, be disgusted, and wince but when separated from the left major side cannot tell you exactly why one does that. Events fed to the disconnected left hemisphere, when embarrassing, will cause the split-brain patient to blush. When asked why he's blushing, the person will make up a story to explain his behavior. This is precisely the case in neurosis. There are forces at work for which the neurotic has no conscious understanding. To rationalize his behavior he must contrive reasons for it that have nothing to do with his real hidden motivation. The split in consciousness renders one ahistoric. It makes one a victim of hidden forces and buried motivations.

Any kind of feeling experience always changes the brain-wave amplitude more in the right hemisphere than in the left. Part of our ordinary consciousness disappears during orgasm and orgasm, it happens, is predominantly a right brain function, as are ecstasy states. Ideational states, such as a belief in the devil, turn out to be left-brain. The right brain is mostly concerned with second-level consciousness, the left brain with the third.

First-level consciousness can function even while we're completely "unconscious" on the higher levels. A person in a coma will still try to brush away a painful stimulus on his chest. When you massage or hold the hand of a person in a coma, there are definite physiologic changes, as if needs are being fulfilled while totally unconscious. People who are unconscious, drugged, anesthetized, or comatose react unconsciously to their environment in a physiologic way. For instance, the traumas of surgery galvanize the body and lower brain into frantic activity even while the mind seems totally tranquilized or anesthetized. What is worse, that trauma remains in the system.[5] It would not be a bad idea for someone who is having surgery to be caressed at the same time, because both the hurt and the caress are being processed unconsciously.

The person in a deep coma who nevertheless responds to external painful stimuli is responding on the first level with no other level participating. Whether he can explain his behavior or not, he is *reacting* and *behaving* in response to a stimulus on a certain level of consciousness. Not all behavior and reactions are of the kind we can explain. The body puts out more hormones or less. It reacts to stress and

[5] Surgeons should be very careful not to overtraumatize a patient during operating procedure under the false belief that the patient cannot feel anything. What they do not feel then they will have to feel later, or suffer from inexplicable tension.

other stimuli again in its own way. Behavior is not just how we deliberately act in the world.

Consciousness is shaped from the time the nervous system begins its formation. From just a few weeks after conception, any stress to the mother can be transmitted to the fetus. These traumas are stored in the very rudimentary nervous system. They will have an effect on adult consciousness.

Great Pain laid down in infancy and during gestation will be mediated by the only mature consciousness available—namely, the visceral. Later events can trigger off those early traumas and the result can be agitated visceral reactions and bodily distress whose source remains unknown and inaccessible. Colitis may well begin with these early blocked experiences. Indeed, as a rule of thumb, one can say that the deeper in the body a symptom exists, the more likely it is to have resulted from very early trauma. As we grow, Pains have an impact first on the internal reactions, then on the feeling level, and later on intellectual development and cognition. To some degree we will become unaware of our bodies, blocked from our emotional life, and unaware of aspects of the world around us.

A newborn under stress does not respond with intellectualizations and ideas, but rather with midline responses. He becomes colicky, asthmatic, has severe stomach distress, etc. These reactions are commensurate with how the baby's brain has developed. His reactions have to do with the internal organ system.

Heredity certainly plays a part in determining which organ systems may have weaknesses. But disorders traditionally considered hereditary may have more to do with circumstances during conception and gestation than with the genes we inherited.

The predominant trauma affecting the first physiologic level of consciousness is that of birth. Birth traumas stay in the nervous system and the body wreaking havoc for a lifetime.[6]

The vulnerability and malleability of the nervous system during the first weeks of life means that events can be stamped with a permanence which is greater than that of events occurring later in childhood. The fact that first-line traumas are often life-and-death matters means that the valence or charge value of the stored memory will be high, and that the force it exerts on later behavior and symptom for-

---

[6] These traumas direct later conscious awareness and conscious behavior with enormous force. When these traumas begin to break through into conscious awareness, their effect on cognition, perception, logic, and problem-solving is dramatic. It is another way we know of the great impact of very early trauma on what we ordinarily consider "consciousness."

mation will be considerable. This is precisely why prenatal and perinatal care of infants is crucial.

All of the emotional experiences that happen to us after we differentiate ourselves from our surroundings and develop emotional relationships to our parents are second-level or feeling events. Criticisms, humiliations, rejections, scoldings, and punishments are "remembered" on this emotional level.

Later, the development of the symbolic intellect or third level will not only integrate the lower two levels, but also *keep them apart*. If ideas and concepts can quell Pain, they can also shield *against* consciousness rather than act as a force for it. Ideas can be developed to keep us from knowing what is going on below the level of conscious awareness. Because the third level is quite plastic, it can deceive, manipulate, and condition itself. It can misrepresent feelings to distract the self from recognition of feeling.

Third-level consciousness begins its formation between the ages of five and seven and becomes solidified after the age of thirteen (when there is a qualitative shift in the brain-wave pattern). Simultaneous with this shift is an increase in the ability to inhibit, reflect, and block emotional responses. It is then that one can shift from emotionality to intellectuality and respond in terms of rules, regulations, and mores. It is at this point, in the early teens, that prohibitions are internalized, where proscriptions of the church and rules of the classroom are adopted and become part of the youngster. Because of the evolving brain, the child can begin to live on the level of ideas and symbols rather than impulses.

If the child grows up with very little Pain, the third level will evolve normally and transmit feelings directly to consciousness. But if there is too much Pain early on, the third level is transformed. It must now misinterpret feelings and motivations and deal with the past in terms of a variety of symbols, none of which correspond exactly to the past.

Real consciousness is not the same as awareness. There are many kinds of awareness but only one consciousness, that is, only one *full* consciousness. Full consciousness is an enduring state of the organism with fluid access among various brain structures.

Consciousness has a structural connotation. Awareness does not. Awareness is discontinuous and momentary. It is only an aspect of consciousness. It is important that we do not make the mistake of treating an attribute of consciousness as consciousness itself. Thus mental illness is not just "mental." It is a profound alteration of consciousness; consciousness being the sum total of all the processes of the brain as they affect and are affected by the body and external reality. It is an organic, psychophysiologic state.

To the extent that the levels are not fluidly interconnected there is false or at best incomplete consciousness. A person can be very aware of his surroundings, quite perceptive, yet have a false consciousness. The awareness may only be third-level deep. It may be accurate in terms of external reality but it does not accurately reflect inner reality. The ideas that we are occupied with, our special areas of interest, our choice of occupation, the newspapers we read, the stories that intrigue us are often part of that false consciousness, merely symbolic of what is really going on within us.

The more connected one is among the three levels, the more objective one can become; that is, the more one can judge and perceive the self—and others—realistically and undistorted by past Pain. Thus you can increase awareness by deepening consciousness. But you can never deepen consciousness by trying to increase awareness. In fact, the more one *tries* to be aware, the more unconscious one becomes. The more you give in to the unconscious, the more conscious you become. The problem for neurotics is that at best they can only be aware of the self, never conscious of it. The deeper that consciousness—the more access one has to lower levels—the more structural relationships change. One can see this in Primals where amplitude, frequency, and hemispheric relationships change.

As a person gains access to his early Pain, he restores the connections between his body, his feelings, and his intellect which were lost due to repression. He has an explanation for the intensity, quality, and direction of his previous behavior. He begins to regain consciousness— not just awareness but an organic fluidity of levels and structures of the brain which have been strangers to each other for many years.

4: The Gated Mind

NERVE cells and their connecting points facilitate and inhibit the transmission of information in the brain. This process is electrochemical. The inhibition of information is called gating, a normal brain function. The gating system works throughout the brain but is concentrated in certain key areas that organize the Pain response.

It is the gating system that separates the three levels of consciousness. In neurosis, the gating system acts continuously to keep us unaware. The uppermost level of consciousness ordinarily gives us the significance and meaning of Pain, its causes and its magnitude. When it is gated, we are unaware of the significance of events.

When the third level is severed surgically, for example, from the rest of the brain—as in an orbitofrontal lobotomy—the person has a diminished understanding of Pain and is relatively unaware of suffering. He knows he is in Pain, cannot tell just how much, and doesn't care in any case. It has lost its *meaning*. The higher centers not only can integrate the Pain experience but can be extremely effective in suppressing it.

The gating system is the agent of repression and controls input all the way down the nervous system. Thus, Pain information can be blocked off at the most basic level of the neuraxis. Once gating and repression set in, neural circuits are functionally disconnected and seem to take on independent lives. Thoughts, disengaged from feelings, have a viability of their own. The energy of the feelings, meanwhile, reverberates or travels in loops on the lower levels of the brain. This energy is distributed to the body as though it had nothing to do with its cognitive counterpart. The person may feel tense and have no idea as to why.

Gating operates on the overload principle. More Pain than the body can integrate stimulates the gating system into action. This principle is illustrated in electrostimulation. Electrical implants in the spinal cord, when activated, can shut off the most intense bodily Pain. In short, when the system is flooded with electrical impulses (overloaded), the gating system goes into action. There seems to be an optimum level at which nerve cells respond and a critical level above which they can no longer react.

Gating works in two directions, keeping lower-level information from the higher levels and preventing ideas and concepts from affecting our emotional level. When we say that someone has lost touch with reality, it should be understood first and foremost that gating has disengaged one level of consciousness from another. One loses touch with the outside world only *after* one has lost touch with the inner one.

When we see how gating works on an everyday level, we can understand it better. For example, all of us make resolutions (I'm going to stop eating, smoking, drinking . . .) that we never carry out. Resolutions on the third level seem to stay there and do not affect our emotional selves. We still eat too much *no matter what we tell ourselves;* in other words, the third level is having trouble communicating with the second and the first. There seems to be some barrier that prohibits any mental resolution from having a real effect.

There is a force below the level of immediate awareness that makes willpower irrelevant and ineffective. It is a Primal force. It is possible to know exactly what that force is and to resolve it permanently; not by reaching down from the top but by letting the force on the lower levels ascend. That is the way the brain develops; and the way Pain is laid down. It is a logical progression that feelings proceed from where they are organized to top-level awareness.

Another example familiar to many of us is that of insights achieved in psychoanalysis. No matter how much we know and understand about our behavior, no matter what the quantity of insights piled up, our behavior is still the same or nearly the same. We understand it better; we accept it, we come to terms with it, but it remains. The attempt at third-level comprehension *strengthens* intellectual processes, enhances gating, and produces *more* unconsciousness, not less. In that sense, mental comprehension *by itself* reinforces repression and neurosis. Thus analysis and insight deepen the sickness in the name of progress.

There are many graphic examples of gating at work. In football, players can often go an entire game with broken bones without being very conscious of Pain. It is only afterward, when their attention has shifted away from the intensity of the game, that they suffer. The same is true of any shocking experience, such as an auto accident. We may not feel the pain of an injury for some time.

Getting drunk is another example. After a night on the town, a person may have no memory of what he did or why. His third-level consciousness was not functioning. He was operating on a lower level so that he was warm, laughing, angry, belligerent, or sexual—all the things that the third level usually prevents him from being.

We are all familiar with someone who either talks or walks in his sleep. These are rather complex functions performed without the activation of top-level consciousness to help produce this complex behavior. There are those who have had seizures who can still drive a car and yet have no idea how they got to a certain place. They manage to drive the car, select the streets, make turn signals, all the while unaware of what is happening. What is more, they have no memory at all of the trip. They were not strictly "unconscious." They were operating on a different level of consciousness.

The gating system allows us to feel one way and act another. It helps us forget our childhood when it is overwhelming, and keeps us from remembering our own early experiences. We might remember innocuous dates and recall facts from our reading but be totally blank when it comes to the memory of emotional scenes from childhood. The reason is that it is first our suffering that we gate or repress and that will drag with it associated memories that might trigger it. Eventually, whole scenes, places, days, and months will be totally buried. The repression of suffering is a key concept because the unblocking of suffering liberates a substantial amount of memory and association. Memory will be liberated only to the extent that suffering is tapped; and gating will allow only as much suffering into consciousness as can be integrated. That is why something as catastrophic as incest may be remembered by a daughter only gradually, in stages.

The lifting of the lower, more primitive gates may account for the return of bruises in patients who reexperience the agony of being battered during birth. Access to the suffering brings up all of the associations, mental and physiologic, which were gated away originally. I have discussed elsewhere how those taking morphine are not likely to bruise until they go into withdrawal. The mechanisms which operate the gating system work with the endorphines or internally created morphine substances. Opening the gates is literally, physiologically like going into withdrawal. The gates are down and suffering pours forth with all of its concomitants.

Patients who finally become conscious of very early Pain have radical changes in a variety of physiologic functions. This means that unconsciousness is not just an absence of consciousness but is a very active process; the brain works hard to keep itself unconscious, and the amount of work it undergoes is a way of telling how much unconsciousness there is. When the unconscious becomes conscious that amount of work is no longer there.

Unconsciousness is not a watered-down version of consciousness. *Painful early events were never conscious in any way.* The processing of them is subconscious, though they may give rise to ideas which merge into conscious awareness. These ideas and notions form part of what is known as "false consciousness."

Gates exist because nature in its wisdom sees to it that we don't suffer too much. They mustn't be tampered with. One must have a thorough knowledge of their mechanisms before interceding in their work.

5: The Imprint of Pain

To SEE how traumatic experience can affect the brain itself, we need to understand how the Pain is engraved into the brain once the gating or filtering system has done its job. A study by Morpurgo and Spinelli helps to clarify this stamping-in process.[1] They show that, as a result of Painful experience, more and more of the brain becomes involved in dealing with Pain.

The *anatomic area* of the imprint *becomes larger* with more Pain. "New circuits become engraved by the ongoing painful experience so that more and more of the neuromachinery is prepared to recognize as painful, stimuli that would go completely unnoticed in a normal subject." Once committed to the pain, neurons are not so easily changed.

Morpurgo and Spinelli believe that the characteristics of single neurons are very dependent on the nature of their early experience. In other words, the way neurons behave later on depends on what happens to them early in life.

Once Pain is imprinted, the brain becomes largely a Pain-processing machine; because not only is an experience engraved, but *the imprint is physically larger when the experience is painful than when it is neutral.* As early Pain becomes compounded, more and more of the brain is converted so that less is left to do the real work of perceiving, thinking, and problem-solving.

The fact that the brain area involved with Pain is much greater than the imprints of innocuous experiences has at least two implications. It means that the threshold for reacting to Pain is lower. It

[1] C. V. Morpurgo and D. W. Spinelli, "Plasticity of Pain Perception," in *Brain Theory Newsletter*, Vol. 2, No. 1, October 1976, p. 15.

means that something normally trivial or neutral is perceived as painful.

Neurosis allows the system to adapt to threatening levels of Pain, but as a result the brain is thereafter less well adapted to normal, nonthreatening stimuli. There is a diminished repertoire of responses. One grows rigid in the ways one handles situations and therefore one is less adaptable to change. The neuronal cells that should have been committed to dealing with life are now processing Pain. Though the original adaptation was needed for survival, continued repression makes the brain less well adapted for survival. *To alter neurosis we must do something about the imprints which have physically altered the brain.*

The Morpurgo and Spinelli work shows there is a basis in the brain for misinterpreting events as a result of engraved Pain. Their work takes the gate theory a step further because "the neurocircuits that perceive Pain are *themselves* structured, both in quality and number, by past experience."[2] That is to say, the neural machinery that takes care of Pain is itself a product of early experience and how the brain deals with later Pain depends on what happened to it very early in life. There may in fact be a special brain organization that operates the same as other senses to facilitate or inhibit the transmission of impulses, and this organization is built up through experience. Pain produces an integrated network *of its own* to process still more Pain. Because more and more ordinary events come to be perceived as painful, the areas involved in this network come to dominate our lives.[3]

E. Roy John of the New York Medical College, an important research investigator in the field of neurophysiology, has written an essay titled "The Model of Consciousness,"[4] in which he defines consciousness as a result of outside events combining with past memories and developing into perception. This is important to Primal Therapy. However, John arrived at this conclusion based on research using the tracer technique. This technique involves a stimulus presented to an animal at a characteristic rate of repetition. Electrical rhythms then appear in different brain regions at the frequency of the stimulus. These reactions are called "labeled responses." They reflect the processing of that incoming information. After an animal has been

[2] All quotations from p. 15, op. cit.

[3] Part of the entire organization and development of the massive human cortex throughout history may have had something to do with the continuous necessity to process Pain.

[4] Found in G. Schwartz and D. Shapiro, *Consciousness and Self Regulation,* Vol. I, Plenum Press, New York, 1976.

conditioned by this stimulus, it is then placed in a similar situation but without the usual stimulus. The brain of the animal still makes its characteristic representation even in the absence of the stimulus. It acts "as if" the stimulus were present. The brain produces a facsimile of its history. Apparently, *previously stored electrical patterns—and probably biochemical patterns as well—are released to drive a specific behavior.* Behavior is driven by memory *exactly as if the original stimulus were present.*

The old memory is prepotent. This is precisely the case in human neurosis. Input early in life can create certain patterns—reverberating circuits—which are reactivated later in life when a stimulus evocative of the original one is present. The person than reacts to the past instead of the present.

John has discovered that it is the perceived *meaning* of a stimulus that evokes a specific pattern of electrical activity. This point may eventually tie in with the Morpurgo and Spinelli findings of an expanding imprint of Pain, inasmuch as meaning makes psychological Pain what it is, and increases the likelihood that ordinary stimuli will be perceived as having meanings related to Pain.

The process by which an electrical stimulus from the outside evokes electrical potentials from the past demonstrates just how important past influences are. As neurosis becomes more severe, historic electrical patterns must predominate and one sees less and less of reality.

When Pain becomes compounded, much of the brain, and therefore of the body with which it is integrated, becomes altered and converted to defensive maneuvers and life-salvaging operations rather than the process of living. A network of Pain spreads its tentacles around memories of infancy in a most suffocating way. One can see the end result of this in psychogenic epilepsy, where a clap of hands or a flash of light can set off a seizure. The most neutral of stimuli become enmeshed in the Pain apparatus, instantly resulting in a symptom. The receptive-reactive surface of the brain is greater than it should be. This larger surface area is almost literally the area representing neurosis.

All of the various adaptations the body has made throughout history persist. The reason the imprint of Pain is so difficult to root out is that it is a *memory of an adaptation.* The body is reluctant to give up its life-saving memories.

The imprint of Pain fixes a permanent imbalance in brain biochemistry—an imbalance that arises to meet early life stress. The trauma is stamped in so that an exact duplicate of that original event lives on in the brain. The body and brain then react "as if" the original situation were always there and the biochemical imbalance is maintained. The more compounded the trauma becomes by later life circumstance the greater the disharmony and the deeper the mental illness. There are more dopamine receptors in the brains of psychotics because there is more Pain and therefore more places must be constructed where the Pain can be "received."

The lopsided biochemical arrangement continues throughout life and forces the person to construct a neurotic environment so as to remain in synch with his altered system. For example, his personal tempo is speeded up to meet an activated brain. Thus, an environment constructs a new brain system which produces a new environment. In this way the dialectic process channels both personal and historic evolution.

Perhaps this is a good time to explain how that brain imprint is changed. When a trauma occurs very early in life there are changes in the cells, biochemistry, and neuroelectric systems. So, for example, cells genetically programmed to mediate feelings become altered to mediate repression. New nerve pathways, rerouted ones, are utilized to shunt the Pain message away from centers that are overloaded, and cells change in their permeability, firing patterns, and reactivity. These processes are *how* the memory is fixed. The genetic program has been aborted. Under the blitz of Pain the DNA molecule which transmits the genetic code may become a new template so that the cell utilizes a different code. Ordinarily, the bank of options from which we draw to develop and handle ourselves in the world is controlled by the DNA molecule. Pain has "changed the rules" so that we now go to that same bank and draw new currencies.

An example of the change in the genetic code is found in a recent study on female rats.[5] They were given substances which lowered serotonin levels (a Pain-blocking neurotransmitter). This produced a premature menopausal state. The normal genetic program for these animals was shortened by a rearrangement of brain neurotransmitters. This also shows the possible relation of Pain to alteration of menstrual function.

When Pain is removed from the system in Primal Therapy there is a normalization of the processes I have mentioned and the imprint is no longer "held" as it was. Let me reiterate: the transmuted system *is* the way the imprint is engraved as memory. The reexperience of the trauma changes all of that and resolves the imprint. Even what happens in the womb is shaping the brain biochemistry of the fetus and developing certain critical vulnerabilities to later stress.

[5] *Science,* Vol. 206, November 16, 1979. Review by Jean Marx.

Clearly, the focus must be on that brain imprint which holds the imbalance steady. Resolving its force changes the inner environment so that the brain can finally right itseif. It is when that equilibrium takes place that we see dramatic changes in height, growth of feet and hands and other musculature such as the jaw, chest, and the shoulders. These physical changes are evidence of the change in the transcription of the genetic code so that it can now unfold toward its original destination. Thus in retrospect, a person's height and the size of breasts and limbs can be an index of neurosis. The changes that we see in our patients occur at the point where there was a block in the original developmental sequence.

Evidence that the genetic code of a species can be repressed was reported recently by scientists from the University of Connecticut. They combined embryonic mouth tissue of the mouse and the chicken, which is toothless. These combined tissues were cultured for several weeks. At the end of that time fully formed teeth developed in the culture "with root development in proper relationship to the crown." The teeth formed were reptilian, which indicates that the genetic blueprint for the synthesizing of teeth was never lost during the evolution of birds but "only repressed."[6]

It is assumed that given an environment where teeth were absolutely necessary, they would not have disappeared in the evolution of birds. The ability of the chick tissue to make teeth would indicate that toothlessness for avians was not the result of a wholesale change in genetic coding but rather of some interference with the expression of the genes for making teeth. In short, birds, which are an evolutionary development from reptiles, retained the genetic blueprint for teeth and presumably for other earlier evolutionary structures. The brain of the bird and the brain of the reptile are almost identical and one might consider birds "flying lizards." The implication of this is that species never really lose anything in evolution. It would seem that we as humans have inside us the history of all species that went before.

The code for the various species, then, is selectively repressed and opened but never eliminated. The notion of an evolutionary tree with various branches is not so much a matter of branching as a selection of a group of potentials which are turned on and off. Thus there is a bird in every mouse and a reptile in every bird, a salamander in every human. It has long been known that human development parallels much earlier forms, as in fetal gill slits. Even the way we are born shows the influence of earlier forms, as seen in our S-shaped reptilian

[6] *Brain-Mind Bulletin,* April 7, 1980, p. 1.

movements. At various points the genetic code turns off the old and turns on the new, and we become human.

The fact that the genetic code for all species along our path of development exists inside of us means that we are our own archaeological find. It may be more fruitful to dig down into our own nervous system for our roots than to excavate in Iran and Africa. Ontogeny not only recapitulates phylogeny but contains it at all times.

The unraveling of genetic instructions can be blocked not only in the course of evolution, but also in individual life. We see in the physiologic and biochemical changes resulting from Primal Therapy a form of unlocking of that code so that patients can resume the fulfillment of their genetic potential, and in that sense become truly fully human. It is literally a way of getting one's self back.

The Darwinian notion of evolution ascribes to chance the way new species come into being. It is quite possible that another factor operates in evolution to account for the development of new structures and indeed new species. That factor is the dialectic interplay between organisms and their environment, which seems to produce structures to cope with that environment, while suppressing those that become obsolete.

Psychotherapy thus far has addressed itself only to the modern systems in evolution and has neglected those ancient systems of which we are captives. We can not only learn about phylogeny by the study of individual man and his personal development, we can learn more about individual pathology through the study of phylogenetic evolution. Man himself is the biologic imprint of that evolution.

The effect of imprinted, inaccessible memory is that personality development must form around the imprint instead of in cooperation with it. An elaborate superstructure of personality is *formed around* blocked feelings. Those feelings are not utilized for one's maturation. Major segments of the brain are "off limits" and consciousness must struggle along without the help of all its potential faculties. The hidden memory is no longer part of the person's available orienting frame of reference. Rather, the repression of memory serves to shut off proper perception and cognition and to leave only substitutes in its wake.

Let us take an example. If, as an adult, you cannot accept help because you have a great deal of Pain over never being helped, your answer to an offer of help may be an immediate, "I can do it myself." Or, "Do you think that I'm helpless?" "I'm not a dummy, you know." The retorts are varied but invariably neurotic because the early Pain is so largely represented that even ordinary simple statements set it off.

These findings tell us in part how the brain shapes personality, how we become what we are, and, further, how we can change what we have become.

The late-acquired brain, the cortex, under siege from Pain must shore up the defenses *against* experience instead of elaborating upon it. It changes the *meaning* of experience, and it changes it in accordance with imprinted Pain. Thus, the neurotic may derive strange meanings from perfectly neutral conversations and, as a result, his behavior and responses are out of keeping with reality. He is responding to a past event of which he is totally unaware. This is the essence of maladaptation.

The fact that neurons are conditioned very early in life by trauma means that forevermore perceptual apparatus sees the world through a screen of Pain and that the literal perception of reality is circumscribed by those altered neurons. The process continues until we later see what doesn't exist. In psychosis, for example, a harmless person walking down the street is perceived as somebody who "is laughing or plotting behind my back." In a lesser way in neurosis the same is true. The third line has a certain accurate perception: "There is a man or woman." Mixed with this perception are old unconscious first- and second-line memories, which add suffering to the perception and change it. What the neurotic then sees is an old meaning in a new situation and he responds to that meaning first.

As less and less cortex becomes involved in Pain, defenses diminish, the mind clears, perception is lucid, and one sees the world as it is. Less and less will be considered threatening and the person will be more open to his world. Being "open-minded" is a *biologic state, not an attitude.*

6: The Loss of Meaning

WHEN we become detached from our feelings we also lose the meaning of our experience. Since it is the *meaning* of our early experiences that makes them overwhelming, repression is called in to render them meaningless. People overwhelmed by Pain cannot see what is in front of them and they lose the sense of the situations they are in. As repression mounts, more meaning is lost until one leads a meaningless life.

One of the ways that meaning is shed from experience is through the silencing of those areas of the brain that deal with meaning. In the brain are primary centers for our sensations, such as smell and touch. These sensations are elaborated and take on meaning through adjoining areas called secondary association cortex. A great many of these secondary nerve cells are uncommitted at birth but as experience is stamped in they weave a texture around it, providing scenes, memories, context, and a sense of what is happening. Meaning is predominantly organized in the temporal-parietal regions which also have the greatest amount of secondary association cortex around them. This is the area where past events receive their meaning—"They don't love me. There is nothing I can do to make them want me."

Ordinarily, information is carried upward in the hierarchy of the nervous system, or neuraxis, via stalk-like vertical units. This information reaches the cortex and spreads out into the secondary association areas. In response to Pain, however, and its massive electric blast, certain of these cells are silenced because the meaning of the event is life-threatening. This silence is protective and is one of the many ways that we can disconnect from overwhelming primary sensations.

Traumas are inevitably electrical, and the brain can only handle so many volts of stimulation. If an event is more than the brain can handle, there must be a shutdown of certain cells. In order to recapture meaning of early events—and therefore meaning in life—one must reengage the Primal agony, reactivate the previously deenergized neurons and reawaken the brain. The agony that is reengaged must be of a specific charge value. Too much insures overload and disconnection, possibly bringing on hallucinations or physical symptoms.

In that agony lies meaning. It is important, therefore, that when agony is released from the limbic storehouse, it be of an optimum amount such that the cortex can integrate and make sense out of it; otherwise there is an overload. A Primal (the active reliving of a specific old scene), when done under proper supervision, seems to discharge just enough electrical energy to open up aspects of the secondary association cortex and yield specific meanings of unconscious events.

In order for the energy of a repressed experience to engage the relevant association cortex—thereby producing a Primal—the amount of voltage released must be highly selective and qualitative in the sense that the release must be specific to the feeling. The amount of overall energy activated will eventually be the same as the original trauma. If the trauma was gigantic, then it will take many Primals of optimum intensity to resolve a single event or feeling and, therefore, the symptoms and behaviors that arise from it.

If the trauma has a relatively low valence, then fewer Primals will be necessary for reengaging secondary cortex.

Thus, a Primal entails both a specific quality and an optimum quantity of activation. Those two criteria are essential for healing and growth. This kind of optimum activation permits *new dendritic growth and resumed maturation of previously silenced portions of the brain*.[1] The vertical functional units will be physiologically unified across all three levels of human functioning.

One can see a direct relationship between silencing or disconnection of the brain and Painful life experience. James Prescott of the National Institute of Mental Health discussed institutional children who suffered great deprivation of physical and emotional warmth in the earliest months and years of life.[2] He believes that this amount of deprivation produces structural damage—fewer dendritic branches and thus less intercellular contact. This damage due to massive overload produces more of the silent areas I have discussed, so many silent

[1] Dendrites are branchlike structures which conduct impulses to the nerve cells.
[2] James Prescott, "Touching," in *Intellectual Digest*, March 1974.

areas that the structure of the brain changes. In other words, "brain damage" has a new meaning. Psychological events can produce a kind of brain damage no less physical or long-lasting than that caused by a blow to the head.

Conversely, when the amount of early input is optimum there seems to be greater growth of neurons. A series of studies reported in the August 12, 1977 issue of *Science* found that rats which grow up in enriched and stimulating environments develop more brain—a heavier cortex and more dendritic connections—with which to deal with the world around them. The authors, R. A. Cummins and associates of Stanford University Medical School, hypothesized that there are groups of neurons within animal brains which develop fully only in the presence of adequate sensory stimulation. When one isolates—and places in pain—an animal, development of these neurons is retarded.

The cortex has a dual function when it comes to Pain. It operates to help us understand the meaning of what we experience, and it also helps *limit* the amount of information we process. It inhibits excess information. Thus, disconnection and silencing is every bit as important to our survival as reconnection later on. Failure of this disconnection can perhaps lead to early crib death or epileptic seizures in which the brain is highly overcharged.

Those who were deprived of physical warmth from the first day of life are overloaded, and this taxes the inhibitory cortex. With weakened inhibition all Primal stimuli impinge at once; the result is distractibility, short attention span, and poor concentration. These individuals suffer from a "failure of inhibition," perhaps due in part to extensive areas of silent cortex—not enough cortex available to handle the constant stimulation from within. It is as though even the disconnecting system is faltering due to its burden.

The secondary association cortex is only one aspect of the disconnecting process. There are other ways the brain disconnects. But no matter what the mechanisms, one thing is certain: with the loss of feeling there is no way to lead a meaningful life.

7: The Pathways of Connection

CONNECTION—making conscious a previously disconnected experience —puts an end to a specific amount of trapped energy associated with an imprinted trauma. Connection is crucial to the healing process because it means that diverted impulses have made a final linkage with their proper and original pathways. Connection means that one has released out of the system the specific energy associated with an early trauma. It means that new situations lose their power to trigger off stored explosions, since there are fewer electrical storms hidden away. It means there are no smoldering forces to impel out-of-control, irrational reactions. Energy that might have been channeled into restlessness, tension in the muscles, stomach secretions, or violent or compulsive behavior is finally properly linked and dissipated.

The linkage of stored memory to higher level cognition means that the person is finally connected to himself in a physiologic way. The system, which had been working hard at maintaining the disconnection, can finally relax. That linkage, when felt during a Primal, has an inviolable solidity to it. It is an unmistakable experience.

If there is not an exact connection, the energy of disconnected Pain continues to activate the system, forcing new channels of release. Some of these channels can be more socially acceptable than others and, indeed, many therapies are engaged in little more than rechanneling disconnected Pain into socially acceptable behavior. Without connection, this is an endless job.

To become conscious when you are neurotic, in the Primal sense, is first to become conscious of Pain. To be unconscious of Pain is to be *unconscious* to some extent. Since there is a biologic system to decrease consciousness, increasing consciousness can only be achieved through dealing with that biologic system. If you are not in Pain, there is no way to become more conscious than you are. You can only become *aware*.

Connection is assured in only one way—by engaging the agony of a feeling or a memory; it is the agony that impels an old memory toward consciousness and resolution. This requires moving down the nervous system so that one is on the level of feeling. There is no conscious, willful way to do that, no matter how strong the motivation. It is a useless task, for example, to try to retrieve memories through verbal means from before one's cortex existed. Consciousness is only achieved through connections made on the proper level.

The patient who relives a Painful scene in childhood has traveled back from the most sophisticated brain functions to the most primitive. In neurologic terms, the cortex has engaged the limbic system to release the store of Painful memories which then activates the hypothalamus to express the agonizing component of the feeling. This Pain activates the neural arrays of which I have previously spoken. The cortical areas previously silenced are awakened to give meaning to the feeling, permitting the entire response to be conscious. Pain contains within it its own meaning and it is through Pain that that meaning is rediscovered.

In reconnection, only some aspects of the entire feeling are experienced during a single session. With each new connection there are new insights, as more and more of the secondary association areas of the cortex are recruited in the knowing process rather than the unknowing process.

As the connection process takes place, all of the original responses surrounding the early traumatic event become evident. As a patient relives a birth trauma, for example, there may be spontaneous gagging and choking. The patient cannot produce tears nor can he utter words. The level of brain organization is specific to the experience. At the point of connection all associated symbolic responses fade and what is left is lucidity, consciousness. The patient feels the feeling becoming integrated.

As the load of Pain decreases, the person can begin to experience those more severe Pains set down deeper in the brain and earlier in the past.[1] He can feel and integrate lower-level Pains because they are

[1] It is possible, of course, to have catastrophic events later in life. But those events, such as the loss of one's parents, are not as catastrophic in one's twenties as they are when one is six or seven. The brain's capacity to handle trauma is not as fully developed in the first years of life as it is later on.

no longer weighted down with compounded more recent Pains. The system begins to relax commensurately. It is apparent to the sufferer subjectively, and it is obvious to an observer. There is considerably less "drive."

We see relaxation resulting from connection in many ways, particularly in the drops in vital sign levels and in the changes in brain activity. The study at the UCLA Brain Research Institute found an 83 percent decrease in neuronal activity of Primal patients' brain waves (amplitude). With connection, dreams change toward less symbolism and symptoms fall away—there is no longer neurotic energy available to produce symptoms and excessive behavior.

It is likely that the insights which accompany feelings occur in two ways. Rapid insights immediately following a feeling are probably predominantly neuroelectric events. But the insight process goes on for days after a feeling and the slower developing kind is most likely due to biochemical transformations of nerve cells which were previously rendered abnormal by Pain.[2]

Integratable agony is the key to understanding connection. Too much Pain released at once (such as with LSD or by forcing the patient) results in excess energy which must again be rerouted neurotically. That means continued suffering. Too little energizing and the cortex is not sufficiently engaged. This often happens in abreaction where individuals will go through the motions of a Primal feeling but have done so "deliberately" from the point of view of an adult trying to be a baby. The thrashing and wailing may be there but not enough of the Pain; connections are not made, except perhaps some intellectual ones which have a very superficial quality to them. A therapist who is not perceptive about his patient may often miss abreaction and inadvertently bolster the defense system.

Both disconnection and reconnection are biologic processes and necessities, each in its own time. Since there is a rudimentary neocortex even at birth, it must be assumed that these traumas which are imprinted deep in the nervous system have some kind of weak correlate higher up. In reconnection, the lower and higher imprints of experience may actually "recognize" each other in a way that makes their later linkage direct and inevitable once the gates are lifted.

Recent research has shown that nerve cells secrete material which

[2] It is possible that delayed insights after a feeling depend in some way upon a gradually restored biochemical balance. To put it differently, Pain originally blocked the completion of certain biochemical destinations of the genetic code for certain neurotransmitters. This prevented the proper appreciation of reality; it may take some time before the reexperience of Pain "rights" the neurotransmitter so that full reality can be perceived again.

determines which other nerve cells will connect with them, although the exact identity of the substance is unknown.[3] When Pain alters the biochemistry of the nerve cells it evidently interferes with the recognition and connection process. Neural cells which have been transformed no longer "recognize" each other enough to meet and form strong bonds. In reconnection the brain's biochemistry is normalized so that nerve projections can find each other again, thus completing a circuit that was originally intended to be. There seems to be a true "home" for nerve pathways that have been disconnected by repression.[4]

One can see the recognition factor on a cellular level. A scientist can place two clusters of heart cells at opposite ends of a prepared dish and two clusters of liver cells at the other ends. The liver cells move toward the liver cells and the heart toward the heart. This cellular recognition is quite similar to our remembering an old friend; it simply occurs on a different level. The recognition of an old friend, sophisticated process though that is, is still the result of a conglomerate of cells working together. Those heart cells on the scientist's dish have two separate lives. They pulse at different rates. But when they come together, they pulse as one.

Cells seem to be inherently able to reconnect with similar cells. For example, severed nerve cells in the leech's central nervous system can reconnect with their normal contacts—even when they have to pick them out from among hundreds of other cells. It takes about two to three weeks for impulses to pass again from a cut nerve cell through the severed segment to its connecting cell. Thus, nerve cells in the leech heal by reconnection. This very process of physiological reconnection may be a model for how neurochemically disconnected nerve cells are rejoined in the human brain.

After the development in human history of a higher cortex, there may have been a tendency for every experience to search out higher level connections for meaning. Pain blocked on lower levels strives toward conscious connection. Neurophysiologist Steven Rose explains that "many aspects of the coding for the wiring of the central nervous system operate in a similar way. They are genetically specified so that certain connections are obligatory."[5]

---

[3] Review by Jean Marx in *Science,* Vol. 206, October 26, 1979, p. 437.

[4] A report in *Brain-Mind Bulletin,* January 1, 1979, indicates that memory storage relies on *connection,* not on individual cells. Memory deficit is based on "flawed connections."

[5] Steven Rose, *The Conscious Brain,* Weidenfeld & Nicolson, London, 1973, p. 170.

William Gevarter of the National Aeronautics and Space Administration has emphasized the importance of connection to deep-lying processes in the brain when it comes to neurosis. He says, "The only therapies providing enduring change are those that permanently defuse old brain programs." He points out that psychoanalysis, because it usually changes conscious judgment rather than the unconscious, offers "new-brain insights and knowledge . . . rather than a cure." Dr. Gevarter believes that old-brain programming must be attacked by permanent modification of the "reverberating circuits" of old emotional charge.[6]

What Dr. Gevarter called the modification of the reverberating circuits we call connection. Connection is the core of Primal Therapy. To be connected means at the same time to be freed from the impelling forces of the unconscious. Indeed, there is no unconscious, as such, to the extent that a person has felt his unconscious needs and Pains. Connection doesn't eradicate or fulfill infantile need. But it does reduce it to an old need, something in the past. This frees the person to fulfill adult needs for love and affection because he is no longer filtering childish needs through an adult body.

Once joined, a circuit remains connected, a physiologic fact. That connection endures and is why, when enough connection has taken place, one does not become neurotic again. With each connection one makes one has more of oneself. The more connections, the more whole a person becomes, the more he is himself. That is what "being yourself" really means.

[6] *Brain-Mind Bulletin,* September 18, 1978, p. 1.

IV: A SCIENCE OF BEING HUMAN

1: A Science of Feeling

MANY people assume that "feelings" cannot be converted into hard information that scientists can readily study and share. After all, "I feel blue" has dozens of different meanings in as many people. But today feelings and emotions *can* be measured. So long as this measurement capability did not exist, psychologists had little choice in what they measured: "If all we can measure is behavior, then psychology must be the study of behavior." Psychology put itself in a circular trap, studying only what it could see and seeing only what it could study.

Yet behavior is only one aspect—the end result—of what goes on in the psyche. What takes place in the brain and body—in consciousness—is at the root of how we behave. It is time to lay to rest the myth that how we behave is what we are.

A fundamental reason why we have failed to study feeling is that feelings have always been suspect. They have been viewed as a danger to society—and to science. Emotions are said to lead scientists astray and keep them from being "objective." Emotions "blind," and feelings are "irrational." "Emotions sway judgment." In an important way, this is true. But the precautions against allowing feelings to sway a scientist's judgment should not then blind him to feelings as a subject of study. It is the very existence of unconscious emotions that sway judgment, and judgment can be in error precisely because emotions are held under control.

Too often there is a tendency in scientists to distrust inner life, because, cut off from themselves, scientists can treat a patient or a subject in the same way—as someone who behaves apart from internal driving forces. An acknowledgment of feelings would go a long way toward enabling scientists to recognize those forces in their patients.

Neurosis is *not* just a behavior, but a form of disease. The changes that take place in the presence of neurosis are the same as happen when an alien germ or microbe invades the system. The person runs a fever in both cases, the lymphocyte balance changes, as does the white cell count. There are germs in the atmosphere that cause physical pathology; and there are pathological situations and pathological parents that cause children to become abnormal psychologically and physiologically.

When any external event superimposed on a human being distorts or impedes natural processes, it is an alien force. It forces all subsystems of the body to compensate for the intrusion. If it is natural to express your feelings but parents stifle you every time, then that intrusion is an alien force that eventually produces disease processes. If a surgeon cuts deep into the body and traumatizes it beyond its ability to respond, that alien force may contribute to the disease of neurosis. If a baby is not ready to walk but is nevertheless forced to try every day, that is an alien intrusion on a naturally developing system which must then compensate for this intrusion. If the infant expresses herself in the only way she can by crying and no one comes to comfort her, another intrusion is made on what she does naturally until she learns to do what is unnatural—not cry when hurt or uncomfortable. She is shutting off a necessary and vital function with far-reaching physiologic effects. It is not simply that she has stopped crying and acted grown-up. That simple act has changed her biology. The restoration of deep crying, then, is not just a nice thing to have happen. It means restoring a vital physiologic function. There are changes when our responses are taken away from us, and changes again when they are returned.

Pain is an interruption of natural processes. The alteration of the self extends down into the tissues and cells. The fact that someone cannot express his feelings isn't simply a matter of a lack of vocabulary. It affects the total system. The end product of this alteration is disease.

Our task is twofold. First, to find out whether repressing an event at age five can result in disease at age twenty-five, and, if so, how. One of the ways we go about the task is to study alterations of normal function. An excessive accumulation of Primal Pain overtaxes normal systems to produce permanent alterations of function. The system then is in a constant state of compensation in order to keep an equilibrium. The subsystems, in response to Pain, become fixed in their distortion and neurosis sets in. There is a new kind of system: a neurotic one with characteristic biologic patterns. We look to the biologic patterns for the evidence of neurosis.

Neurosis is the pattern of enduring, critical alterations of both psychologic and biologic functions in the absence of current stressors. It is real to show the stress reactions when we are in current danger. But it is neurotic to show those same reactions when we are not in danger. Of course, the neurotic is in danger, but it is from his past. He is in danger of becoming conscious of his Pain and of being overwhelmed by it. He frequently exhibits physiologic responses as though his life were in continual danger.

All of the stressors that originally altered his systems are still there, and these changes can be measured. They are chemically engraved in his cells. His body reacts constantly to the imprinted engrams (memory traces) of that original Pain from his childhood. That is the meaning of neurotic stress. *The cure for neurosis is expressing finally the full response to those Pains that have caused alterations of function.*

THE CURE FOR NEUROSIS

It is rare indeed that the word "cure" is used in psychotherapy. Psychotherapists are more comfortable with such terms as "remission of symptoms." Indeed, any therapist using the word "cure" is immediately suspect. Perhaps this is due to the despairing feeling among professionals that rooting out causes is practically impossible. Therefore, one must be content with "beating back the devil."

But so long as we are careful about the meaning of cure there is no reason not to use the term. Indeed, if one can make an enduring change in a person's psychophysiology by dealing with the deep-lying drives behind neurotic states of being and neurotic symptoms, one is warranted in using the word "cure."

Unfortunately, psychotherapists cannot agree on any way to measure cure or therapeutic improvement. To compound the difficulty, almost every psychotherapeutic system has a different notion of what improvement is. Their idea of improvement is in accord with the theory propagated.

The behaviorist Joseph Wolpe, for example, noted various standards for therapeutic improvement: symptomatic improvement, increased productiveness at work, improved interpersonal relationships, and enhanced ability to handle reasonable reality stresses.[1] Albert Ellis, in ra-

[1] Alvin Mahrer, *The Goals of Psychotherapy*, Appleton-Century-Crofts, New York, 1967, p. 131.

tional-emotive psychotherapy, states that his very different goal in treatment is to give the patient a method of self-observation and self-assessment that will keep him from being anxious or hostile. He redirects the patient through philosophic understanding and a kind of conditioning of behavior, toward a more rational acceptance of his situation.[2]

The existentialists, on the contrary, believe that psychotherapy is a process in which a patient is set free to "actualize" his unique self in a unique life situation in accordance with reality. In all of these the more insight a person has, or the more maturely a person behaves, the better the therapeutic improvement is supposed to be.

However, such criteria offer no reliable way to measure therapeutic improvement. Each of these theories is pretty much a case of "shoe-makers seeing only shoes in the world." The behaviorists study behavior. The Rogerians measure attitudes, and the existentialists extol "commitment." Indeed, the more vague and self-limiting the theory, the less precise the measures of therapeutic improvement. But such is the state of the art of psychotherapy today.

A recent survey in psychology discovered that the great majority of psychologists are eclectic in their approach, meaning that they have no special approach to the patient.[3] In eclecticism, the practitioner pays total allegiance to no one theory of personality, yet employs "useful information" from all of them. If this situation appeared in any other branch of science, it would be ludicrous. Can you imagine ten different theories about the same phenomenon in nuclear physics? And that the physicists claim allegiance to no special theory but to *all* of them?

Clearly, until now, psychotherapy has been an art, not a science; that is why it has been a "matter of taste," so to speak, as to which therapy one enters, and a matter of personal judgment as to whether one has improved in psychotherapy or not. I believe that eclecticism rises in popularity among mental health professionals when nothing seems to work. No one approach accomplishes much, so the belief is that if one throws in more and more, something is bound to work; hardly an auspicious way to treat a sick person. The problem, of course, is that so many professionals do not know that these neurotics are really physically sick.

Can you imagine how confusing all this would be to the seriously ill person? He doesn't need a supermarket of approaches; he needs one consistent approach based on a thorough understanding of what is wrong. Apply this approach to child rearing and the point becomes

2 Mahrer, p. 218.
3 *American Psychologist*, August 1978, p. 753.

clear; for the first two years the parent is passive, the second five years authoritarian, and then the next five years passive and nondirective again . . . a sure way to make a child neurotic.

We now know what to do, and the procedures are specific and becoming more refined by the day. The approach varies, not from one theory to another, but from one technique to another within a single comprehensive theory. If the mishmash approach were really valid, why hasn't someone put all of the best into one theory and developed that? I think it is because all one would get is a more elegant mishmash.

Psychologists cannot even agree on what mental illness is. Thomas Szasz believes that mental illness is a myth, that people who deviate from the norm are only labeled "abnormal" by the so-called "normals." Yet, by recognizing that "mental illness" is a biologic state of suffering, as we have found it to be, one could never reach Szasz's conclusion.

Psychologic processes are biologic. Since all biologic systems have a normal way of functioning, the brain must have a normal mode of operation as well.

Thought processes cannot be normal if the lower brain mechanisms are distorted by repressed Pain. The way to evaluate those functions is to measure them against "normal" brain processes which occur in the absence of Pain or after its resolution in Primal Therapy. Thoughts will correspond to external reality if one resolves the early distortions which made thoughts correspond to *old* realities. Since we cannot measure Pain directly except by verbal report, the best we can do at this point is to measure it indirectly in terms of the processing mechanisms of the brain and body—for example, via body temperature.

Without biologic standards psychologists must average out responses of well-functioning neurotics (the conventional idea of a normal) to establish their norms. They must often rely on psychological tests to tell them about the existence of mental illness. The various test questionnaires, such as the MMPI (The Minnesota Multiphasic Personality Inventory), ask hundreds of questions, such as: "Do you sleep well?" "Do you shake a lot?" "Do you find yourself in a corner alone at parties?" "Do you suffer from frequent loss of appetite?" These really ask someone only to list his neurotic symptoms. Then the scores are added up, a neurotic index is created, and if you score high enough, you are "neurotic." You are fed back what you feed in. The language you feed in is not half as sophisticated as that which you get back, so it seems scientific and somehow utterly different from what you put into the test. You get one description for another.

The verbal tests are standardized among thousands of individuals.

Somehow "normals" are found, usually in college for some reason, and then your neurosis and its severity is measured against those norms. The problem is that "normal" for these tests implies someone who adjusts well to his neurosis. The degree of a person's neurosis, nevertheless, is how much he deviates from these college students. They have decided that what is average is "normal" but they have no idea what is "healthy." To discover health we must apply biologic indices to these "normal" populations.

What most of the psychological questionnaires really measure is how effectively repressed someone is; that is then called "normal." If you don't shake, suffer anxieties, or eat or sleep poorly, and are not moody, you are fine. If you do suffer all of these symptoms, you are not so fine. Yet from our perspective, it may be just the opposite; you are fine as you get closer to feelings and not so fine as you leave them. It is not pleasant to shake, but it is a sign of being closer to being human than if you had Pain and didn't shake. Being human is in feeling, sensing, experiencing—being open to the great joys and agonies of life. The person who is conventionally "well adjusted" may be killing himself through compulsive overwork. The good neurotic rarely considers that he is working too hard. He is simply carrying out the normal work ethic.

When Pain is laid bare, we can see the unconscious at work. We can make direct observations of the *underlying motivations* of behavior. We understand that perception, cognition, attitudes, and interpersonal interaction are not separate aspects of human behavior so much as inextricably interwoven emanations of feelings. "Seeing" the unconscious is an entirely new idea in psychology.

CRITERIA FOR A PRIMAL: THE PROBLEM OF MEASUREMENT

To judge the efficacy of Primal Therapy we need to be very clear as to what a Primal is. There are subjective and objective criteria for the Primal experience.

The Subjective Experience of a Primal

A Primal begins with an increase in the depth of breathing while the body may twitch and shake.[4] The whole system acts as one unit

---

[4] Not everybody experiences a Primal in exactly the same way but there are several common characteristics.

deeply encompassed by an overwhelming experience. The person is transported into his childhood, is engulfed by it. He is experiencing a Pain he has not fully experienced before. His face and posture show his agony. Generally, vivid, old scenes pass through his mind. He is descending to a level of consciousness where emotional tone is organized and where images are sharper than ever imagined. He is not rehearsing, nor dwelling on what he is going to say. He is overtaken by the sights, sounds, and the sense of the past. He feels a great upheaval. Tears and sobs usually occur and there is agony. The body is often out of control, sometimes writhing and thrashing around. There may variously be screams, groans, whimpers, grunts, moans, and deep, tearful crying. The emotional tone is of great pathos and misery. The patient is expressing his needs, "Hold me," "Love me," "Be good to me." There is not a deliberate quality to what he is saying, the words just pour forth. There is a total lack of willfulness. Sometimes there are no words, just moans and sobs. The Primal may go on for an hour or more. Slowly, as the feeling subsides, the person comes back into the present.

The feeling after a Primal is not like any other. It is a profound feeling of deep tranquility, relaxation, and very acute perceptions— suddenly everything is crystal clear. The patient often doesn't move for a long time after—he is filled with new sensations and insights which continue as the feeling settles in. His breathing is deeper and clearer. He has been in a "conscious coma"; he has not only been conscious, but superconscious—not of an external world, but a deep, internal one. He knows where he is, he knows where he has been, but in a reversal of his normal experience the usual consciousness remained in the background, dimly lit, while the lower levels of consciousness moved to the foreground.

The patient may say there is a knowing and then there is a real *knowing.* It is a different magnitude of knowing, a different kind of experience than the cerebral type one is used to.

One cannot try to have a Primal. When one makes deliberate, conscious efforts to have a Primal, the less access one has to oneself. That is because the top level of consciousness is making an effort, is more active when it should be less active.

Objective Criteria for a Primal

There are physiologic changes which characteristically occur when a person is having Primals and there are psychologic effects as well, which help provide objective evidence of a Primal.

Not all Primals look or sound alike. What they all have in common, however, is Pain. The processing of ascending Pain by the system has objective signs, such as the sudden increase in heart rate and blood pressure, increases in muscle tension and an elevated body temperature. Here are some of the objective signs:

1. Sudden and marked increases in heart rate, ranging from 120 to 200 beats per minute, and occasionally higher.

2. Abrupt rise in blood pressure into the hypertensive range.

3. In first-line Primals there is extreme increase in muscle tension with a postural bias in extension with arching of the back and extension backward of the head and neck. The face registers agony and is often "scrunched up." Both knees are brought in tightly against the belly.

4. Transient rise in body temperature ranging between one and three degrees.

5. Breathing becomes deeper and deeper as the patient approaches the feeling, expanding to seemingly cover the entire body. If the patient is abreacting or partially disconnected, he will often become dizzy, which is not the case in a true Primal where the patient needs that oxygen, as he is expending great energy.

6. Finally, there is a breakthrough into the feeling, often, but not always, accompanied by full and prolonged crying or screaming. The various vital signs begin to fall.

The Post-Primal State

The energy of a Primal is often released over a period of an hour or two. It is liberated in the form of deep crying. It is also liberated in the extreme physical movements often exhibited during a Primal. After a Primal session:

1. The heart is usually slower than the resting pulse by ten to twenty beats. It can happen that it can drop by thirty or forty beats per minute below resting levels.

2. Blood pressure falls steadily so that a typical post-session reading would be 100/50.

3. Facial pallor is replaced by profuse sweating and a reddening of the skin.

4. There is a profound decrease in all muscle tension. Electromyographic readings of neck tension after a Primal indicate major decreases. One need only inspect the patient to see that the entire body seems limp. He could not be tense again even by an act of will.

It would be extremely difficult for him to even mimic the muscle strain he showed an hour or two before. His face is relaxedly alive and clear-looking.

5. The access to tears—some of our patients have not cried in decades or for as long as they can remember—is associated with a decrease in pupil size.

6. The core body temperature falls below the patient's usual "normal" reading.

7. Urinary urgency ceases.

8. The breathing is light, steady, and calm.

For all he has been through, the patient often appears markedly refreshed. It is due to feeling. There is that sudden surge of lucidity which has been buried with the Pain.

There is an ineffable but unmistakable quality to a Primal. It is a moving experience. You feel for the patient and often you are brought to the verge of tears yourself. This is never the case with abreaction, which moves no one, least of all the patient, and which has a hollow ring. The crying and screams are forced and shallow and often they go on too long to be justified by the so-called feeling one is in.

PAIN IS PAIN IS PAIN

In our research, we have had patients rate their Primals—complete, incomplete, abreaction, just sobs but not Primal, etc.—with a matching questionnaire for the therapist to fill out. It is surprising how rarely the patient and therapist will disagree—this, of course, without discussing it with each other. These reports were then matched against the objective criteria of a Primal.

There are characteristic changes in all vital signs with Primals, including brain-wave patterns. They do not occur in simulated Primals, mere screaming, abreaction, physical exercises, or hypnotic states. We have been searching for objective methods of differentiating a Primal from abreaction. We have also wanted to find some instrument that would quantify Primals in terms of intensity. In this way we hoped to measure the resolution of Pain and Primals. Dr. Michael Holden, director of research of the Primal Institute, has developed a "Resolution Index," which is essentially a mathematical treatment of changes in the key vital signs and the alpha amplitude during a Primal session. It is a way of measuring, for the first time, neurosis and its resolution.

A true Primal experience is a two-phased event: a sympathetic nervous system crisis with vital signs markedly elevated, followed by a parasympathetic nervous system recovery phase. The recovery phase is marked by a continuous drop in all vital signs below the starting baseline values.[5]

What is important about the processes is that no matter what Primals different patients are having, their biologic systems move toward a common denominator. There is the same movement downward of the vital signs even though one patient is reliving being abandoned while another is having the experience of being humiliated or criticized.

Pain is Pain. No matter what the external circumstance and no matter what the mental labels, Primal Pain is processed in the same way by the same mechanisms with the same results. The analysis of the multitudinous external circumstances in psychotherapy is not at all necessary. Once they arrive inside they are *exactly the same* so far as the body is concerned. It is to those internal processes that any psychotherapy must address itself.

As the biologic indices become more homogeneous within the Primal groups, patients are free to become more heterogeneous psychologically. Thus, as they move toward the biologic mean, dialectically, they diverge psychologically to become an individual personality.

A Primal session is characterized by several surges of the feeling, or at least several bouts with experiencing pieces of the feeling. Thus, we characteristically see several pre-Primal peaks in a session followed by one very high peak before the person falls into the feeling and begins his recovery phase. The beginning of the feeling is the beginning of the recovery phase biologically. To feel is to recover—to recover one's sanity, one's self, one's ability to rest and repair. When we still see elevations of vital signs after a session, we know the person is still defended and has not fully felt.

The hallmark of the Primal breakthrough is weeping. Yet weeping does not constitute a Primal. Hysterics weep all the time and make no therapeutic progress. The weeping must be connected to its original source. Primals have been characterized as "weeping fits." Restoring that natural function to someone has many beneficial results. Indeed, weeping is essential to the healing process. The therapeutic benefits of weeping have largely been overlooked in the psychiatric literature, even while it is obvious that *what all psychiatric patients have in common is misery.* It should have been logical to allow patients to weep

[5] E. Michael Holden, "A Quantitative Index of Pain Resolution in Primals with Discussion of Probable Relevant Biologic Mechanisms," *Journal of Primal Therapy,* Vol. 4, No. 1, Winter 1977, pp. 37–52.

out their misery for long periods of time. Yet, any crying that goes on too long or too deeply is often suspect in conventional therapy. It is considered hysterical or disintegrating; often tranquilizers are prescribed or the therapist rushes in to comfort and thereby shuts off the feeling. The history of psychiatric disorders is nothing else than the history of sadness; yet *no one drew the conclusion that sad people need to cry.*[6]

There is a good deal to be learned in the study of tears, for they have roughly the same ingredients as the blood system without the red cells. We are engaged in a study of the biochemistry of the tears of our patients in cooperation with William Frey, biochemist at St. Paul University of Minnesota, Biochemistry Department. Dr. Frey has studied the chemistry of tears and has discovered in them high concentrations of stress hormones. This does not occur in tears resulting from irritants such as onions. Clearly, if there is indeed a release of stress hormones with tears, then the blocking of that release may result in the buildup of stress hormones. We believe that crying is an important biologic function and that the shedding of tears is *central,* not incidental, to the resolution of neurosis. There is no such thing as a "talking cure." The fact of weeping *itself* helps relieve suffering. Tears not only remove toxic substances of the eye, they also have a precise role in the removal of toxic biochemical substances from the entire system.

It doesn't matter how long one has been in therapy for there to be full resolution in a particular Primal sequence. Beginning patients can have just as much resolution as the older ones. The one difference is that the long-term patients have shorter, more "efficient" Primals. They find it easier to get right down to it without a lot of defensive maneuvering. Control groups who did as much exercise as we see in Primals had no resolution at all; indeed, all biologic indices indicated increased body work at the end of the session. Here we have a seeming anomaly. The Primal patient is often moving about violently and his vital signs are *dropping.* There is only one explanation for this and that is feeling; it is the one sole differentiating factor. The body doesn't work when it feels; it works when it doesn't.

[6] Release is important, as both Drs. E. Michael Holden and David A. Goodman describe the Primal breakthrough as a cortical-release phenomenon, where the cortical control (third level) has been lifted naturally, allowing subcortical mechanisms, the mechanisms which produce sobbing and convulsions, to occur. Dr. Goodman writes, "Weeping may hold the key to mental health. Primal tears are the key to understanding the phenomenon. Tears of grief, loneliness, and loss are the solution that dissolves the walls of the unconscious and that dissipates encapsulated Pain." Weeping is a holistic act involving all of the human systems, encompassing all levels of the neuroendocrine axis that begins in the hypothalamus.

One must not lose sight of the simplest points in doing research. The wide swings in all vital sign indicators in a patient lying flat on his back shows that a memory with its original force from the age of two, for example, is still there.

Regression by levels in Primal Therapy proceeds by the reverse order of the development of the brain. We descend not only in personal time in Primal experiences, but in anthropologic time as well. We are eventually controlled not just by our infant brain but by the brain system of animal forms which existed millions of years ago. The slithering, fishtailing movements we see in first-line Primals are truly amphibious. It is virtually the same brain as the salamander.[7]

The swimming birth movements in some patients are organized in the deep nerve tissue of the brainstem, exactly where the swimming movements of the salamander are also organized. These movements by patients are scarcely play-acting nor can they be copied voluntarily. They indicate control of our system, *for that moment,* by a brain system more than 300 million years old. Here is where the earliest infantile (and even prebirth) traumas are stored, and here is where we must go if we are to connect to and resolve them. There are no words during this period; and if there are, if the person is merely describing his state, he is not really there; he is in his head—millions of years later, *talking* about an experience instead of *having* it.

A Primal has the appearance of a seizure, yet is physiologically and emotionally far from it. Interestingly, however, the aftereffects of a seizure are not altogether different from those of a Primal; slowing of pulse and respiration, dilation of superficial blood vessels, profuse sweating, and the fall of the temperature and blood pressure. *One might say that the epileptic has had a Primal equivalent but without the connection or the relaxation.* A seizure is a random discharge of tremendous—usually first-line—energy. The great difference is that a seizure is *dis*integrating; it fogs consciousness, produces a transient amnesia, and leads to a state of general confusion.

STRESS

An important consideration in measuring neurosis and recovery is the amount of stress in the system. Stress is convenient to measure,

[7] The hypothalamus of the human brain comprises much of the anterior brain of the salamander.

both because previous research has illuminated many of its biochemical aspects, and because we would naturally suspect that stress is created by Pain.

There has been a good deal of research on stress, particularly since World War II when studies were done on soldiers who had been in lengthy combat. For almost all of those years since the war, Hans Selye has been conducting research on stress, particularly on the ways in which the human system handles stress.[8]

Selye's important discoveries have to do with hormone changes that occur during stress. The pituitary secretes a number of stress hormones including ACTH (adrenocorticotrophic hormone), causing the adrenal cortex to change raw materials into stress hormones which are then distributed by the blood system. The adrenal medulla also secretes the stress hormones *adrenaline and noradrenaline.* Noradrenaline transmits messages of activation. These two neurotransmitters work in compensating fashion so that the depletion of the repressant serotonin results in an increase in noradrenaline, and vice versa. The brainstem overarousal, produced by increased noradrenaline, puts enormous pressure on control mechanisms and can render them ineffective.

Adrenaline likewise increases blood pressure and heart rate as well as body temperature. It also increases the energy turnover of the body. The effects of increased adrenaline are anxiety states, restlessness, and sleeplessness. The long-term effects of adrenaline overproduction may be decreased reserves for emergencies and, therefore, a shorter lifespan.

Low noradrenaline animals are more lethargic; low serotonin ones are more agitated. Noradrenaline is clearly an activator; serotonin a suppressor. Low serotonin animals are more frightened and anxious. One might say, in biochemical terms, that an anxiety state is one in which serotonin is low and noradrenaline high.

Selye lists behavioral and symptomatic indicators of stress, including irritability and hyperexcitation, pounding of the heart, dryness of the mouth, trembling, easy startle reactions, teeth grinding, insomnia, sweating, frequent need to urinate, diarrhea, and indigestion. These indicators are largely signs of sympathetic nervous system arousal and of leakage in the gates against Pain. A reduction in these obvious effects means to the conventional psychiatrist that the person is getting over his neurosis. It is mostly a case of anxiety reduction. If you take, as a starting point in research, a reduction in the most obvious indices

[8] Hans Selye, *The Stress of Life,* McGraw-Hill Book Company, New York, 1976.

of stress, it will appear to mean an alteration in the neurosis, when all it may really mean is an improvement in the defense system.

Neurosis is not synonymous with the obvious symptoms of stress as listed above. Therefore, we have measured stress on the most fundamental level possible, such as that of hormone production. Scientific knowledge of how pain is processed would indicate that the burden of Primal Pain on the hypothalamus is distributed to the pituitary, which converts the Pain message into hormone secretions.

From our work, we understand that stressors are implanted in the neurophysiologic system with early trauma, and that these stressors then *chronically* create the same biologic havoc that Selye sees. The difference from the acute stress reaction is that the stressors are unseen; they are historic and not at all obvious as is usually the case in stress research. Yet all of the stressors that originally altered the system are still there. Until resolved, Pain is a *permanent stressor*.

Primal stress is an odd thing. It is not as though someone pinches you, you hurt, they stop pinching, and you stop hurting. It is as though someone has pinched you, and then you go on hurting from it for a lifetime. People wonder later on why you are suffering so and why you have all those physical ailments for "no apparent reason." "It must be in your mind." "It's psychosomatic"—the favorite phrase of physicians who have no concept of inner stress. It is in your mind, all right, right smack in your brain; as physical as a tumor, as forceful as being plugged into a light socket.

In a sense, the body doesn't know that there are no longer any forceps traumatizing it, no longer any parent ignoring its needs or terrorizing it. It receives the constant imprinted message of danger and responds accordingly. A part of the brain doesn't know what the danger is; all it knows is that it must mobilize itself to meet some unknown threat. That is why so many of us get up each morning feeling a kind of dread or apprehension. At that moment we just happen to be less distracted from ourselves, from what we feel all of the time.

Biochemical research can detect the presence of stress. There are biologic parameters indicating stress and these exist irrespective of what a person notices about himself. Many of our patients never report a feeling of being "under stress." They often do not feel the stress as such. They just feel dead, dull and lifeless. But our measurements reveal a paradox: the "mind" is unaware of stress but the lower levels of consciousness are very aware of it; and dealing with it continuously.

Oddly, one can read volume after volume on stress and never see the word "pain." Stress is always considered to be external and in the here-and-now. There are numerous studies on job stress, marital stress, school stress, but not on the stress of imprinted Pain. We all suffer from chronic stress—Pain—but nobody talks about it *because* everyone suffers from it.

The neurotic is in a constant state of alarm. The alarm reaction causes the release of stress hormones and the burning up of energy. As long as one is young enough to organize one's life to keep pace with the flow of energy, things may be fine. But with age and insufficient outlets, the energy begins to be absorbed by the organ systems; that is when the heart and other organs begin to falter. (Retirement frequently kills because the same amount of excess energy suddenly has still fewer outlets for release.) It is a sign that Pain is causing the mobilization of energy reserves usually utilized for daily living.

WHAT IS "BETTER" IN PSYCHOTHERAPY

Until now it has been possible to treat patients with almost any kind of approach ranging from poetry therapy to psychoanalysis and have numbers of reported successes. Is it possible that every approach has something to offer? We will never know until we establish proper criteria for progress in psychotherapy. And we shall lack those criteria so long as psychotherapists insist that only *mental* illness exists, and that neurosis is not a biologic disease.

Patients in a wide variety of therapies believe that they have improved, and by all subjective indices they have improved. They "feel better." At least, they *think* they feel better. They have made better external adjustments and social adaptations. It is possible, however, to produce better social adaptation without once touching the neurosis.

Some researchers have looked for biologic change but on a very selective basis. They have measured either blood pressure or adjustments of the biochemistry, but because they have lacked a holistic approach, their findings are one-sided. For example, the interpretations of findings from certain kinds of meditation and biofeedback are incorrect. They contend that high amplitude waves indicate relaxation. We have found that high amplitude alpha is a sign of high repression which produces a *self-deceptive* state of relaxation.[9] The person is simply well defended. It is impossible to become relaxed so long as there is a significant amount of Pain in the body.

[9] Specifically, high-amplitude brain-waves indicate repression when they are measured in the occipital-parietal region of the brain.

In other therapies it is possible to produce a lowered blood pressure or a remission of another particular symptom. Often the improvement is only for a short period of time. Even when results are lasting they can be deceptive, if the therapist has investigated only one dimension, such as blood pressure, and left out the fact that the whole body and brain work as a compensating system. Thus, it may be that there is a price to pay for the lowered blood pressure in terms of the increased work load on another system. It is something one would not see unless one approached the patient systemically. Pain elevates blood pressure —and body temperature *and* heart rate. Each system shares its part of the load, or overload. Even if all of the standard vital functions are lowered through various forms of conditioning, one must look at brain functions; for they too form part of the compensating system, absorbing more of the work load as other subsystems are diminished in their response range.

We must ask what is the role, if any, of suggestion in patients' feeling "better." I believe that anyone who goes to any therapist or even a place of worship (which too often is what the psychiatrist is) has expectations and is self-suggesting even before any words have been spoken or promises made. He expects help, obviously. The wise therapist with all the proper therapeutic accoutrements *is by the fact of his existence "the promise."* His surroundings, his mannerisms, are invested in it. The more desperate the patient, the greater his expectations, the more he will overlook realities and place all his trust in the therapy or the doctor. The doctor need not make any overt promise for it to exist in the mind of the patient.

Long-term research offers the advantage of minimizing suggestion and expectancy as factors in therapeutic improvement. Suggestion therapy, directed daydreaming, and hypnosis are all dependent on suggestion and their results are transient. One has to continue to perform the ritual to ensure continued change. They are helpless methods before the truly major maladies such as epilepsy and psychosis.

When most people leave a therapy they expect to feel better and to be over their anxiety and depression. If they leave feeling good, is the therapy a success? If they leave feeling badly, could the therapy still have been a success? Is it possible that someone could feel better, much better, and not *be* better? Does it matter so long as the patient is satisfied? Can someone get well no matter what approach? Are they really better? And what is more, could you ever convince anyone who felt better after psychotherapy that he really wasn't better? And, while we are at it, what really is "better"? Subjective reports by patients in any therapy are not always trustworthy. There are just as many people who have turned to religion with their problems and claim cure as there are in psychotherapy.

But if we are talking about something other than transient feelings, something that produces profound biologic change, we enter another realm of discourse. For what all other methods have in common is *a lack of permanent change.* You have to keep on jogging to reduce tension. You must meditate frequently to feel better continuously, and you are required to be physically manipulated often if muscle tension is to be diminished. Reconnecting with pain does not just *reduce* tension, it progressively eliminates it. That is why former five-year patients have similar and permanent alterations in brain-wave patterns and characteristic vital sign changes.

Not everyone knows how he feels. The existence of Pain and repression indicates, by definition, that a person is unaware of his true feelings. If a person could *feel,* he would know. If he cannot feel, all he can experience is gradations of tension. Less tension feels "better." Belief itself reduces tension and makes the person feel better, which again makes him believe in his therapist and therapy. It is a self-perpetuating cycle of belief—tension reduction—belief.

There are no external cues to tell if a person is better or not. These can only tell us the ways in which a person *behaves* differently. The only proper cues for "better" are the internal ones; and, in truth, no one ever really gets "better," they just become themselves.

2: Measuring Sickness and Health

TRUE health or sickness can be at odds with how a person *thinks* he feels. One can feel "fine" and yet not be healthy. Only when key biologic indicators—temperature, heart rate, blood pressure, and brain wave patterns—reflect minimal Pain is a person truly healthy. Then we know that his statement, "I'm feeling good," is an accurate report of his inner state.

In Primal Therapy, we measure a person's vital signs before therapy and at various times thereafter. Frequently people show striking decreases in body temperature, heart rate, blood pressure and brain-wave activity as the result of our treatment.

BODY TEMPERATURE

The body temperature reflects the heat of the body as it works. Pain affects body temperature. Yet this notion has been given little consideration in the literature of medicine. Body temperature increases rapidly as a person becomes more conscious of his Pain. The closer Pain comes to consciousness the higher the body temperature.

To come near first-line Pain before a Primal feeling usually drives the temperature above 102. This indicates increased metabolism. If fever is a sure sign of illness, then the fact that those in the pre-Primal phase run a fever bolsters the argument that neurosis is a biologic disease. Further evidence of this is found in psychotics, who often have an elevated body temperature. Their systems produce more heat in counteracting Primal Pains. Those with inadequate repression and defenses usually have a higher fever.

When a patient is monitored with an electronic thermometer his temperature increases with deepening access to Pain. When the patient resolves his feeling, however, the temperature begins its descent to below the starting values of the session. This implies that the neurotic is running a slight fever and that there may be a "governor" that keeps all of his vital signs within manageable limits in the interests of survival. If this were not the case, most neurotics would be running a constant temperature of 100 or more (and a markedly elevated pulse rate). Indeed, in Primal Therapy, when we begin to weaken the defense system and render repression less effective, a fever develops that would be *manifest all of the time* if the defense system were not working. An oral temperature of 98.6 is *not* a valid standard of healthy body temperature; it is, at best, the *norm among neurotics*. Rather than being an accurate index of health, it simply reflects the system's ability to keep temperature from reaching lethal heights in response to Pain. When the system has less Pain to handle, temperature decreases permanently by one half to one degree.

Body temperature, like all of the vital signs, is regulated by the hypothalamus. Early catastrophic Pain evidently determines a specific setpoint of body temperature, some of us having a slightly different setpoint than others. (Many readings of patients taken after deep firstline Primals showed a rectal temperature of 96.) This setpoint determines one's average body temperature throughout life and is based on the Pain one has experienced.

If, for example, the first prototypic trauma was suffocation by drugs given to the mother during the birth process, the setpoint may be low; whereas if the trauma has to do with a major effort to get out of the canal during a prolonged labor, a higher temperature setpoint would be imprinted by that sequence. This is not to say that constitution and hereditary factors never play a part. But our observations suggest that they play only a minor role.

The drop in body temperature is an index of *overall* change in terms of less body work and the slowing down of the metabolic rate. After therapy the body is not exerting as much effort. It does not need to. What has changed, by virtue of the therapy, is the Pain. Therefore we must assume that a great deal of bodily effort goes into repression. *Repression is a very active, energy-consuming process.* Someone who feels comfortable and is "well adjusted," yet runs a constant temperature of 100, all else being equal, is under stress. In this sense, body temperature is an excellent biologic indicator of the state of neurosis. It is the key sign of increased cellular work over the entire system.

HEART RATE

One important function of the heart is to fuel the cells by providing a more rapid delivery of oxygen to every cell in the body. It helps mobilize the system for battle.

The heart rate is directly related to Pain and responds chronically to imprinted, enduring Pain. Under pressure of Pain, the heart will increase up to double its "normal" resting rate of 72 beats per minute. Given catastrophic first-level Pain, it may reach 200 beats per minute or more.[1] Pulse rate is an efficient index of sickness. In almost every case Pain causes the heart to beat faster.

Our patients sometimes begin sessions with high rates. However, the defense system, strained to its maximum, finally fails. After repeatedly entering and reentering the Primal feeling over one or one and a half hours, heart rate at the end of the session is typically below the baseline rate.[2] Over time, the resting heart rate tends to decrease permanently with continued feeling.[3]

BLOOD PRESSURE

Blood pressure is a very good index of the strain the system is under because when we take pressure—or Pain—out of the system, blood pressure automatically drops—permanently.[4] Blood pressure attempts

[1] The body of a person in a Primal will never choose the option of dying. A Primal is a reexperience of a trauma that one has *already survived*.

[2] The trauma that is forcing the heart rate up to 200 is an infantile trauma. If an infant had to endure that kind of heart rate he would surely soon expire. Repression can be a blessing in keeping down soaring vital signs.

[3] There are those who come to Primal Therapy with a very low heart rate, sometimes in the 40s and 50s. They usually experience an increased rate within a Primal but return to baselines higher than before they began to feel in the Primal. Their general resting baseline tends likewise to rise over time to the 60–68 range.

[4] Recently a survey was done of seven of our particularly hypertensive patients. There was a mean blood pressure drop of the group of 30 millimeters of mercury or an average drop for the group of 24 percent in blood pressure read-

to guarantee adequate perfusion of blood to all cells during stress.

We have seen many borderline hypertensives whose readings for hypertension, after one year of Primal Therapy, have dropped significantly. The relationship of Pain to blood pressure is underscored in medicine because pills designed to repress Pain also lower blood pressure—and, conversely, many antihypertensive drugs act as tranquilizers.

BRAIN-WAVE MEASUREMENT

Brain-wave patterns must be considered among the vital signs. The vital signs cannot be understood without reference to what is going on in the brain. All of the vital signs act as internally compensating systems. If one subsystem does not respond to Pain or stress, another will be recruited. That is why it is necessary to measure all of them as an ensemble. Otherwise, it is possible to get false or misleading results.

We have done research on brain waves for more than six years. In addition, a scientist from the Brain Research Institute at UCLA studied our patients' brain-wave patterns for over a year. He included in his study patients who had begun their Primal Therapy up to five years before.[5] After eight months of Primal Therapy, he found in these patients a permanent decrease in electrical voltage (amplitude). After three to five years of Primal feeling, the resting alpha amplitude dropped by half. In addition, there were indications of decreased cortical work—thus, a less busy "mind." The Primal patients' brains were working less hard to push down Pain. This was particularly true of the left-frontal region of the brain, which is the true executor, carrying out orders from all over the brain. It is the part that translates ideas into the neural basis for action.

The consistent drop in alpha amplitude tells us that amplitude is a sign not of relaxation, but of repression. And indeed, it is a direct sign of the amount of Pain internally. Patients in first-line Primals have been known to increase their EEG amplitude up to ten times the starting values. Rises of 300 to 500 percent are not uncommon. These are considerable rises in key vital signs. After the resolution of Pain, amplitude typically drops below starting levels, ten- to twenty-fold

---

ings. The group as a whole came from hypertensive to normotensive. The sample is too small to be statistically significant, but the survey is indicative of the trend we have seen for years in Primal Therapy. See also the 23.5 percent average drop in blood pressure recorded for Primaling patients in the Goodman-Sobel study.

[5] The report was summarized in the Brain Information Bulletin of UCLA.

from the peaks. There is a direct relationship between the increased access of Pain toward consciousness and the additional recruitment of cortical neurons to aid in repression. The best lie detector test may be one that measures only one dimension—amplitude—for it takes a lot of neurons to hold down the truth, or reality, or Pain.[6]

There are characteristic EEG voltages (amplitude) of those who are anxious or suffering. They are consistently higher than normal. Lower-level activation by Pain produces a breakthrough into the cortex, causing a higher level of activity. The cortex, less able to inhibit the ascending Pain, therefore, has the subjective feeling of suffering. The person cannot pinpoint his Pain but he feels agitated, irritable, and on "pins and needles." Invariably, we see these high readings in the pre-Primal phase with readings continuing higher as the patient begins to come closer to feeling. When under attack by Pain, the brain galvanizes itself toward repression by recruiting as many neurons as possible. With a therapist there to minimize that repression and at the same time make it safe to feel, the patient opens himself totally to the agony until the suffering turns to Pain—until amorphous misery becomes the exact old feeling it is.

Not only does alpha amplitude change in Primal Therapy, but amplitude is greater in those sectors of the brain dealing with feeling. The resolution of Painful feelings causes changes in the feeling or right side of the brain. A current study by Erik Hoffman, assistant professor of neuropsychology at Copenhagen University, is examining these changes by measuring the differences in the hemispheric relationships of the brain during Primal Therapy.[7] The right side of the brain is chiefly involved in mediating feelings. Whether the feelings are bad or good, pleasant or unpleasant, Primals produce a better balance in amplitude between the hemispheres—a sign of a more integrated mind. This points to a normalization process in Primal patients.

When Pain is taken out of the system, amplitude and hemispheric relationships change. There is a disappearance of neurotic or even psychotic ideas—psychological consequences of the neurologic changes. Decreased brain metabolism is eventually translated into psychological

---

[6] A study by C. R. Chapman at the Washington University Medical School underscores the point. In experiments using electrical stimulation to induce pain, it was found that: "The size of the brain waves correlates nicely with the amount of pain the subjects reported subjectively. So now we have a physiological correlate of pain and a means of objectively measuring the effectiveness of an analgesia." *Science News*, October 14, 1978, p. 267.

[7] Done in conjunction with Professor Leonide Goldstein, chief of the Department of Psychiatry, College of Medicine of New Jersey, Rutgers University.

processes—less philosophizing, intellectual rumination, and obsessive reading. There is less uncontrolled thinking and planning and less of a "racing mind." Energy relationships within the brain have psychological consequences—more energy, more mind work; less energy, less mind work.

Since brain-wave functioning reflects Pain and its repression, we can begin to see specific pathologic or neurotic patterns of brain waves. Phobic and manic patients have characteristic brain-wave patterns, as do those with inadequate inhibition: for example, those who have taken many LSD trips. We can see in their (low-voltage, fast) EEG patterns indications of the breakdown of repression, the shattering of the defense system, and reduction of the effectiveness of the cortex as a defensive bulwark.[8]

IMPLICATIONS OF VITAL SIGN RESEARCH

We recently monitored a young woman during a Primal of being held back at birth by a nurse until the doctor arrived. Struggle as she might, there was nothing she could do to bring about her own birth. During the Primal her vital signs rocketed until an apparently critical point at which the body gave up. She then fell into a Primal feeling which had no name, just its physiologic concomitants and the feeling of complete futility. Later on that nonverbal experience would have words to describe it, such as "despair." The resolution of that despair, which she had felt sporadically throughout her life, required the reexperience of the early life-and-death struggle with all of those threatening vital signs. The original memory of birth later evolved into a psychological state of despair and drove a great deal of her adult behavior—forcing her, for example, into prototypic patterns—feeling futile the moment she faced a significant obstacle. This experience changed her body temperature, her blood flow, her muscle tone, and her hormone output. Reliving the experience helped to resolve her tendency toward despair while lowering her vital signs. The registration of her Pain was not an inert force but an active, dynamic power.

[8] Cerebral blood flow measurement corroborates some of our observations. Psychotics usually have less blood flow in the frontal area of the brain and more flow in the parietal region. This may indicate that there is not enough inhibition relative to the amount of Pain activation. Greater blood flow in the frontal area is found in subjects exposed to physical pain stimuli, reflecting frontal cortical repression of Pain.

Reaction to stress and Pain is the same whether the stressor is a parental criticism or a bacterial infection. In both physical and neurotic disease the system responds to insult with elevated vital signs— blood flow redistribution to the muscles, heart, brain, and kidneys, and the release of white blood cell reserves into the general circulation. By "insult" I mean anything which interrupts the normal balance of the system.

Up to now we may have been accepting vital sign norms applicable to a largely neurotic population and making those our standards of health. It may be that much of the population is sick beyond our ability to see it. Also, because of our limited knowledge, we may be simply measuring the averages of an unhealthy population, rather than real health. We will never know until we have a different set of subjects with a different set of values to compare.

The most precise standard of health that we can develop is probably that of a healthy range of variation in vital sign values of our advanced patients. Before therapy, for example, we see a very wide range in blood pressure readings among patients, e.g., from 80/40 to 180/120. After some time in therapy, the range narrows, suggesting that a healthy individual would have a blood pressure between 90/55 and 115/70, a body temperature between 97 and 98 degrees (measured rectally at noon),[9] and a heart rate of around 60 to 64 beats per minute. There may not be a particular blood pressure or pulse reading that is an absolute signal of health but there is almost certainly a healthy range. The range of variation in the absence of Pain is likely to be quite narrow.

Even though post-therapy vital sign readings indicate standards of reduced Pain, they are probably not identical with the kind of readings one would get with a person who had a healthy, loving upbringing. Despite the low readings we find with our patients after taking Pain out of the system, these people are still ex-neurotics. They are not like others who grow up healthily, with two loving parents.

THE BIOCHEMISTRY OF STRESS

A systematic biochemical analysis of our patients will enable us to see just what chemical systems are associated with Pain. Toward this end, we are uncovering evidence that growth hormones may be related to stress. The same is true of the sex hormones. This developing profile

[9] Current medical norm for rectal noontime measurement is 99.6 degrees.

will eventually be integrated with neuroelectrical data and vital sign information.

The first biochemical experiments to measure stress hormone levels of Primal patients were carried out in 1976 in conjunction with Dr. Malcolm Carruthers of the pathology laboratory at the Maudsley Hospital in London, England. This study, lasting only three months, produced information that showed decreases in the plasma adrenaline and noradrenaline levels—stress hormones.[10]

One young man in our study, who had been convicted of rape, experienced a 90 percent drop in overall levels of stress hormones. This suggests how much stress he had been under and how much pressure had forced him to act out impulsively. Over a three-year period of therapy this man has not acted out any tendencies toward rape nor does he feel the impulse to do so. *Therefore there may be ways to measure physiologically the tendency to commit a crime.*

The addition of physiological factors in evaluating inner stress is certainly a help to those who are charged with evaluating the tendency to commit a crime on the part of mental hospital patients or prison inmates.

Biologic measurements of stress are terribly important when we consider how the tendency toward dangerous behavior is shrouded in mystery and mysticism. A study by Harry L. Kozol, a Massachusetts psychiatrist, of 304 men arrested for sex crimes, led to the following conclusion: "No one can predict dangerous behavior in an individual with no history of dangerous acting-out."[11] It doesn't have to be that way. The stress hormone levels indicate pent-up pressure forcing impulsive behavior.

PAIN AND BIOCHEMICAL CHANGE

In early 1978, Drs. David A. Goodman, neurobiologist, and Harry Sobel, biochemist, of the Newport Neuroscience Center undertook a one-year study of biochemical changes in Primal patients. Dr. Sobel selected the following hormones for study in Primal patients because he believed they may be most responsive to stress:[12]

[10] There was also a lessened variation of values around the mean, suggesting strongly that we were measuring an actual biologic process. The subjects, independent of where they started, ended toward a single value.
[11] Peter Schrag, *Mind Control*, Pantheon Books, New York, 1978, pp. 99–100.
[12] The following passages are quoted from Sobel and Goodman's research proposal.

Corticosteroids—Elevation of these in the plasma and urine is the hallmark of the generalized stress reaction. Corticosteroid levels rise in infants left alone by their mothers for one hour. Early experience alters an organism's reactivity to stress. These early experiences may also alter patterns of sexual maturation, adrenal functioning, and the rhythms of corticosteroid release.

Catecholamines—Central catecholamines regulate food intake, mood, body temperature, systolic blood pressure, and motor activity. Alterations of the catecholamines have a profound effect on behavior.

Growth Hormone—This is known to be altered by a variety of stressful activities such as exercise, fasting, surgery, maternal deprivation, and insulin injection. Growth hormone spurts out in episodic surges related to the daily rhythms of the body. Chronic stress can change the secretion rate; if persistent, it lowers the levels.

Testosterone—This is a steroid hormone vital to all phases of male development. Stress can suppress testosterone secretion and alter behavior. Sufficient suppression can lead to lack of libido and sex organ atrophy.

Cholesterol—Cholesterol levels in the blood are affected by diet and by stress. Various investigators have reported that acute stress, such as illness, may elevate blood cholesterol. There are reports, too, that a chronic stress, such as cold, can raise cholesterol blood levels in laboratory animals. There are shared structural chemistries of cholesterol and the ACTH-activated corticosteroids (stress hormones).[13]

The researchers gathered biochemical, behavioral, psychological, and physiological data on Primal patients, who were ranked according to the time of onset and the frequency, depth, and patterning of their Primals in their therapy.[14] In other words, patients were differentiated

[13] The Goodman-Sobel biochemical study population consisted of twenty-five patients, eighteen males and seven females, who entered the experiment in January–February 1978. The researchers took blood sample readings on the various biochemicals as follows: twice in the pretreatment week, and on the Friday of the first, fourth, thirteenth, twenty-sixth, and, finally, fifty-second week after therapy began. Results reported are after six months. The one-year results, still in press as of this writing, confirm the six-month trends.

[14] The ranking according to Primal onset, frequency, depth, and pattern led to the formation of five subgroups of quintiles. These were then isolated into two main subgroups and their responses compared. First quintile were the early Primallers and the fifth quintile were the later Primallers. (Please see appendix for further information regarding research methodology.) The early Primallers

according to when they first began crying in therapy; how often they cried or felt; when they first began to Primal; the frequency of their Primalling; and the depth or level of their Primalling. Evaluations of these variables were made by the patients, who kept a diary, by the patients' therapists, and by an independent investigator, an experienced Primal Therapist who was unaware of the biochemical findings in each case.

Growth Hormone

For more than a decade we have been observing soft tissue growth in our patients and have had no way to account for it. The results of our growth hormone studies begin to offer some answers.

At the beginning of therapy there was no difference between early and late Primallers in levels of human growth hormone. At the end of twenty-six weeks, there was an average increase of 206 percent in growth hormone values of those who felt deeply early in therapy. This increase was especially evident in female patients. At the same time, those who didn't have deep feelings until later in therapy showed an 80 percent decrease in this hormone. The difference between those who felt deeply and those who did not amounted to a ratio of ten to one. Growth hormone continued at a high level in Primal patients through the fifty-second week. Thus, feeling and resolving Pain *liberated a healing force* (the growth hormone), providing striking evidence that the more pain was felt, the more healing took place. (There has been a good deal of research evidence linking growth hormone to repair and healing processes.) Interestingly, also after fifty-two weeks, when those Primalling late in therapy began to feel and resolve Pain, they began a similar movement toward higher growth hormone levels—and normalization of the other hormones studied—suggesting further that Primal Therapy was the factor leading to change.

A model for growth in Primal patients is the growth seen in victims of "deprivation dwarfism"—children who grow normally only when they have been taken out of institutional settings and placed in real homes. The growth of these children depends on a change in their environment. In neurosis, a Painful environment is imprinted in the

---

had Primals during the initial year. Patients in this group vividly described their Primals. The later Primallers were those who had very slow going in the initial six to twelve months. But by the twelfth month they were still not deeply Primalling.

brain, so that the adult still lives in that environment. When Pain is resolved, the environment changes and growth can occur.

Cortisol

Nine Primalling patients who started out with high initial levels of cortisol showed a definite and persistent decrease across all the measuring periods. The average decrease for the group was 19 percent, indicating reduced stress throughout a period of feeling. At the same time, nine Primalling patients with the lowest initial values in cortisol showed a 21 percent increase during the six months. It begins to look as though cortisol may not be only a stress hormone in the neurotic sense, but also a hormone that helps a person deal with the world, so that *it is* possible to be too low in cortisol, with inadequate mobilization for adaptation to the environment.[15]

Among Primalling patients, those with high cortisol levels reduced their levels and approached the group mean; those with low values went up toward the mean. Overall, there was a change among these patients of approximately 20 percent either up or down toward the mean. This normalization of cortisol levels with Primal Therapy indicates the possibility that early trauma skews the functioning of the hypothalamic-pituitary structures in two directions—high and low—altering hormone output.

The direction of change in hormone output (high or low) seems to depend upon the prototypic trauma in and around birth. If the trauma is such that there were no viable behavioral options against threat, chances are the direction will be toward a low rate of output. If the trauma involved fighting to get out of the canal or other active behavioral responses, the chances are the direction will be toward higher output.

There have been studies in psychotherapy of various stress hormones. But there is no correlation of these studies with particular stressors. It has never before been said, therefore, that "X is the cause of this particular stress reaction." Even if psychotherapists found that their patients have levels of stress hormone reduced in psychotherapy —which has not been the case—they still would not know which particular stressor had to do with reducing the stress hormone. That is be-

[15] The late Primallers showed an appreciable increase in cortisol after the start of therapy, which is what we would expect when the patient's defenses are threatened but are not yet yielding. The late Primallers showed an increase of 41 percent over beginning values at thirteen weeks.

cause the fountain of wisdom is the therapist, who tells the patient what is troubling him. Therefore, the stressors have to be theorized about. In Primal Therapy the stressors are felt and experienced. The patients know them absolutely.

Cortisol levels above the mean indicate a measure of defensiveness against feeling. More importantly, as cortisol rises in the suffering neurotic, growth hormone decreases, indicating that stress and healing are antithetical forces. The higher the cortisol or stress levels—when they are considerably above the mean—the lower the concentration of growth hormone, and vice versa.[16]

Testosterone

Testosterone was measured in males only.[17] Late Primalling males had high testosterone levels at the start of therapy. In this group, after twenty-six weeks, there was a mean decrease of 8 percent.

In the early Primallers who showed a high initial value of testosterone—i.e., a value above the mean—there was a 32 per cent decrease at the end of twenty-six weeks.[18]

The Primallers who began with a low initial value of testosterone *increased* their level by 16 percent at the end of twenty-six weeks.

Therefore, those with low initial testosterone values rose by the twenty-sixth week while those with higher initial values dropped toward the mean. For example, a patient 155 units below the mean at the beginning of therapy rose to 27 testosterone units above the mean. Another patient, 111 testosterone units below, rose to 32 above. A patient with an initial value of 306 testosterone units above the mean moved downward to 66 units above the mean. Another case which was 211 units above the mean dropped to 73 units above the mean.

[16] In addition to the first study of the stress hormones noradrenaline and epinephrine undertaken with the Maudsley Hospital, Goodman and Sobel conducted an independent study of epinephrine in the Primal group. In the third to sixth month of therapy there was a 25 to 40 percent drop in epinephrine in Primallers, again showing that stress hormone levels normalize as a result of resolving Pain. The drops in the stress hormones in Primal patients are due, in my opinion, to one key element: the decrease in the amount of stored Pain.
[17] Thus the same quintiles or subgroups, based on the entire study population, do not apply here.
[18] Especially impressive to the researchers was the consistent drop across all the measuring dates—21 percent after the first week, 28 percent—below starting values—after four weeks, 26 percent after thirteen weeks. The mean decrease across all the measuring dates through twenty-six weeks was 27 percent.

These are considerable changes and indicate a *normalization* of testosterone values.

In the non-Primalling patient subgroup, there was essentially no change across the twenty-six weeks. Among the entire group with high initial values, there was a net difference of 39 percent, at the end of twenty-six weeks, between those in the group who Primalled and those who did not.

Since testosterone is responsible for the primary and secondary sexual characteristics and for aggressive and sexual behavior, we would expect to see changes in these dimensions when testosterone levels change. Indeed, we do. Those who are "oversexed" normalize to a more moderate level of sexual activity, whereas those who are "undersexed" move up to a more balanced amount of sexual activity.

High levels of testosterone may well protect against feeling and may be another sign of defensiveness. When feeling does take place, there also is a drop in this hormone level. Our research gives some basis for the fact that when men do cry they do reduce testosterone levels and are hence less "macho" and less defensive. One indication that high testosterone is tied to the "macho syndrome" is the fact that women have very low testosterone levels.

Additionally, macho societies are more violent ones. Any society which is systematically able to lower testosterone values possibly may lower the tendency toward violence.

Cholesterol[19]

Despite a lack of basic change in diet among these patients, the Primallers with high cholesterol values significantly reduced their cholesterol levels, while the lowest values increased. Again, low values increased toward the mean, high values showed an appreciable decrease toward the mean. Thus cholesterol is another biochemical which does not simply become reduced when Pain is taken out of the system, but which becomes *normalized* toward a narrower range of variation than we observe in the neurotic or pre-therapy population. Rises in cholesterol levels, in and of themselves, may not be harmful.

Among other tests made in the study were blood pressure measurements. The early Primallers showed an average drop in blood pressure

[19] Cholesterol, unlike HGH (growth hormone), cortisol, and testosterone, is not a hormone. It is, of course, an important biochemical for study and one which is probably related to hormone output.

of 23.5 percent by the twenty-sixth week, compared to a 5.2 percent drop for late Primallers.

Each patient was administered an adjective checklist, which required the patient to mark which adjective best described the way he felt. Half the adjectives were considered positive and half negative. The scale ranged from —4 to +4, so that +8 or —8 was the greatest change that could take place during this study. The early Primallers showed a change of +5.3. The late Primallers did not show a significant change.

The fifty-two-week results show that the phenomenon of normalization seen earlier was valid—an unprecedented finding in the history of psychotherapy. Hence the postulation: connected Primal experience changes the organism biochemically.

High levels of cortisol are associated with impaired functions of lymphocytes, the cells which are the major producers of antibodies and which determine the effectiveness of the immune system. Thus whether one suffers from an infection or psychological stress, one is healthier and better able to heal when cortisol levels are normalized.[20]

Pain and distorted hormonal output are clearly related. It is not a great stretch of the imagination, therefore, to suppose that hormone-related diseases can be Pain-engendered.

Further, many people are either above or below the norm in hormone output, though not clearly observable, and these slight deviations may well cause general irritability, impulsiveness, anxiety, fatigue, depression, and many of the so-called "psychological traits."

THERMOGRAPHY AND PERIPHERAL BLOOD FLOW

Thermography, sophisticated heat-sensing photography which has been variously applied in industry and medicine but rarely if ever in psychotherapy, was used to measure peripheral blood flow in the faces of Primal Therapists, Primal patients, and in a control group. The study, conducted by Dr. David A. Goodman of the Newport Neuroscience Center with Dr. Michael Holden of The Primal Institute, found significant evidence that those who had been feeling Primally

---

[20] Also, as is generally known, lymphocytes have a "surveillance" function which minimizes the occurrence of latent cancer. An individual with high cortisol values would have impaired lymphocyte function and this might predispose him to the development of certain cancers. Conversely, normalization of cortisol may allow lymphocytes to perform their normal function.

for the longest time (the therapists) had the warmest faces and, by inference, the greatest peripheral blood flow, and that subjects who had begun Primalling (the patients) had warmer faces than non-Primalling controls.

Thermography is essentially the measurement of heat radiation and the conversion of the measurement into pictures; it is an infrared photography technique. It has been used in medicine to screen for breast cancer, to observe blood flow in the skin after plastic surgery, to find evidence in the facial blood flow of occlusions or blockages in the brain, to find thermal evidence of inflammation in the joints of athletes, and so on.

The study examined 52 subjects—13 therapists, 22 patients and 17 controls. The tests were controlled for outdoor temperature, physical activity, and whether or not a Primal had taken place. Evaluations of the lightness scale (lightness or brightness indicating warmth and, causing the warmth, degree of peripheral blood flow) for eleven carefully defined regions of the face were made by independent observers who did not know whom they were grading.

In Primal feeling a defensive constrictive process gives way to a more free-flowing "open" blood system. Over the long term in therapy, patients become more relaxed and more normally balanced in terms of blood flow. It is the sympathetic nervous system excess that mediates constriction of the peripheral blood vessels, making the face colder and darker. The parasympathetic system is the one that takes over when a Pain has been felt and resolved, and brings with it vasodilation and a lighter, warmer reading on the thermogram.

Therapists were lighter and warmer than nonpatients and also had a better blood flow than patient groups. Over time in Primal Therapy the peripheral blood flow system becomes better.[21]

The saying, "He keeps his cool," may not just be metaphor. The person who effectively represses his Pain *is* cooler, *on the exterior.* One can often see the signs of repression in the facial tone of the neu-

21 Thermographic data helps us to distinguish real connected feelings from abreaction. Even though the abreactive person was "letting off steam" his post-session thermogram was darker than before the session. Feelings clearly improve the health of the blood flow system. It is healthier because warmer skin temperature indicates parasympathetic system influence and this in turn means better tissue repair, skin tone, and healing. Sympathetic nervous system dominance can keep the peripheral blood vessels constricted to one half of their maximum diameter. If this turns out to be true of the most inner of the internal vascular systems, one can readily see implications for high blood pressure, migraine, and heart disease. The blood system, in any case, has an active role in the repression of Pain.

rotic, in the complexion; restricted peripheral blood flow can make someone look "cold."

The person who is ccoler on the outside is also hotter internally. That is, as we might expect, repression galvanizes the body, making it work harder. This work is reflected in higher body temperature.

The results of thermography, when examined alongside changes in vital functions and biochemistry, indicate that the vascular systems become more normal in therapy, so that a person is profoundly more relaxed.

QUESTIONNAIRE SURVEY

Our biochemical and vital sign studies provide us with the first comprehensive measurements of psychophysiologic changes in psychotherapy.[22]

The initial step in our current psychological research has been the 1979 Primal Institute questionnaire survey.[23]

This survey shows that there were significant indications of improvement in many different symptom areas. These included symptoms such as skin disorders, muscle tension, teeth grinding, nail biting, hemorrhoids, tension headaches, migraine headaches, stomach disorders, frequent urination, attacks of heartburn, frequent colds, tense, strident voice, throat disorders, allergies (which showed a relatively lower rate of improvement), smoking, alcoholism, drug abuse, obesity and overeating, use of prescribed medications, rapid heartbeat, menstrual difficulties (also a relatively lower improvement rate), excessive startle reaction, hypersensitivity to heat or cold, recurring dreams, nightmares, insomnia, chronic oversleeping, impotence, frigidity, premature ejaculation, excessive masturbation, habitual desire for pornography, homosexual fantasies, homosexual activity, inappropriate anger, agitated depression, melancholic depression, obsessions, compulsions, phobias, paranoid ideation, difficulty speaking in public, workaholism, introversion and shyness, social withdrawal and self-isolation, difficulty in asking for what one needs, difficulty in crying, difficulty in

[22] According to a report prepared for us by the Biomedical Documentation Group, Carlsbad, California: "There does not appear in the literature a discrete matrix of biochemical and psychological parameters."

[23] See Appendix B for details of the 1979 questionnaire; complete results for all symptoms are included in the table.

discussing problems with others, and difficulties in functioning independently.

Several of the results in the table are suggestive concerning the way in which Primal Therapy effects change. For example, the self-reported improvement rates for sexual symptoms are interesting, assuming that the trends hold up in further study. In Primal Therapy patients relive nonsexual traumas dating from long before sexuality was organized but which have a profound effect on sexual functioning nevertheless.

The population sample for homosexual activity admittedly is small, but of those reporting first-line feelings, 70 percent reported a disappearance of homosexual acting-out, while 56 percent of those feeling only on the second line reported disappearance of acting out. Change is a function of experienced Pain.[24]

The average frequency of sexual activity before therapy was fifteen times per month. After therapy the average dropped to ten times per month—a drop of 33 percent. Our own discussions with patients suggest that it is not so much that *sexual desire* diminishes with Primalling, but a generalized Primal drive underlying sex activity has been resolved. The Goodman-Sobel biochemistry data also suggests that sexual drive does not simply drop—as we once thought—but normalizes toward the mean.

More than 90 percent felt that Primal Therapy had changed their lives and that they were more in control of their lives. Some 94 percent had not engaged in another form of therapy since Primal Therapy. Over 90 percent felt that Primal Therapy held up over time.

Fully one third of those respondents failing to Primal after one year had previously been in mock Primal Therapies—therapies conducted by untrained personnel. When we isolated information from those who had been in mock Primal Therapies, we found statistically that their chances of gaining access to their Pain were only one half that of the other respondents.

The patient in mock Primal Therapy is brought near to his Pain but, once again, just as in the original situation, is not given a proper chance to respond in a natural way. This situation often leads to development of a second or compound neurosis.

Having first-line or very early Primals is important in the resolution of certain symptoms but it seems as though any reduction in the level

24 In some cases, those who are Primalling on the second line only sometimes feel worse and report exacerbation of symptoms. These patients often have first-line "intrusion." That is, first-line Pain is beginning to ascend, which raises the patients' general anxiety level and makes them more symptomatic.

of Pain, first or second line, can bring a person below the threshold of symptoms.

Results for "Veterans"

One of the ways in which the survey was analyzed was by comparing results from the general study population with those from the group of former patients who had begun Primal Therapy in 1975 or before. This group consisted of 62 of the 200 Primal respondents. One reason for this particular analysis was to see whether changes in Primal Therapy hold up over time, as reported by the patients themselves. Precise results can be found in the comprehensive chart.

For most symptoms, the "veterans" show a strengthening of the trend of improvement reported by the study population as a whole.[25]

The results for veterans support the idea that symptoms are resolved progressively as one descends levels of consciousness and particularly as one continues to Primal over the years. The result indicates that patients continue to improve after having left therapy, implying that the therapy is a tool which they have mastered for use by themselves. The results for the veteran Primal patients indicate continuing progress the longer they are out of therapy.

The 1979 survey included a control group of 50 prospective Primal patients who mirrored our survey population in all major respects except one—the fact that they had not yet undertaken Primal Therapy. We wanted to know whether Primal Therapy was indeed bringing about the changes reported by patients.

For almost three decades there has been a controversy in psychotherapy concerning whether or not therapy makes for real change and, specifically, whether patients might not achieve the same results without going into therapy. The controversy began with a study by H. J. Eysenck, who found that subjects had about a two thirds remission rate whether they were in therapy or simply on a waiting list for therapy.[26] Twenty-six years and at least fourteen related studies

[25] The significance of results varies according to the number of responses. The small size of the veteran study population means that, in most cases, their reported rate of improvement is simply of interest and has mainly heuristic value, as an indicator of possible trends which call for further research. Confirmation of these trends would require increased numbers in a longitudinal study.
[26] Of course, it is important to keep in mind that the two thirds improvement rate was defined in terms of criteria selected by Eysenck—"psychological" criteria which did not encompass the biopsychological dimension. H. J. Eysenck, "The Effects of Psychotherapy: An Evaluation," in *Journal of Consulting Psychology*, Vol. 16, 1952, pp. 319–24.

later, the controversy was still unsettled, and the best that the defenders of psychotherapy could say was that the two thirds remission rate reported for people on a waiting list is much too high—that there is a remission rate for those not in therapy, but a much lower one than Eysenck reported. As for the improvement rate in therapy itself, a review of the studies since Eysenck suggested that there was only modest change in psychotherapy patients.[27] In addition, a review of some 38 studies came to the conclusion that no one traditional psychotherapeutic method was more successful than another.[28]

The Primal Institute survey found not only that patients report high rates of improvement in therapy, but that the control group of waiting patients reported their symptoms becoming *worse* in the same period, without therapy. This finding indicates that it is Primal Therapy which is responsible for the changes reported in the survey.

Biochemistry and the Psychological Dimension

We isolated those patients in the survey population who are also part of the biochemical study.[29] We found significant differences between those who were feeling early in therapy and those who were not.

The trends in this study consistently indicated that certain biological changes are associated with psychological improvement. For example, those who were feeling early in therapy had considerably less depression than those who did not have access to the feelings. They had fewer physical symptoms such as diarrhea and tics, and enjoyed a general feeling of relaxation. Thus we think it will be possible by biochemical studies alone to infer certain psychological changes.

As a result of our research and that of others, we are developing a frame of reference for study of psyche and biology as a single entity. We are approaching the time when we can observe certain biochemical states and have an idea about the nature of the person's feelings and attitudes—a time when we will be able to see neurosis in the blood. We cannot say what the person's specific ideas will be because of the diversity and plasticity of ideas. But we do know that those

[27] Allen E. Bergin and Michael J. Lambert, "The Evaluation of Therapeutic Outcomes," in Sol L. Garfield and Allen E. Bergin, eds., *Handbook of Psychotherapy and Behavior Change,* John Wiley & Sons, New York, second edition, 1978, pp. 142–52.
[28] Ibid., p. 162.
[29] See Appendix A.

ideas rest upon a substratum of just a few attitudes—the emotional vehicles upon which a variety of ideas ride. If we can pinpoint attitudes by both biochemical and psychological analyses, we can describe a range within which an individual's ideas probably lie. We may not only analyze the criminal, for example, in terms of his "mental" state, but we will be able to "ask" his blood chemistry if his ideas and impulses are deeply changed.

The initial skewing of the biochemistry due to early trauma probably sets up a predisposition to associated psychological distortions. Someone may not only act neurotic, but will have a "neurotic" biochemistry. He may both look neurotic—in terms of his bone structure, skin tone, growth patterns, hair distribution—and act it.

The Biology of the Mind

Primals are neither infantile regressions, play-acting, role-playing, hysteria, catharsis, or abreaction. Each of those states I have just mentioned can be defined within certain biologic boundaries. We know what hysteria looks like psychologically and biologically. Disintegration is not just a term for psychoanalysts to bandy about—it is a biologic reality.[30] Corroboration of the point I'm making is that we have discovered an almost one-to-one correlation between long range mood change and alterations of growth hormone. Over the first thirteen-month period of therapy as primalling increases, so does the release of growth hormone. It may be that the biologic meaning of the psychologic state called "feeling good" is a system in a repair and healing phase with a proper hormone distribution.

The more that we can *biologically* quantify the changes that take place in a *psychotherapy,* the more precise we can be about the effects of that therapy. We are better able to monitor the progress of the patient independent of the therapists' personal persuasions and prejudice.

The registration of Pain is a dynamic force with widespread biologic sequelae. Neurosis is a concert of reactions, a total biologic configuration of responses that ultimately drive a wide variety of behaviors and symptoms. As has been shown, you are not necessarily healthy if you have no obvious psychiatric signs: You may only have

[30] The brain of those who have taken hallucinogens, for example, suffers from permanently opened gates. The brain-wave pattern shows a disintegrated defense system—the amplitude first "going through the ceiling," often rising tenfold, and then collapsing into a permanent defenseless low amplitude fast pattern.

very well-functioning "gates." You are not necessarily healthy if you act in a well-adjusted manner to the society you live in. However, you *are* healthy if your entire biologic system, including the brain, functions properly.

Even though I have discussed scientific, objective methods of understanding neurosis, the ultimate truth about neurosis lies on the level of experience and no amount of scientific evidence or statistical data is going to help scientists understand what feelings are. Indeed, feelings cannot be adequately understood in terms of ideas and the more one uses ideas for understanding, the less one will comprehend. Those who cannot feel, need a great deal of cerebral, statistical proof. Yet, those who cannot feel need a proof they cannot accept because they still have no idea what a feeling is.

When a person stops being a prisoner of his history, he emerges with a changed individual physiology. The designation "prisoners of Pain" is neither just semantics nor mere imagery. The chemical chains that bind us are as real as any of those made of steel.

3: Restoration and Renewal

CHRONIC disease of whatever kind hastens death. If we want to live, the body must remain healthy. That means it must be as free as possible of chronic Pain.

Our time in life is cut short by neurosis, the most intangible, devastating, and widespread of diseases. Many of the diseases which we think of as natural causes of death are hastened and perhaps even generated by this underlying illness.

Repression works to keep us alive. But as we grow older, we begin to pay more and more dearly for having buried our Pain. Primal Pain is a continuous burden which increases metabolic work, which eventually wears down the body to produce disease and ultimately a premature death.

Systems which metabolize at a faster rate burn out and die sooner. Certain rodents with a very high metabolic rate, such as the shrew, live only a year or so. Yet species of tortoise with an exceptionally slow metabolic rate live for more than a century. By lowering the general metabolic rate of our patients, which we have been doing through Primal Therapy, they will, I believe, be able to attain a significantly longer natural life-span.

Unlike other diseases, which usually confine themselves to one or two organ systems, neurosis is a disease of the total person. What happened to us as infants and children didn't just happen to an arm, a leg, or a lung. In fact, nothing happens to us that way. It happens as an *experience*. That is why working on symptoms, especially a single symptom, must fail as therapy, for the body will manifest a different symptom as long as the neurosis is left unresolved. In fact, if no other symptom can provide a "spillway" for Pain, I believe the person may die even sooner from the increased metabolic burden.

Symptoms are a language all their own. The primary meaning of any symptom is to indicate physiologic disequilibrium and to shout out the need for restoration of the proper conditions for fulfillment.

In the end, it is only a matter of which system is vulnerable to stress and which system has become the target for absorbing stress. That probably depends on heredity as well as on which systems were most involved in the prototypic Primal situations. Thus a constant banging against the pubic arch during birth may leave one susceptible to headaches under stress, while those drowning in birth fluid may later be more susceptible to chest and lung conditions.

As a general rule, Pain results in constriction, whether of muscles, blood vessels, or pupils. It's the way physical systems withdraw from danger. Chronic Pain adds a burden of constriction to the blood delivery system.[1] Afflictions such as strokes may result from changes in the blood system produced over time by Pain. It also may have a good deal to do with chronic migraine. I believe that under massive first-line trauma, the blood system constricts so much that the constriction process finally fails, resulting in a "rebound" vasodilation and a severe migraine.

If we remove Pain from a physical system and a disease disappears permanently—and, furthermore, if this happens often enough—we may say with some assurance that the basis of the disease was Pain. Of course, this is no longer just hypothesis, as the questionnaire survey points out that many disorders, including migraine, have been eased or eliminated with the resolution of Pain.

PAIN'S PATH FROM THE BRAIN TO THE BODY

The ancient brain structure, the hypothalamus, translates pain into changes in the inner organ systems, in heart rate, temperature, and blood pressure. A close relative of the hypothalamus is the pituitary, which is responsible for the output of key hormones. Both these structures are mature at birth and are responsible for integrating the earliest Primal Pains. The maturity of these structures of the brain at birth helps explain why reliving traumas from the earliest days of life

[1] See section on Thermography in part IV, chapter 2, "Measuring Sickness and Health."

can produce such remarkable changes in vital functions and hormone secretions. It also explains why some people have to endure chronic elevation in blood pressure and pulse without seeming cause. These primitive structures are under constant stress from hidden and inaccessible stored trauma.

The hypothalamus and pituitary supply hormones to the body throughout life. If cells can utilize hormones for repair, healing is enhanced and aging presumably retarded. If the hormone system has been altered and is now inadequate, repair does not happen as easily and the system breaks down more quickly. The changes we see in hormone production, indicated by the Goodman-Sobel results, are indicators of better repair facility. This is also indicated by our observations that men in their twenties and thirties begin developing plentiful facial hair for the first time, while some women resume breast growth.

I have discussed elsewhere how Pain is literally an electric input to the hypothalamus. Animal studies at New York Medical College showed that electrical stimulation of the hypothalamus caused changes in the major coronary arteries of rats.[2] In these studies the cause and effect relationship between Pain and heart disease is evident. Reversing the hypothalamic load may also reverse the many forms of heart disease or, better, prevent heart disease in the future. We have already seen reversal of disease in several heart patients we have treated, particularly in those with angina pectoris.[3]

There has been a good deal of evidence concerning the relationship of high levels of cholesterol and heart disease. The Goodman-Sobel research points to the conclusion that cholesterol levels are related to Pain. Experiments with rabbits fed a high cholesterol diet again implicated the role of Pain. One group was given periodic electronic stimulation of the hypothalamus (as might happen from Pain) and the other was not. After three months the stimulated group showed much higher fat content in the blood and at death had more severe atherosclerosis. Perhaps some of us who eat a certain diet develop high blood cholesterol, while others eating the same diet do not. The cause may lie in a combination of diet and amount of Pain affecting the hypothalamus. High cholesterol producers can watch their diets but still may be vulnerable to heart disease unless the hypothalamus is restored to normal function. The relationship of Pain to heart disease is illustrated in the work of J. E. Skinner.[4] He conditioned pigs—which have

[2] *Brain-Mind Bulletin,* February 20, 1978.
[3] A case from Primal Therapy is reported in detail by Dr. E. Michael Holden in the *Journal of Psychosomatic Research,* Vol. 21, pp. 333–50.
[4] As reported to the Society for Neuroscience, November 1978.

a cardiovascular system similar to humans—to anticipate pain. He traced this anticipation through the various brain structures and found again that the message was transmitted to the hypothalamus, which then regulated the heart and cardiovascular system. Skinner also blocked the coronary arteries of pigs, put one group under stress and left the other group unstressed. The stressed animals died within minutes, while the unstressed ones did not. Skinner concluded that psychological factors were paramount in the development of certain kinds of heart disease.[5]

Recent research on aging suggests that there is a "clock" in the brain that controls the speed of aging, and that the "clock" probably lies in the hypothalamic-pituitary centers. Changes in the hypothalamus trigger changes throughout the body.[6] Pain may account for those changes in the hypothalamus and thus for the systemic cascade effects. Research in the Soviet Union[7] indicates that it may well be the hypothalamus which begins the deterioration of vital functions in old age.

Another theory currently being studied in research at the University of Southern California and California Institute of Technology posits a "death hormone" triggered by the hypothalamus and then secreted by the pituitary at a critical time when the endocrine system breaks down. A feedback mechanism monitors the body and tells the brain when it is beginning to wear out. Then the hormone is secreted.

Another piece of evidence regarding the hypothalamus, Pain, and aging comes from experiments of Paola Timiras at the University of California, Berkeley, cited by Albert Rosenfeld in *Prolongevity*. Timiras believes that by withholding a substance called tryptophan from the diet, aging could be slowed. Tryptophan is a building block of serotonin, one of the body's major neurotransmitters that helps repress Pain. Timiras concluded that by slowing the production of serotonin one could greatly retard the clock of aging. In short, lessening the forces of repression seemed to keep aging in check.

[5] Since Skinner, several more studies have suggested a link between Pain and heart disease. For example, a study at Ohio State University found that rabbits which were cuddled developed only half as much arteriosclerosis as rabbits which were fed the same diet but not cuddled (*Science News,* September 15, 1979). A nineteen-year study of the town of Roseto, Pennsylvania, concluded that the town was relatively immune to heart disease only as long as its families and clans recognized the importance "of being appreciated, of belonging, and of being supported unconditionally" (Stewart Wolf and John G. Bruhn, *The Roseto Story: An Anatomy of Health,* University of Oklahoma Press, Norman, 1979).

[6] In Albert Rosenfeld, *Prolongevity,* Alfred A. Knopf, New York, 1976.

[7] At the Petrov Research Institute.

Pain is the factor which could account for the serotonin production in the first place. Pain stimulates production of serotonin, which would then affect the hypothalamus, resulting in faster aging. In strict experimental terms, this is speculation. But confusion in the field is only increased when changes in hormones and neurotransmitters are seen not in terms of the total person but as entities apart. Thus we see studies of serotonin as it affects aging, but not of what may have caused the production of serotonin.

Some evidence points to the thyroid as a critical structure in aging. Rosenfeld points out that "the heart rate, the metabolic rate, the time of gestation, the time of puberty, and the time from puberty to death . . . all these time events" may be governed by the thyroid, because it is the "rate-controlling" gland. In Primal Therapy, many patients with thyroid deficiency have achieved normal readings after resolving some of their Pain, and are able to stop taking thyroid pills; some had been taking as much as four grains per day. Improvement with the resolution of Pain isn't surprising, since the thyroid is another structure in the endocrine chain controlled by the hypothalamus and pituitary.

The lowering of temperature in almost any life form extends life. Experiments with fish show that even a slight cooling considerably increases longevity. An experiment at Purdue with monkeys involved direct alteration of hypothalamic temperature centers. Their life-span was increased over that of the control group. The lowering of our patients' temperature may well have important implications in their longevity.

I have already noted how the changes in repressive hormones (serotonin) seem to have changed the genetic code in rats. With excessive Pain and therefore heavy repression, the genetic code that controls hormone release may be blocked from its natural denouement. Since repression acts globally and not just on ideas, it would seem that with the lifting of repression the genetic code is allowed its natural development, and hormones which have been blocked are finally released. This permits the system to right itself and for blocked growth to finish its original destination. That is why we see changes in jaw structure, shoulder and chest measurement with the lifting of repression. This also may mean that there are no longer deficiencies or excesses in hormone release which eventually produce catastrophic disease.

Many diseases which are not usually considered psychologic in origin may be. One school of thought has it that diabetes is inherited. We believe that Pain has an important role in this affliction, judging by the diminished insulin requirements of our diabetic patients. As yet, the number of diabetics undergoing Primal Therapy has been too small to provide a clear demonstration of the relationship between Pain and this disease. The trends are encouraging.

Certain cellular distortions resulting from emotional trauma may underlie all immune deficiencies from asthma to cancer. Robert S. Picard has found that "certain patterns of long-term emotional experiences produce a state of immunological incompetence, which may be involved in cancer." Early-life traumas which remain in the system may make one cancer-prone. Studies suggest that it isn't just an alien force intruding on a system that brings about catastrophic disease. What seems to be important is a person's resistance capabilities. There is very good evidence relating the immune system to the development of malignant tumors. The resolution of Pain seems to have a definite effect on the immune system, judging by the permanent resolution of allergies and asthma as a result of Primal Therapy. Just as with any other system, it is possible that the immune system undergoes maturational arrest as a result of global repression. Thus, in the presence of alien forces such as antigens, a person does not make sufficient antibodies resulting in various symptoms.

A study in the 1960s conducted skin biopsies in random fashion in a so-called healthy population and discovered numerous cancer cells in many subjects without the presence of cancer disease. The implication was that we are in constant balance in combating these dangerous cells and it is only when the immune system is incompetent that there is a breakthrough of the actual disease itself. Perhaps trauma affects the development of the immune system so that these cancer cells escape immune surveillance. The resolution of Pain may allow maturation of the immune system so that it can perform its proper surveillance.

To be familiar with Pain and its incredible destructive force is to realize that we simply do not have to "grow old" in the usual sense. Aging—*as we know it*—is unnecessary. Death at the ages we accept as natural is in fact not natural in the fullest sense of the word. We can affect aging if we isolate the factors which hasten or slow down our decline. One major factor is Pain, and something can be done about it. For example, with age the brain deteriorates first in those deep interior areas involving functions which were mature at the time of birth and infancy. We grow and age from "inside out." The older person loses his drive, his motivation, his hunger, his awareness of inner states and all of the psychological consequences of a lower drive state —such as decreased ambition and "push." The earliest days and months of life were the time of our greatest Pain; to feel that early

Pain is to remove tremendous pressure from those corresponding areas of brain function. The resolution of Pain removes pressure from the inner areas of the brain which manifest the first strong signs of aging. Removing the burden of Primal Pain from these structures is the single most important thing any psychotherapy can do. This is not to say that other factors besides Pain do not play a role in aging, as, for example, nutrition and exercise. They can never be as helpful as when the system is free from this tremendous burden.

Feelings never grow old but, when they remain unfelt, they make us old before our time. We can reverse the tendency toward premature aging by frequent visits to our childhood.

V: IN EVERYDAY LIFE

1: The House That Pain Builds

ALL MAMMALS go through cycles, alternating between two kinds of states: the sympathetic and the parasympathetic—energy-expending *versus* energy-conserving. These states, governed by the hypothalamus, are modes of metabolic regulation. A healthy person maintains a proper balance between them, so that the cycles alternate regularly. However, this balance can be upset by early painful events, and one mode or the other will predominate thereafter.

The sympathetic system is the workhorse. It galvanizes, mobilizes, alarms and alerts, expends energy and increases the work of organ systems. It elevates temperature and other vital signs such as heart rate and blood pressure. It increases urine production, can produce bowel spasms and churn up the viscera. This system regulates peripheral blood flow so that under anxiety the hands and feet are cold, the face pale. It is this system that triggers secretion of the steroids, the stress hormones. It mediates nervous sweating and dry mouth, high-tension muscle states, taut face and jaw, and higher voice. It is the agency for impulsive behavior. It determines vigilance and pushes toward externalizing behavior rather than toward reflecting on events.

The parasympathetic system, as the energy-conserver, is dominant in feeling, in deep sleep and full relaxation. It is responsible for the anabolic or repair functions and serves to lower the vital signs. It dilates certain blood vessels so that the skin is warm, the eyes and mouth are more moist, the muscles more relaxed, the voice lower, with a general slowing of movements. Parasympathetic responses are predominant during rest and during recovery periods following stress.

The two systems are complementary, but early-life Pain skews the balance. These hurts, particularly those just before and during birth, put an excruciating burden of Pain on the hypothalamus and stamp us with a particular mode of response for a lifetime.

The reason that this particular mode of response is important is that it not only shapes internal responses but also forms a personality type. The original catastrophic trauma set off a concert of physiologic reactions known as the prototypic response. Any later severe stress tends to set off the prototypic reaction, which is a permanently engraved memory that includes the characteristic life-saving response that occurred at the time of the life-threatening trauma. Thus, if the womb were terribly constricting at birth, and the fetus had to fight to come into life, then the characteristic life-saving response would be fight, aggressiveness, anger, and drive. If the fetus were heavily drugged at birth and could do absolutely nothing except try to breathe, the life-saving response might be resignation, passivity, and sensations—not yet conceptualized—of futility and despair. The continuity of reactions persists because of the memory trace. The prototypic trauma is highly charged, usually a matter of life and death, carries an enormous force, and causes one to react forever to the old situation over and over again when an anxiety-producing stressor occurs in the present.

The importance of sympathetic-parasympathetic dominance is that it is the substructure out of which ideas, attitudes, values, interests, emotional tone, drive, ambition, and many other psychological characteristics are built. It forms the boundaries in which one will characteristically react. The sympathetic dominant person is rarely despairing or futile, but is full of aggressiveness and drive. The characteristic response of the parasympathetically dominant person, on the other hand, is to give up when life is too much, to give in—submit, succumb, and be resigned.

Later childhood events obviously have a great deal to do with one's responses, but for the moment let's concentrate on the prototypic birth trauma. When does the trauma end? Is it while the struggle is still going on or when the body begins to fail and die? Does it end soon after it begins or after many hours of agony? How does it end? Abruptly, or over a long period?

Also critical is the nature of the trauma. Too great a dose of anesthetic? Breech birth? Overlong, hard labor? The question is, when does the infant or newborn get out of the trauma sequence? Does he get off the "trauma train" almost dead from drugs and needing to be revived by ice water, drugs, smacks, etc.? Is he lifted out by Caesarean? Or is he born while he is still fighting for his life? In short, when the trauma ends, is the baby in the sympathetic or parasympathetic mode? All of this will determine much of a person's personality. Has he struggled and failed, struggled and won, not struggled at all? Has he been close to death or, for a moment, actually been clinically dead?

If the labor was long and difficult, if the fetus had to struggle interminably, if she had to be on constant alert to survive, if she had to fight her way out, then the sympathetic system will tend to predominate. For the "sympath," to be on the go is unconsciously life-saving. She had to force her way out at birth or death would have ensued. Every second was a matter of life and death. The system "remembers" this life-saving reaction and continues it no matter what the later circumstances. This early life-saving reaction becomes neurotic because it is no longer appropriate to the situation at hand. Someone may be overly aggressive, overly driven, too quick to anger—all inordinate responses to situations that no longer threaten the person.

If the fetus is heavily drugged—via the mother's anesthetic, which passes through the placental circulation—his respiratory system may be smothered and he is near death. That response is also stamped in and the system will be skewed toward parasympathetic dominance— the "parasympath." This kind of response not only begins to shape personality, it shapes physiology and anatomy.[1]

The sympath is optimistic. He is certain the future will be good *if he tries hard enough* because it was, originally. Contrarily, the parasympath is pessimistic. He has an almost permanent sense of foreboding and doom because the end of his "trauma train" was a disaster. He is constantly looking forward to a doom that has, unbeknown to him, already happened.

As each of us wakes up in the morning, we are still functioning on the lower levels of consciousness and, hence, closer to our prototypic feelings. Thus, the sympath may wake up in a more mobilized, ready-to-meet-the-world state than the parasympath. The sympath bolts out of bed because he wakes up in the sympathetic mode just as he did at birth. All of his arousal hormones, including cortisol levels, are quicker to increase than the parasympath who doesn't reach his peak until much later in the day—sometimes not until night.

The parasympath will be "hypo" both as a personality and as a physical system. He will tend to wake up "down." His body "remembers" how it was and tells him unconsciously that there are no al-

[1] There aren't many parasympaths around, at least as pure types, since many did not survive at birth. Most of us fought like hell to live and obviously we succeeded. But having a cord around one's neck or being held back by a nurse until the doctor arrives, or being heavily drugged allows a newborn nothing he can do to save his life.

ternatives, that the future is not very bright. The physiologic and psychologic systems dovetail so that the lack of energy and lack of physical mobilization produce a kind of "what's the use" attitude. He is not one for physical exercise.

Under stress the parasympath tends toward low blood pressure and slow pulse, replicating the engraved dying response. Taken by themselves these signs might indicate a healthy physical system. But the brain-wave activity shows a change toward higher amplitude. This means that the cortex is under stress. These readings mean that the parasympath is more likely to suffer from dizziness, fainting spells, and vertigo, as well as hypothyroidism and hypoglycemia. He is more prone to migraine. He may live longer than the sympath, because of his energy-conserving tendencies, but he carries a great burden of Pain and a constant memory of physical suffering or death deep in his unconscious. He may dream of actually being dead, something the sympath never does.

Anger is slower to build in the parasympath because his system physiologically is not geared for it. It is not, as Freud thought, that he has anger turned inward into depression; rather, he hasn't the physical wherewithal to organize anger as easily as the sympath does. His neurotransmitter and hormone imbalance impede the easy flashes of anger that are so common to the sympath. Again, these are not attitudinal differences, these are profound biological states. The parasympath isn't going to "get over it" and become more ambitious and less phlegmatic just based on some decisions.

In addition to biological differences there are also differences in appearance. The passive person is more likely to look soft physically; his anatomy accommodates to his psyche. He appears defeated, walks and holds himself that way. His system is in "retard" position. The sympath, on the other hand, has a more aggressive stance. He is ready to do battle with even the slightest provocation, his stride is more determined and certainly a lot quicker. If there's a choice of drugs, the parasympath will choose uppers and needs a good deal of coffee to get going in the morning.

The pure sympath and parasympath are not always evident. Most of us combine qualities of both but tend toward one type or the other. Nevertheless, determining a tendency toward either type is more than mere classification. It implies that one is more likely to have one disease than another and it tells us a good deal about how the person will defend himself under stress. By and large the parasympath will be the depressive. It will take a far more hopeless situation before the sympath becomes depressed.

Depression and its treatment vary according to where a person is on the continuum from parasympathetic to sympathetic dominance. The parasympath wakes up in the morning feeling totally engulfed by inner forces. The subjective experience includes slow heart rate, retarded breathing rate, and the feeling that the limbs are heavy or sluggish and that the flow of thought is confused, unclear, and not very alert. These are already the makings of depression. The idea of death or suicide is often a comfort to the parasympathetic depressive because at least if offers a way out. When all else fails the parasympath can kill the pain by the *thought of death*. It was and is a solution to agony. The system constantly veers toward either the thought or the act of suicide because death is the only real alternative to that trauma. The *solution* to Pain, remember, is also encoded as a memory. Death pops into the mind almost immediately when life gets tough.

Even the kind of death one is preoccupied with would seem to depend on the birth process. The person who is drugged at birth may choose pills while the person who strangled on the cord may opt for hanging. These "conscious choices" remain an outgrowth of early imprinted memory. There are reasons or motivations behind whatever choice we make as adults. Clearly, chance factors are important in how one chooses to kill oneself, but the person who has thought out suicide, buys a gun and shoots himself in the mouth is making a decision and that decision is based on earlier experience, by and large.

The sympath-parasympath continuum has important implications for the treatment of the various states of depression. It is necessary to bring each type of person into the Primal Zone where conditions are optimal for feeling. The sympath needs to come down from his agitated state, the parasympath must come up. Sometimes just a bit of coffee is enough to bring the parasympath into the Primal Zone.

Restoration of the balance between parasympathetic and sympathetic modes begins to occur within the Primal session itself. The sympath comes in anxious and agitated, with all vital functions raised. When the sympathetic defense is strained to its utmost there is a shift, the defense fails, and the patient falls into the feeling where the parasympathetic system takes over. The patient then feels greatly relaxed and the system has begun to work in harmony. The sympath's post-session vital signs indicate a shift toward the parasympathetic side, compared to his baseline readings. Conversely, the person in parasympathetic excess is able to come up out of his generalized suffering and finally react to the Pain which caused it. He engages the sympathetic system for his expression of the Pain and when the session is over his vital signs will shift toward the sympathetic side, compared to baseline.

On a psychological level the normalized balance between sympathetic and parasympathetic modes is illustrated by fewer bouts of depression and moodiness, and fewer extreme highs and lows. The parasympath is able to express his anger and all his feelings more readily, while the sympath has greater possibilities for reflection and introspection. His whole system is more moderate. Nothing could have restored the balance short of changing the imprint of Pain which skewed it. Once that is done, the person tends to be neither a sympath nor a parasympath. He is a more "stabilized" human being. The mentally ill have been called the "mentally unbalanced." Now we see why.

THE NATURE OF DEPRESSION

What is depression? It is another form of neurosis, not a separate disease. It is a repressed state. It occurs because any Pain that cannot be felt engenders an equal amount of repression to control it. The subjective experience is exhaustion, labored movement, a feeling of heaviness and futility, sighing and feeling "down." These are the results of an internal war where Pain is combating the forces keeping it from consciousness. The person feels *repression* at work though the subjective experience is *depression*. Depression is repression moved to a higher plateau. Depression, in and of itself, is not a feeling, it is the result of many feelings compacted and unexpressed.

Depression generally results when outside events render someone hopeless or without enough options to act out his neurosis. This hopelessness sets off the original feeling and the Pain begins to move toward consciousness. If the Pain completed its circuit upward, there would be an acute feeling of anxiety and perhaps impulsive acting out; but what happens instead is inhibition. The Pain is pushed down automatically; the site of this downward thrust is the frontal lobe. This is the area which ingests ideas from parents and society which block feelings, impulses, desires, and needs. It is the neural center for guilt, self-discipline, rigidity and inflexibility. It is the major site of behavioral inhibition, an inhibition that eventually can lead to depression. It is almost certainly the area of Freud's "superego."

The impulsive person who acts "out" and the depressive who acts "in" are not suffering from two separate diseases but have two distinct ways of dealing with the same Pain. The one who acts out merely has less effective frontal inhibition. This can be due to a number of reasons but generally is because of the immense, compounded first- and second-line Pains.

It follows, then, that whatever decreases or attenuates frontal lobe activation will help ease depression. Frontal lobotomy, severing the connection from the frontal area to lower structures, *absolutely* stops depression. To put it another way, depression and thoughts of suicide require a high level of frontal brain activity. You can't have either inhibition or thoughts of suicide without a certain level of brain development. Depressive cycles usually begin in the late teens after the third level has been solidified and a maturational leap has taken place from the child to the adult brain. The adult brain is not merely a larger one but is qualitatively different from the child's. If one were looking for the superego of Freud, one would have to wait until the teens—not between the ages of six and eight, as he thought. It is only in the later teens that we could locate the superego in the frontal section of the brain, the neural basis for depression.[2]

Any substance which acts as a metabolic poison—alcohol, barbiturates, and carbon monoxide—will decrease repression and therefore depression. Electroshock is also a means of combating depression. As a massive blow to the brain, it literally shuts down consciousness while radically increasing serotonin supplies. It prevents the retrieval of memory and, in so doing, prevents access to Pain. There is yet another way that third-level cognitive function can be manipulated and that is if the depressive turns to mystical, religious, or other "in-group" dogmas. The energy of feelings can flow outward so that the person feels lighter and less depressed. This energy becomes attached fanatically to a series of ideas which offer relief. The same pressure is at work but now there is an outlet.[3] Indeed, the expressions of almost any feeling helps depression. Both rage and crying are helpful cathartics.

[2] Eric Courchesne studied the brain-wave patterns of teenagers and children and found a qualitative difference. (From "Neurophysiological Correlates of Cognitive Development: Changes in the Long-Latency Event-Related Potentials from Childhood to Adulthood," in *Electroencephalograph and Clinical Neurophysiology*, 1978, Vol. 45, pp. 468–82). The fourteen-to-seventeen-year-old patterns were substantially different from younger children; particularly wave forms increasingly shifted to the frontal areas (demented children without a well-developed cortical function do not become depressed).

[3] What really is happening in this case is that the person is in the manic phase of a manic-depressive cycle. The manic aspect of this cycle represents a breakdown of repression and a breakthrough of Primal Pain, wrapped in ideation that gives it shape and form. The person who is now "blissed out" is an example of what I mean. He has unconsciously rearranged his third level so that it is not the fixed, rigid repressor that it was before.

This has probably led to the common theory that depression is a matter of rage turned inward, involving self-hate and self-loathing.

Depression is going to be compounded, clearly, when the outlets in one's early childhood are severely limited and where the general atmosphere is exceptionally repressive—in strict schools, rigid churches, and a family life that carefully circumscribes every move the child makes. If the child's head is filled with inhibitions, warnings, and prohibitions almost every minute of his life, sooner or later he's going to suspect his own feelings and impulses. That is the beginning of real "self-hate" where the ideational or cognitive mind cannot tolerate the feeling one. The denied feeling self becomes addicted to alcohol and drugs, and the intellectual self "hates" the addicted one. The self that is hated, paradoxically, is the one that needs so much, and so the person comes to hate his needs.

The difference between an acutely anxious person and a depressive is that the anxious person has less effective gates against Pain. The anxious one has more access to the frantic anguished component of the Pain. In fact, the very anxious person and the depressive are often dealing with exactly the same breakthrough of first-line Pain but the difference is that the depressive can contain it. He constantly feels the pressure of the Pain, even though he cannot delineate it.

Depression is an accumulated sadness, a summation of all the little hurts that have never been expressed. Confusion is an important part of this syndrome because the motivating forces cannot be singled out. It is as if one were presented with all of one's past all at once.

It seems paradoxical to say that the treatment for depression is Pain. But it is a fact. The experience of Primal Pain is the best antidote for depression.

2: Long Night's Journey

EVERY night's sleep is a voyage back in time. Each night we return to our childhood and to the childhood of mankind. In sleep we journey down through our brain circuits to link up with an ancient brain, older than man's own existence, a brain that never truly sleeps until we die. On the way down we encounter old, infantile Pains that lie beneath the surface, so well buried, to keep from troubling us during the day—but not well enough hidden to prevent anxiety-ridden dreams.

We are not really unconscious during sleep; we are simply operating on a different level of consciousness. If we understand these levels, then dreams and nightmares are not such a mystery.

The progression of the brain is from instincts to emotions and then thoughts. This is true in the development of a single brain and in the history of the human brain. We relive this development all in a single sleep cycle. When we wake up each morning we return to full consciousness via the levels of the brain evolution. We come out of the deep unconscious onto the second or emotional level and finally return to wakefulness and the third or cognitive level. We sink into sleep in the opposite order from the way each strata of consciousness was laid down, turning out the lights of consciousness and then slowly turning them back on again.

Dream sleep did not evolve until fifty million years after deep sleep. In the same span of time, the jump from primitive reptilian forms of consciousness to the mammalian was made. But this jump indicates that they represent two different stages in history, two different structures, with very different functions. It means that dream sleep made its appearance in early mammalian forms over one hundred million years ago, and it was only millions of years later that we developed the capacity to interpret dreams. This capacity involved new brain structures, and tells us why it is that interpreting dreams in psychotherapy is not efficacious in terms of changing the basic processes giving rise to them.

In the gestation and birth process, man re-creates his entire evolution from fish to monkey to human. The implication, to me, is that we never radically change—or become "new"—we truly evolve. Sleep seems the time when the species collectively assimilates its experience and deposits its learning into the general hereditary bank.

One might well ask why we must go back through mankind's entire history every night in our sleep. We could just as easily ask why it is that in every human birth we have to go back through the phylogeny of man before we can become human. Man himself is the encoding of all his history. There is something in our constitution that requires a constant return to our roots. We have never left those roots entirely; indeed, each level of development of the brain remains almost intact and each has its own history, its own historic function. During sleep the latest acquired brain is active, followed by a lower brain, and finally we return to the earliest brain of mankind. It is as though each level of brain organization is "unaware" of the other level; it is simply doing "its own thing."

The return descent down the neuraxis is the body's cyclical attempt to heal, for it is the most primitive physiologic brain organization that is responsible for healing. It is during deep sleep that growth hormone (largely responsible for healing) is released.

The brain is arranged in a hierarchy. It is man's inherent capacity to go back down along that hierarchy that releases those healing forces, even as nightmares are always attempts at healing; that is, an attempt to bring the most deep-lying memory trace to consciousness for connection and ultimate resolution. It is not the newly acquired cortex that is responsible for repairing and healing; it is busy adapting. This tells us a bit about why cortical insights cannot heal the wounds of neurosis.

Animals who have been systematically deprived of dream sleep develop lesions or damage down to the cellular level of the most newly acquired areas of the cortex. The implications of this are that one has to descend periodically to the deepest portions of the brain involved with healing in order to maintain the integrity of the entire brain. Interestingly, the higher levels of the brain evolved out of Pain and, while Pain was producing all of these changes in the neural structure, it was also, at the same time, providing the mechanisms by which the brain could solve its traumas.

We always "begin at the beginning" in terms of the imprint of experience. Primals usually start at the beginning of a scene or memory; and man's neurotic struggle is but the symbolic attempt to go back to his beginnings and resolve unfinished business.

Each of our previous—or lower—brain systems was peculiar to a distinct kind of animal form and served the requirements of that form. But the elaborate cortex is most particularly human and serves human needs in a special way. It cannot do so when Pain is pushing. It must sleep well if we are to have a restful night.

When the cortex sleeps, there is automatic regression—to our childhood and to the brain system of the childhood of humankind. Sleep gives us an opportunity to understand regression. It is as though putting the cortex to sleep automatically initiates a form of regression, because access to the second or emotional level provides instant access to childhood.

When we go to sleep we do so in the opposite way from how the brain was formed. We become "unconscious" selectively. At night there is little use for concepts or ideas so the third level falls asleep first. Emotional relationships are suspended and the second-level brain rests. But the first level never sleeps. If it did, we would die. We must go on breathing. Our hearts must pump. We must stay aware of whether we have enough oxygen, whether there is too much heat or too much cold in the room.

The quality of sleep is circumscribed by the levels of consciousness. Researchers have concentrated on the sleep phenomenon as though it were something special and apart. They have not seen it as part of one's general behavior. They have measured levels of sleep without reference to daytime conduct. We cannot sleep on levels which do not exist. The very same levels of consciousness in wakefulness dictate the kind of sleep we have and the kind of experiences we can have on certain levels. We cannot have complex linguistic or abstract ideational night terrors any more than we can have verbal birth Primals.

Neuropsychologist Erik Hoffman describes the relation of sleep to levels of consciousness in terms of stored Pain: "As a person falls asleep, his state of consciousness takes a regressive course, or he descends into the lower levels of consciousness. As he goes from third- to second-line consciousness, he enters light sleep. Neocortical functions are reduced, and the limbic system (the repository of childhood memories) takes control. As the individual passes into deep sleep, first-line consciousness and limbic activity decline and the vital body functions are now governed by the brainstem and the inner brain. In this state the slow delta waves predominate the EEG. Limbic activation during dream sleep helps churn up old feelings which require dreams to screen them from consciousness."

Since sleep is so important to the repair of our systems, it is necessary that repression continue its activity to protect this vital process. As Pain is resolved, sleep becomes just that—a form of rest without the need to suppress Pains.

The deeper the sleep the more likely one is to be in touch with catastrophic Pains, hence the need for greater repression. Deep sleep involves an *active* brain, where deep-lying neurons hold down the earliest traumas. It is here that repression is at its peak; and where large, slow brain-wave patterns indicate great neural forces pushing up from below. The forces seem to be Primal, because this same brain-wave pattern occurs when patients are about to have first-line Primals.

Though the three different brains in our skulls evolved at different times and have different sleep cycles and patterns, they still cooperate so that when one is in dream sleep with a high degree of agitation the muscle system remains inactive so that we do not wake up and act out our dreams.

It is possible through electrophysiologic technology to visualize the various segments of the brain during sleep. For example, when the brain shifts from dream sleep to deep sleep, the hippocampus of the limbic system also "goes to sleep" by decreasing its activity. The thalamus, on the other hand, which sends feelings to the cortex, becomes quite busy during dream sleep.

Graphically, deep sleep resembles an infant's brain-wave pattern. Given our hypothesis that deep sleep puts us in touch with early preverbal consciousness, that finding is not surprising. This pattern begins to give way to faster wave activity, indicating lesser repression, as one begins dream sleep. It is like a shift from low to second gear—from greater to lesser repression.

Critical in the process of repression is the inhibitory neurotransmitter, serotonin. It is found in large quantities in the limbic system, where childhood Pains are stored. Serotonin levels are highest in deep sleep. They are lowest in psychotics—who rarely have periods of deep sleep—neurotics who impulsively act out, and agitated depressives.

Increases in brain serotonin accomplish two things: they quiet anxiety and they increase deep sleep—thus decreasing dream sleep.[1]

If serotonin is artificially lowered in the lower medulla, there is decreased repression, more access to Pain, and less deep sleep.

[1] L-Tryptophan, when taken by mouth, acts as an excellent tranquilizer.

Repression depletes serotonin supplies, causing Pain impulses to rise during phases of sleep. After a long period of deep sleep, serotonin is diminished and the system gives way to dream sleep. The rapid depletion of serotonin during deep sleep allows for nightmares. It is as if, during deep sleep, all the biochemical resources are rushed in to help hold down the force of the first-line Pain but they can only hold on for so long before caving in.

The reason that such a large percentage of strokes and heart attacks occur during the last, long dream phase of the night is that the system is rallying its forces once again against Pain. The system caves in. It has responded to a memory time after time, ringing the alarm, putting all systems into action, but the enemy never fully shows itself. It keeps hiding and attacking. The defenses that kept us alive very early in life by burying the Pain finally bury us.

The neurohormones involved in dream sleep are predominantly of the stress hormone variety—the catecholamines. Dream or REM—rapid eye movement—sleep is predominant in newborns, which makes me wonder if it would not be much less if the newborn did not have an overwhelming birth experience. As we age and our brains and defenses mature, the proportion of deep sleep increases.

Dream sleep is the phase when repression is less effective and feelings move toward consciousness. This is when Pain is symbolized and some of its energy is discharged. This catharsis of excess energy is essential.

Since dreams emanate from the same sources as our waking behavior, a sleeper can walk, talk, think, imagine, carry on conversations, and create. A level of consciousness is very active in dreams.

The symbolism of a dream is but a more delineated and abbreviated form of one's waking symbolic acting out, which is why measuring changes in sleep is so important. Dream experiences happen in a relatively short period of time, are circumscribed, and *really are* the same symbolism, by and large, which is acted out in larger scope during the day.

We should consider each level of consciousness as a general underpinning below waking *and* sleep behaviors. The same forces drive both; the same resolution of those forces affects both. That is why sleep is such an excellent index of progress in therapy. Those with very effective repression, for example, experience distance not only from their feelings but also from even the awareness of them. This is apparent in their inability to remember dreams. An increasing ability to recall dreams, and to feel the feelings in them, is one of the standards by which we judge a patient's inner access. Changes in sleep patterns, changes in dream styles and symbolism have implications for waking behavior.

The resolution of giant terrors during a Primal means that a person will have reduced night terrors and also diminished phobias during the day. The resolution of a fear of one's father in a Primal has implications for how one treats other adults in general and points toward lessened dreams riddled with fears about awesome male figures of one kind or another.

If we consider how the levels contribute to dreams and waking life the point becomes clearer. Dreams begin with sensations; to these sensations are added images and emotions, then a story and a meaning. The meaning is an explanation for the images, and the images help to make rational the sensations. All of this is an elaboration of a basic encoded feeling, need or Pain. The central function of a dream is to cover up reality in order to protect sleep and to keep consciousness from being flooded by stored reality. Its purpose is to keep away a direct linkup with higher centers so that the dream is not transformed into Pain and then into waking. If it were not for dreams, we would all be very, very tired and a bit more neurotic.

Freud believed that dreams process the events of the day preceding, especially disturbing events. This sometimes happens, but in the main dreams process old feelings which may be set off by even small unresolved problems during the preceding day. The higher the charge value of the buried feeling and the closer to consciousness it is, the less the stimulus during the day needed to set it off. Conversely, a powerful current event can set off even the best-repressed feeling. It is very much a balance. The greater the Pain, the less it will take to set it off, and vice versa.

As a feeling is on the rise we select out of the environment those things which are most associated or similar and react to it in neurotic ways. We overreact and do not distinguish well between the past and the present. This also happens in a dream. We wake up out of some dreams convinced of their reality. Everything in them seems real; in fact, it's the feeling that is real.

Intimately associated with Primal feelings are hundreds of scenes, events, and memories. In a dream they are fused together. They are intermingled and condensed. Many random events may shape the details of the dream. But the denouement, the way it unravels, is determined by our history. It is the same predictability as in waking life where people go on acting the same way year after year. Feelings form the continuity of personality and hence the continuity of dreams.

Dreams make rational unconscious feelings. They buffer the feeling while allowing release of some of its energy. One who has felt lost most of his life may dream of losing things or of being lost in strange lands. Those strange lands are creations to meet the feeling. If the person really felt, "Mommy, I'm lost. I don't know what to do. Help me!" he would be in agony instead of dream sleep and those feelings would change his dream life.

Contrary to Freud, the symbols in dreams *cannot have universal meaning.* They flow idiosyncratically out of one's own experience. They have meaning only in terms of the particular feeling they symbolize. The same symbol, even in the same person, can have two very different meanings in two different dreams. Symbols differ radically in meaning for different people. To one person, for example, books in a dream mean a way of "finding out." To another they represent anxiety about being forced to perform. Drowning can mean being overwhelmed to one person and be an actual re-creation of an old event to another.

Since dreams are condensed replicas of trapped and reverberating messages, it follows that *the feeling in a dream is always right.* It is always truthful in the way it reflects our past. That is why feeling the feelings of dreams—rather than analyzing the symbols—can lead us to the unconscious Pain. Dreams in one sense are the royal road to the unconscious—not through their analysis, as Freud thought, but through their emotional experience. The agony component of a memory, remember, must also be retrieved.[2]

Feeling the feelings of a dream allow one to recapture agony; it is agony, remember, that is also part of the entire memory that must be retrieved and connected. No intellectual exercise in the analysis of dreams can possibly recapture the exact agony trapped within that dream.

There are times when one must not only recapture agony but absolute terror because the original situation was terrorizing. The night terror is different from a bad dream. The bad dream evolves slowly out of a developing story. The night terror, on the contrary, is sudden and unexpected. It erupts into consciousness and makes us awake. It arises out of first-level sleep often accompanied with screams, ex-

---

[2] Sleep is in some ways analogous to the process of a Primal. The difference between the two is higher connection. Although dreams symbolically express Pain on the lower levels, dreams, by definition, lack connection. In fact, in Primal Therapy we turn dreams into Primals by tapping the feeling and making the connection. Since feelings organize both the dream and the Primal, the stronger the feeling the more force to both. The nature of sleep changes with the resolution of Pain, and our preliminary evidence indicates that the overall amount of dream sleep changes radically.

tremely fast heart beat, and a feeling of nameless dread. It is a shaking experience. The shattering Primal forces have temporarily escaped their cage. Sometimes the second level is pressed into service to provide symbols for the terror such as a dragon or a monster, but the impulse is from the first line.

Charles Fischer found that night terrors were often accompanied by what we now know are birth terrors—feelings of choking, smothering, being crushed, falling, and dying.[3] In other words, what we see in Primals when a person is into the first, deepest level of consciousness is exactly what one sees in night terrors. The person with night terrors is, by and large, poorly repressed and has weak defenses.

Night terrors are formless. This is because the Pains are preverbal and undelineated; they occurred when there wasn't enough cortex to intellectualize them. Though the pulse can double and terror will mount, the person usually has no idea what is the matter or where the terror came from.

The bad dream is usually a second-line Pain where the force is not nearly that of the night terror. If the second level is sufficient to control first-line intrusion, what you get is a very bad dream with a high charge value but sleep continues. If the second level is inadequate to handle the first-line force, then there are night terrors or sleepwalking, which also often comes out of deep sleep. The Primal forces strong enough to move someone around the house during sleep must be very powerful indeed.

Recurrent dreams and nightmares have a special significance in dream life because it is as though one great feeling or event is fixated as a reverberating circuit climbing periodically to the surface. "I'm walking through the woods," one patient dreamed, "and I'm grabbed by a bony hand, black eyes and a hood. I'm hauled brutally to a clearing, pinned to an ice-cold marble table by seven other skeletons. I cannot move. Then suddenly one of them stabs me in the chest. Time stops. I can't breathe. Time passes. Suddenly I breathe in with a gasp and I'm back again." This dream went on for many years before he arrived at the feeling of the dream. It was the re-creation of an event at the age of two; of being anesthetized on a stainless steel table prior to surgery. A mask was put on his face by other masked doctors. He remembers their "bony hands." Experiencing the repressed feelings surrounding this event finally freed him from this nightmare.

Many of us have nightmares where we can neither speak nor call

3 Charles Fischer, et al., "A Psychophysiological Study of Nightmares and Night Terrors," in *The Journal of Nervous and Mental Disease,* Vol. 157, August 2, 1973, pp. 75–96.

out because the level of brain organization, the level which is totally in charge of organizing the dream or nightmare, has no words. Even though the second level is involved in a first-line dream in terms of producing images, the first-level involvement sees to it that we cannot scream nor open our mouths. The reason is that the trauma occurred when there were no words; nor, if it happened during birth, were we able to open our mouths. The suffering that goes on in the womb is all in silence. That is partially why we cannot believe that the newborn has been in excruciating agony. He may let it out slowly over the years in the form of a constant whine but rarely will he express that agony at a single time. The agony may begin to surface later on in the form of recurrent nightmares—a message which tells us that something important has been left unresolved. This is the message of every major nightmare.

The reason that a nightmare is so clear, simple, direct, and unsymbolized is that it usually reflects a single catastrophic event. The feeling comes up in pure form. Whereas the second-line dream involves many years of the same kind of seemingly innocuous traumas which combine into a single feeling and a dream. The dream weaves and contracts many events and scenes and ties them together with symbols. It is not one event that makes the feeling so strong but many similar events that compound into a deep feeling; as, for example, years of subtle rejection where a parent won't look directly at his child or call his name. Or years of constant criticism. Here the dream may be of being chased without surcease by unrelenting figures as a symbol of the parent never letting up, never getting off the back of his child.

Those patients close to first-line traumas have immediate, direct, and uncomplicated free-floating anxieties. They experience all the feelings that others might experience in a nightmare. They might feel suffocated, crushed, or disoriented, the content of the daytime anxiety and the nightmare being the same.

It is not just the Pain that comes up during the night but one's whole history. To paraphrase a famous saying, "He who has not *felt* his history is doomed to relive it." Trying to understand a dream is like trying to understand one's history through analyzing a few symbols. Much better to *experience* that history first and then the symbols will clarify and explain themselves.[4]

[4] Sleeping pills allow us to sleep by putting repressive forces to work against our history. When effective, they, like tranquilizers, render us "ahistoric" and disengage us from our roots. The pills act on specific levels of consciousness. Some act on the arousal centers, the reticular activating system, shutting down general arousal; others act on the muscle system, forcing relaxation. Sleeping pills enhance the repressive system. That they aid sleep is again evidence of the importance of Pain to sleep disturbance.

Even though the whole country is tranquilized day and night, few recognize the fact or would admit it. Society has made it convenient not to feel. We have cigarettes, alcohol, tranquilizers, stimulants, and sleeping pills to help us remain unfeeling. So here is the paradox. We cannot sleep because we are suffering from a Pain we can't feel. We push it down before we can feel it so we remain unconscious of exactly those forces which could finally liberate us. If the intellectual level didn't provide a racing mind, if the feeling level didn't produce dream images, we would all recognize the problem for what it is.

When Pain is suppressed at night with pills, there is a price to pay. For there will be a rebound, perhaps subtle and unnoticeable, but what is held down during the night will spring forth during the day, making one a bit more grumpy, edgy, and irritable. Then more pills and tranquilizers will be used during the day to push back the very same history we had to deal with at night. It is a truly vicious cycle.

The neurotic must be neurotic in his dreams. He has no other choice. Depriving him of dreams prevents him from having a primary neurotic outlet. Certainly he will be more anxious when dream sleep is interfered with. Dream sleep is a release state. The dreamer is discharging energy in constant movement, perspiring, mumbling and mental activity. He will wake up refreshed if, first, he has had enough deep, restful sleep and, second, he has had enough dream sleep to discharge neurotic tension. With insufficient deep sleep more dream sleep is needed.

Dreams are the steps just below a Primal. They are the ladder we can sometimes use to arrive at Primals and are the harbingers of Primals to come rather than special, mystical phenomena.

Our history is always trying to declare itself. We scream during sleep and imagine that it is the quirk of some kind of dream. "It's the dream, not us." We are plagued by recurrent dreams and nightmares and do not understand that there must be some recurrent underlying *force* producing them that is not the property of the dream itself. We have a mystical idea about dream life because the unconscious is such a mystery to us. Sleep has become some encapsulated event that bears no relation to who we are as people.

If we are to understand ourselves, we must understand all our experiences—which we will do when we look at the entire human system that mediates them. The discovery that Pain profoundly affects sleep processes and that the resolution of Pain changes them again may help to demystify the study of sleep and to save it from being a separate compartment in psychology. We must study ourselves as a whole.

3: The Sexual Prisoner

A REAL "SEX" problem is a rarity. The problem of sex is a problem of a human being with a particular upbringing. This is true even of those who indulge themselves sexually, and seem to enjoy it. There is a quality to the act that is missing; something that those who concentrate on technique alone miss.

People don't just have a pocket of neurosis here, a bit of neurosis there. Everything a neurotic does will be neurotic. But there are degrees of neurosis, and the effects may be felt in one area more than another. Any degree of repression of feeling will involve repression of sexuality, which is a feeling state. The first major trauma, the birth trauma, may already produce a great amount of bodily repression. When the child is old enough to have moral ideas drummed into his head, more repression will take place regarding sex.

Pain is rerouted into sex impulses in the hypothalamus; this process takes place unconsciously. What is discharged through sex is tension, yet the person is unaware of it. This release feels good, as does any effective tension release; and it is this good feeling that is often confused with sex. Many sexually active people seem to enjoy "sex" very much without ever realizing that it is not a sexual experience they are having. So long as there is significant Pain to be released it is unlikely that these people will ever know the true ecstasy of sex nor will they ever enjoy a purely sexual experience. Sex, for those who act out that way, is only the transformation of Pain into sexual outlets: the more Pain, the more "sex" drive.

Why is sex at once such an effective antidote to Pain and such an exciter of it? Orgasm, for example, can be relieving to some while extremely threatening to others. On the strictly emotional level, sex offers a greater potential to satisfy need than other outlets. There is potential gratification for all the senses. But in flirting with gratification, one is brought close to the imprinted feelings of unfulfillment—for a very simple reason. The centers in the brain mediating Pain and pleasure are very close. Feeling is a single phenomenon: if you heighten the level of any feeling, you stimulate all other feelings. The warmth and tenderness one gets with sex bring up the rejection, coldness, and lack of physical affection from earlier life. Just the feeling of being wanted brings with it all the unwanted feelings of early childhood. With that arousal of all of those feelings and *their repression* it is clearly impossible to have a high level of totally orgasmic ecstasy for a repressed person. This is because part of his body is busily engaged in holding down feelings. In sex the Pain that is dredged up is rechanneled into the buildup of sexual tension with the final orgasmic release.[1]

Pain always seeks an outlet. If the sexual one is blocked early in life by parental morality and prohibition, then another outlet will be found. It could be an intellectual one. The child may become absorbed by books. If parents and church are successful in their indoctrination, the child's intellect will act as a brake on rather than a mediator of sexual impulses. The result later on may be a low sex drive. Watch any parent almost anywhere with his or her child. It is rare that one sees constant affection and tenderness. Too often it looks like a war. There are warnings, rules, spankings, reprimands, shushings, apprehensions about this move or that. These are the causes of Pain that can finally end up as a "sex" problem. It is never just what the parents said or didn't say about sex. Whenever the child cannot move freely about, whenever she cannot say what she wants, play with whom she wants, be held when she cries, caressed when she hurts herself, enjoyed for the person she is, repression goes into action. It converts that psychologic event into physical Pain, stores it and holds it. These are the causes of sex problems, as can be seen from Vera's story:

"Not long ago I met a man whom I loved, but with whom I was unable to have orgasm. I had not had that problem for years: with

[1] Orgasm allows for a massive discharge of Primal energy. It is a convulsion that, in its intensity and valence, also mimics the early convulsions during birth. Thus, a person may temporarily relieve himself of the stored convulsive energy of a first-line trauma via the sex act. However, to be forced near an equally severe experience of Pain as he or she comes close to sexual convulsion —orgasm—can result in shutdown, as in impotence or frigidity.

my present husband and other lovers I had been having orgasms successfully for six or seven years. It wasn't necessary for me to feel any strong emotional attachment to a man in order to have an orgasm with him, and I could enjoy intercourse for the sake of the physical pleasure and release and the warm company. But suddenly I found myself blocked from orgasm, with a man I found incredibly beautiful both as a man and as a human being apart from sex, a man to whom I was very strongly attracted and with whom I loved making love. One night after we made love and I didn't come again, I let myself have some of the feelings that were rising; cried, cursed, pounded the bed with my fists. Shortly afterwards we fell asleep, and I immediately had a nightmare from which I woke shuddering with horror. I went to group, but although I felt more of the horror the dream was still ambiguous and puzzling. I still had no notion what it was about or how it related to the whole sexual hassle. So I stood up during a group session, hoping to talk about it some more. But by the time my turn came to talk, the session was almost over, and I was nervous and rushed by the feeling that I should hurry, not take up too much time, if I talked too long people would resent me. I was rushing, trying to explain the dream as briefly as I could then get into the feeling, when suddenly Art interrupted me and said, 'Your time's up.' I stared at him in disbelief. 'It is?' I asked incredulously, and he replied cheerfully, 'Yes, time's up.' I was overwhelmed with anger, indignation, and hurt. The woman just before me had talked much longer than I, how could my time be up? By the time I was back at my place by the wall I was screaming with rage and pain. No time for me, no one wants to listen to me or cares about me—a feeling very close to the one I had about making love with a man, wanting to come soon so as to let him have his pleasure without the strain of going on and on. I cried with pain and rage at having been cut off and put down, and then as those feelings began to abate, I had a strong urge to put my head against Art's chest, and heard myself cry out to him: 'I love you and you hurt me!' which I recognized immediately as one of my big feelings about my father and was then able to say to him. Then it came to me how the men I had loved had always hurt me—except my husband, who loved and cared for me in such a way that I could relax, for the first time in my life, and know myself loved. So with Greg my block had to do with the conviction that any man I loved would inevitably hurt me. Because my feeling about Greg was so strong, on some level I felt again the old certainty I wouldn't be loved, the old fear and expectation of pain. The next time I made love to him sometime after this session at group I had an orgasm, and sex between us has grown more and more delightful ever since."

Children who are not allowed any spontaneous move without first getting parental approval—which is long coming—are not going to grow up to be good sex partners. The spontaneity has been taken out of them. Their sex problem may have begun at age four when they couldn't go out and play with the neighbor children; it continued when they couldn't go out at night until all the endless chores were done, and went on into the late teens when a controlling mother or father had to know the child's whereabouts every minute of her life. Can anyone believe, then, that that lack of spontaneity in sex can be treated here by confrontation sessions where someone now "relearns" to be spontaneous? There is little chance, since those unresolved demands are *still* the constricting, disabling factors. The past is still a *physiologic* internal fact, as we can see from Fran's experience:

"In therapy I relive what happened between my father and me. I struggle with him. He holds me down. He grabs my neck. My hands hurt. I feel like I don't know what is happening or why. Then I have sensations in my genitals and I feel my vagina pulsating and getting wet. My pelvis is jolted up and down. In one Primal, I saw him for an instant, standing over me, naked, and I cried out, 'I'm too little,' and felt a pain in my abdomen and my vagina tighten. I scream 'NO' over and over, but it doesn't stop. I cry out, 'I promise I won't tell Mommy,' then my jaw becomes tense, and my teeth chatter, and my whole body shakes. The intensity of the feeling continues until I start thinking, and sometimes calling out, "There's something wrong with me. I'm sorry. It's my fault. I'll be good.'

"In these Primals I feel the pain of my father raping me at age five. I also relive the way I first defended against this pain. I believed that *I* did something wrong, something shameful that I had to apologize for. I 'forgot' about what happened. I could not feel the painful truth: my daddy hurt me very badly. He does not love me. I still can't stand the pain and still use the same old defenses in many variations. I forget about unpleasant truths. I feel guilty for anything that goes wrong and undeserving of anything good. I seem to be constantly saying, 'There is something wrong with me. I'm sorry. It's my fault. I'll be good,' and especially, 'It didn't happen.'

"I have made many connections as a result of these Primals. One of the most important concerns my own sexuality; to me, having sex and being helpless are identical. In order to avoid being helpless I have avoided sex. I feel ashamed of my body and prefer hiding behind plainness—wearing jeans and a T-shirt and no makeup—to looking attractive."

Sex problems have a history. The impulses behind sexual problems are not particularly due to traumas around sex. Early trauma, predating the maturation of sexuality, affects feeling, which in turn will later affect the ability to feel in sex. Indeed, the deeper one feels and the earlier one goes back the more liberating the feeling is for *adult* sexuality. Sex is not one of our "thinking" kinds of activity. We do not acquire a sex problem overnight; it is not undone in a few weeks of training. These problems are deeply embedded in a neurotic body. *Neurosis* is the problem and its treatment is the solution.

Because opening up to full convulsiveness in sexual orgasm requires being vulnerable to first-line Pains, neurotic sex has to be muted and shallow. Deep-lying sexual problems such as frigidity and impotence may begin with the birth trauma, which shuts down the body instantly; therefore, the final resolution of, say, frigidity, lies in reliving first-line Pains of one kind or another. Women frequently report profound sexual changes at some time after a series of first-line Primals. They remark on the different quality of their orgasms, which are deeper and more encompassing. These spontaneous expressions by women help us to know the relationship of the most early Primal traumas and sexuality which occurs decades later. Women who begin to open up in Primal Therapy can actually feel the shut-down when they begin to have sex. They reach a certain point of excitement and no more before the Pain starts to surface with that excitement. Then repression occurs, which unfortunately shuts down the growing excitement. After some time in Primal Therapy they notice how the states of sexual pleasure augment as repression decreases. After several months of therapy it is not uncommon for a person to begin to have orgasm and then slip into a birth Primal. The convulsions of sex set off the memory. This is another corroboration of the relationship between the convulsions of birth and sexuality.

Often Primals which have nothing to do with sex can be quite liberating. One woman felt that whenever she showed any great feeling as a child her parents shushed her and told her to act "like a lady." She dared not show any excitement in sex. She could not if she wanted to. Her parents had taken excitement away from her and left her with only ladylike motions. She was dainty and proper but not sexual. Her whole body accommodated itself to this Pain. She was tight, rigid, and inflexible. She could not let go. Once she learned to let go of the Pain in her body, she was on her way to letting herself go in sex.

When one girl's father died when she was six, it ruined her sex life later on, even though the event had nothing to do with sex. When she relived the experience several times in Primal Therapy, her sex life became much more satisfying. It has to do with being totally open to a man—her father—who then "left" her abruptly, resulting in the later inability to open up to a man and be completely vulnerable. When she resolved that feeling she could be sexual. She now understood why she could masturbate to orgasm without any difficulty but was otherwise totally frigid. As long as there was no one around she could be sexual, because she was not vulnerable and open to anyone but herself.

A child can grow up with almost no outlets. If parents are cold and rejecting, if they are on him every minute, if they block all expression of feeling, the result can be an incredible buildup of tension. Generally this would be released in sexual activity but if the early mores of the parents are prudish in regard to sex, then all spillways are stopped up. One result of this could be convulsive seizures, the automatic, random release of tension. In one sense, the orgasmic release of sex could be a preventive for psychogenic seizures.

One patient who was sexually insatiable and addicted to orgies was forced to stop her behavior by threats from her husband. She then developed dangerously high blood pressure. Pain took another route, a dramatic illustration of the underlying problem. Her problem and the source of her drive was not getting enough love early in life. Her tension was not the result of sexual frustration, even though she experienced it that way subjectively. When sexual outlets were blocked, she was again left with her early Pain.

The person who acts-out sexually is far less likely to come for help than those who find themselves blocked and either frigid or impotent. But the one who acts out is generally compulsive about it: he must do it. He is not free about sex, though he may pose as liberated. So long as he finds partners, he may not have a pressing problem. However, what is lacking in his sex is a relationship. He is releasing but not relating; the other person is merely the object of an act-out.

For instance, some older men get turned on by very young girls. This choice tells us about the emotional level of these men. They really don't feel like men. They are still little boys unable to relate to real women.

Men who have never had enough mothering need more than any one woman can give, no matter how giving they are. These men are bound to be unfaithful. Women without father love may have the same problem. No man will ever be enough. They are constantly dissatisfied, not comfortable in their skin, searching for something new and different. No one will ever make them feel content and no one should try.

Sexual impulsiveness has nothing to do with sex per se. All of the original traumas were expressed in the form of electrical impulses, and it is the sum total of this charge that produces impulsiveness. Reliving *nonsexual*, first-line traumas takes the pressure off sexual impulsiveness. We have found a high degree of correlation between patients' subjective reports of reduced sexual impulsiveness and radically lowered electrical activity in the brain.

There is still other evidence of the relationship of Pain and stress to changes in sexual activity and sex hormones. A. S. Heritage[2] has recently discovered that the male and female sex hormones are secreted by nerve cells very close to those cells which have to do with stress. Thus, in a neurotic individual with increased sympathetic nervous system activity, there is likely to be an alteration in the regulation of male and female sex hormones. These findings again provide the physiological basis for the incomplete maturation of secondary sexual characteristics in neurotic individuals and also accounts for changes in sexual activity. The hypothalamic centers which carry the burden of Pain also translate that Pain into sex.

We can see clearly in these instances the tremendous pressure the person is under, exactly what that pressure is, and how much there is. That is why it is so disappointing to see the treatment of sexual offenders in prisons by group discussion sessions. They are little more than morality plays. I suppose it is possible through these intellectual exercises to soup-up mental control, but for someone suffering from constant pressure that rarely is going to be enough.

The same forces underlie the less dramatic forms of poor impulse control, such as premature ejaculation. Early-Pain impulses are constantly urging the person on. In sex the general excitement level is heightened, so, of course, will be these impulses. That heightened level puts a strain on the control apparatus, with the resulting premature ejaculation. Treating premature ejaculation simply as a sex problem is missing the point.

How a child had to distort himself for love will inevitably be reflected in sex. The perversion he prefers and the rituals he adopts will reflect a lifetime of buried feelings. Perversions are the same as a recurrent dream, in which a symbol of a feeling is fixed and frozen. The ritual or dream is an attempt to reenact and come to terms with

[2] A. S. Heritage, *Science*, March 21, 1980.

the feeling. It is not only derived from Primal feelings but is a way back into them. If we can stop the ritual long enough we can help the patient into his feelings.

There are those who need pain to get aroused. The higher the level of beatings, pinchings, and so forth the higher the level of excitation. The connection between Pain and the feeling is unconscious but close.

The need to be hurt to enhance sexuality occurs for a variety of reasons, not the least of which is advance punishment for pleasure to come. The timetable is turned around. Instead of enjoying sexual pleasure first, feeling guilty and expecting some kind of punishment, they take their punishment first, which frees them a bit more to enjoy it. They can now feel guilty with a clear conscience.

Repressed need directs sexual choice. The turn-on is automatic. Need is already agitating the system for fulfillment. It has simply been eroticized so that fulfillment is symbolic. When something outside triggers off the need, there is excitement. Need, now sexualized, surges forth. What turns someone on is usually dictated by what happened to need early in life.

The person whose Pain has more of a later childhood focus usually gets turned on by a special need. One patient had a Primal about his mother never showing feeling. He got involved with "dead" expressionless women. They turned him on as "live ones" never did. His symbolic struggle was to take the dead ones and try to get them to show feeling. He never thought about himself much during sex. He was too busy "techniquing" the women so as to produce what he needed—a feeling woman. He discovered after Primal Therapy that he had never really enjoyed sex before. It was a task. It is the infant who needs to have emotional expression from its mother, and the adult who tries to bring it about through sex. There isn't enough sex in the world to fill that need. But that doesn't stop anyone from trying.

In any ritual it is rarely the act itself which is compelling. After all, there is nothing inherently pleasurable about dressing up in a woman's panties or in leather. It is need which is overpowering, and it is neither augmented nor reduced in a ritual. Its force remains exactly the same. When the ritual is stopped the person is in Pain. This is how we know that Pain underlies sexual rituals. The person who wants to be urinated on, whipped, or chained is only trying to match his external world to his internal feeling. He *already* feels humiliated and worthless, as though the only way anyone would pay attention to him is to humiliate him. It is important that the ritual not be treated as a viable entity, as some special disease form, apart from its feeling base. Early experiences shaped the ritual; experience will end it.

One does not act out a ritual every day during the routine work hours. So why must one do it in sex? Because any bodily arousal is global and unhinges Primal feelings. As they come up, they would create agony if felt directly. So the ritual, like the dream, steps in to block the Pain while allowing the continuation of arousal. This is why sex reveals hidden need. A man can deny his need for men during the ordinary course of daily life but when put into a sexual situation begins to fantasize homosexual relationships. A "correct" housewife, when aroused, must fantasize being "gang-raped" because her feeling is that sex is dirty and bad. She must imagine being a helpless victim in sex so that she can enjoy it.

What is healthy sex? Anything healthy people do. What is a healthy person? Someone without overbearing Pain. Variations in sex are not necessarily unhealthy. After all, not everyone is the same nor is everyone aroused by the same things or in the same way. But whips and chains have nothing to do with sex. There is nothing intrinsically erotic about them; they reflect a Primal force in some people. Any continuous kind of sex which avoids direct intercourse reflects the repression of Pain.

Even the choice of a sex partner can sometimes be considered a perversion. A man we saw had a mother who was exceptionally seductive with him. She rubbed and cuddled him constantly, saying, "You are all mine." She was blond. In order to have sex with any woman, he had to have it with a dark one, preferably black or oriental. To avoid the incestuous feelings, he had to get as far away as possible from anyone who reminded him unconsciously of his mother. He was impotent with light, blond women. What looked like a simple, innocent choice of a sex partner was not. But one might never know its Primal base without getting down into the feelings of the early parent-child relationship. He always knew his mother was seductive. The understanding helped him not at all. When he felt what it did to him, how she had aroused sexual feelings in her son, feelings that were terribly confusing to a young boy, he then could see how his own sexual choices were attempts to avoid those feelings. He was then free to make real choices.

The possibilities of perversion are endless. The different ways a mother can be seductive will result in different perversions or rituals. The young boy whose mother straddled him without panties on and then slapped him for looking, set up the ritual of having to have women straddle him standing up before sex could take place. The young boy whose mother left him to go to work everyday left him with the souvenirs of her existence, her panties and hose. So he became erotically attached to them and needed to see and feel a woman's hose in order to get aroused.

Behavior in and of itself is neither healthy or unhealthy. It can be healthy to want a dark or light skinned partner, or completely unhealthy. And the label "unhealthy" is not important except as it reflects buried Pain.

The serious sex problems that most people have are not apparent; they are in the quality of the sex experience. Until now we have had no proper gauge to tell us about healthy sexuality. We have previously taken averages and considered them guidelines for health. But with full access to the self we understand what normal sexuality is. We know what is behind perversions, frigidity, and impotence. After extracting Pain from sex, we have an insight into the nature of real sexual experience.

The most important thing to be said about the sex act is that it is not an *act*.

4: The Last Retreat

Psychosis is another way for the brain to handle Pain. It is no more mysterious or unfathomable than neurosis. Primal traumas are electrical storms that are gated in the brain. Under stress or under weakened conditions, electrical eruptions can spring from those storm centers. Those eruptions can be in the form of rages, crying jags, epileptic fits, migraines, nightmares, and, when the charge of Pain is great enough, delusions and hallucinations.

Psychosis represents the breakdown of repression; energy pours forth from its storage sites on a Primal rampage that cannot be stopped by internal means. It is the last mental operation the brain can perform in response to Pain—the brain's final defense. I think the only alternative is death. The system has gone crazy to defend itself and if the mind cannot go crazy, I believe, the body will, in fatal or near-fatal ailments.

So, the psychotic exhibits sudden crazy movements, sudden darting of the eyes or sudden talking out loud to no one at all, the instantaneous onset of delusions and hallucinations. One can also see these explosions in neurosis, such as rage reactions, asthma attacks, tics, migraine attacks, and so on. These too are signals of the eruptions of internal Pain storms which are not well contained. Indeed, when one gives psychotics and neurotics the very same drugs that blunt Pain and help gate Pain, the explosions are better contained and one no longer sees the symptoms of either neurosis or psychosis.

The symptoms of psychosis are symptoms first of all. They are different in quality from neurotic symptoms because they are bizarre and seemingly have no basis in reality. There really is no one in the television set giving one orders—to quote a current delusion of a patient under treatment. The symptoms are, by and large, ideational or pure imagery. They are bizarre because their source is deep, inaccessible Pain. Thus there is seemingly no apparent connection between the symptom and anything in present reality. In neurosis where the source is closer to the surface, and where the Pain is usually less severe, the symptom seems to have greater justification; someone may act just like one's mother, for example. In psychosis there need be no current event to trigger the hallucination. The source is so remote in the past as to seem nonexistent and it springs forth almost without provocation.

The higher the level of Pain internally, the less the force required from outside to set off a psychotic symptom—a mild illness, a criticism, a look. When one is riddled with compounded Pain, it takes *no* outside stimulus to produce the symptom. The psychotic cannot distinguish between internal and external, since his internal life suffuses his external conscious awareness.

Although the sources of neurosis and psychosis are the same, psychosis is a qualitative leap from the neurotic state. Pain accumulates until one passes into a new realm. Here the behaviors, symptoms, dream life, and biochemistry are different. That the psychotic is different is immediately apparent to all. The look in his eye tells almost the whole story. His glazed look tells us that he is seeing only his past. He is not "here." His responses are strange; one patient thought the therapist changed his clothes from the previous session in order to trick him. His delusion was that this was a plot to disorient him and make him unable to tell where he was; in other words, a plot to delude him. Other patients report that they hear voices coming through the walls, laughing at them or mocking them.

The psychotic cannot navigate well in the world. He cannot hold a job, study, or make appointments. He is forgetful because he is not conscious—he is not (all) there. He dresses poorly and does not eat properly because his mind is engaged with the past—with the Pain. He may be still living on the assumption that someone is going to take care of him. He is often perceptive because he reacts directly off the second or emotional level and has no solid third-level or intellectual defenses to keep him from sensing what is going on. Indeed, he may be in the fix he is in because he has always been too sensitive—to Pain. It is a peculiar paradox. He is sensitive to emotional nuances, yet totally unconscious. He simply lacks the cohesion of consciousness that would take in an entire situation and judge how to respond. His reactions are inordinately inappropriate.

Psychotic delusions nearly always involve some secret and powerful outside source. There may be, for example, a secret conspiracy directed toward him. That "secret force" is usually Primal in origin and though projected externally the content is very much internal. Because the person has no idea that the events of his past are still pressing inside him, he has no choice but to project. The content of the projection—the Communists or Mafia or aliens—simply borrows from what is current or convenient.

The chronic psychotic is fighting a last-ditch battle for control and reason. As he loses again and again to overwhelming internal disruption, his attempts to make sense become ever more frantic and inappropriate and thus increasingly ineffective. Projection is survival for the psychotic.

To externalize Primal fears means something can be done about them. However absurd or incongruous a person's delusion may seem to us, to them it *makes sense*—literally. It imbues an otherwise inexplicable, amorphous feeling with sense and reason.

The external situations can be manipulated so that the person feels he has some kind of control over his life. One can kick in the television set, one can nail up doors, one can avoid people who are "laughing at me." There *is* a method in madness.

When the psychotic is given a drug to block the Pain, he is no longer overwhelmed with a force he must project and, hence, the delusion falls away.

Sometimes the psychosis is not noticed because the person has embraced some mystical or religious notion which merges into an institutionalized ideational structure so well that his psychosis has become institutionalized. With an organizational imprimatur behind him, the psychotic has cachet. So long as everyone in his group believes the same thing, no matter how strange, he probably won't be put away. He can stare into space for hours, but because he is "meditating" or "communing with God" he is presumably sane.

The psychotic lacks cohesion. He may start a paragraph making sense and end up in non sequiturs. Though plain to everyone else, he doesn't sense his fragmentation because he has no cohesive framework from which to view it. He doesn't see the contradictions in his statements because each statement is a thing in itself. His intellect is literally "unglued"; and it has come unglued because of lower-line pressure. He cannot put the various pieces of his life together. He is simply left with various fragments which he attends to serially, rather than globally. It is usually early-life Pain that is dismantling his intellect, but there can be other factors as well, especially in transient psychotic states such as those induced by fever or toxic substances.

In a nervous breakdown, one succumbs to a disconnected, ascending Primal force. It is the beginning of the Primal feeling with all of its terror, but without the ability to connect. Instead of breaking down *into a feeling* (that is, into the Pain), with the help of a therapist, then connecting it to consciousness, the victim of a nervous breakdown breaks down, breaks apart, and perhaps becomes something else—the President or Jesus. When you think about it, what is there to "break down" in anyone? There are only the defenses to break. A person who is without Pain could only break down and become himself—which is health, not psychosis. So whenever we think of nervous breakdowns, we must think of a breakdown of the defense system against Pain. That occurs because events in the present touch off more past Pain than can be integrated.

One lives in madness because one cannot feel it. The psychotic has effectively converted all of his feelings into thoughts and the bizarreness of those thoughts are the measure of the force of those feelings. His imagination, whether of ideas or of images, is the best possible protection he has. One must be very careful in taking those away without dealing with their source.

The infant has a very inadequate conception of space and time. When an adult is bombarded with Pains that happened to him in infancy, he will tend to develop "spacy" ideas, imagining a kind of out-of-space-and-time significance. Astral projection, a feeling of traveling through timeless space, is an example of what I mean. The reason is that when an early preverbal Pain is triggered, the exact early reaction to that Pain also comes up. So, of course, a person has a feeling of nonspace and time. This alone produces confusion and the feeling of disorientation as though one is going crazy. This is because they cannot confine or delineate the experience in any normal way—they have no ordinary labels for it. In that sense, the feeling is "boundless" or "boundaryless."

The content of the ideation attached to early Pains usually has something to do with hurt or death—with threats to survival. The psychotic deals with those feelings by thinking that he is in danger of impending death because someone in the nearby phone booth, for example, might throw a switch that will finish him off. The content of the feeling is right; the framework is wrong and the feeling is unresolved. He feels that he is going to die—that he is going to be killed at the hands of an unknown source and, of course, by now we have a pretty good idea what that unknown source really is. Someone in the throes of a feeling of being strangled by an umbilical cord is usually totally helpless before this memory. He has no idea at all what is happening to him or why. Very few of us even realize that those memories from birth are still there and that they are "feelable."

Psychotics can be treated with Primal Therapy. Psychotic symptoms can be eradicated in an hour *without drugs*. I do not say psychosis (a state of being) can be reversed in an hour, only its symptoms. We have seen full-blown delusional patients come in for a session totally psychotic and leave without their symptoms. This is a result of a connected Primal. It is truly an amazing thing to watch. They will revert to their symptom soon again, as soon as more Pain comes up. But eventually, with resolution of enough Pain, the psychosis will disappear.

It is important to reiterate that the various tranquilizers and neurochemicals affect psychosis—which is a manifestation on the third level, a "thought disorder"—by working on *subcortical* systems. This fact demonstrates the great effect of subconscious or unconscious events on cortical functioning—on thought, perception, and ideation. Cortical functioning, in other words, is very dependent on subconscious processes.

The psychotic is in tune with reality, in a sense. Unfortunately, it is a past reality, one that the conventional psychiatrist might never dream existed. That reality is subcortical and well hidden.

The treatment of psychosis can be approached from any level and achieve decent *transient* results. One can drug or shock a psychotic and block the severe early Pain. One can exercise him and release the tension of stored childhood feelings. One can put him in a tranquil environment and ease present-day, cognitive pressure. But *cure* takes into account all levels. It means an interconnected experience of oneself rather than relief on a single level. So long as there is only that relief—so long as there is no connection—the psychotic, even in remission, is always in danger of a recurrence of his insanity.

Psychosis represents another of the dialectic paradoxes—the closer one gets to reality, the more unreal one has to be. Coming close to the Pains that will make one sane can drive one crazy.

The subcortical springs of psychosis might help to show how neurosis and psychosis are really just different points on the same continuum. With less Primal breakthrough—there are more adequate defenses—the cortex is not driven into its frantic retreat and symptoms are only neurotic. More breakthrough—more prepsychotic and psychotic symptoms. Psychosis, then, is the failure of neurosis.

There is no latent psychotic process in anyone, there is just stored Pain. As the Pain comes up, it forms the stimulus for psychotic ideation and behavior. As the Pain level goes down, it is the stimulus for reduced psychotic thought and behavior. *Psychotic reaction is a reaction,* not a primary process. One has to ask the question, what is psychosis a reaction to? The answer is clear. Pain. One can treat psychotics by concentrating on various changes; reduced vitamin C, for example. Treatment with vitamins, while it lasts, is bound to be helpful in rebalancing the system. But the psychotic is sick everywhere, not just in his vitamin levels. His brain acts and is constructed differently. His biochemistry is different, and his way of thinking is certainly divergent. He doesn't have separate mind and body afflictions. He has a "psychologic" disease that has changed the structure of his brain—a disease that permeates every cell.

It is not very fair that a trauma which lasts perhaps minutes or a few hours at the beginning of life can ruin the rest of one's whole existence on this earth. That is why care of the fetus and infant are so very important.

Feeling is both a prevention and a cure for mental illness. What you cannot feel can drive you crazy.

5: The Feeling Child

ALMOST every book on child-rearing is a "How-to" book. Yet there is something odd about advising parents about their children. It's as if we're talking about people from Mars rather than a stage of life we've all lived through. The tacit assumption in these books is that we are all walled off from our childhood, that none of us can remember what it felt like to be a child. That we cannot feel.

Obviously everything that goes on between the parent and the child is only important insofar as it reflects feelings. That there are books continuously being written about how to rear children is evidence that there is not much feeling going on; so we fall back on technique. But technique is the last resort for someone with depleted, repressed feelings who cannot sense what is right. No one needs rules on how to relate to others if he has direct access to his feelings. The only question that needs to be asked is: "How do you treat people you love?" If you love a child, you'll treat her properly. Not if you just say it or merely think you do but if you really want her around, she'll sense that she's wanted. If you don't want her around, she'll sense that she's unwanted. If you're happy or unhappy to see her, she'll sense that too. If you don't expect her to be anything other than what she is, she'll understand that without any words having to be said.

To feel the child that exists every minute in us is to know exactly what we felt in our youth and what we and children need. Our needs are exactly those of our children. To be insensitive to ourselves is to be insensitive to them. To be sensitive to ourselves is to be tuned in to them. There is no sensitivity that doesn't begin internally. If you're sensitive to your needs to be held, for example, you will sense when your child needs to be held.

No one is going to tell a chronically depressed father to be happy around his children. No one can tell an irritable, edgy mother to relax and be calm around her children. No one can tell an immature mother, who can scarcely take care of herself, to "grow up and be a mature adult with her children." No one can tell a repressed, withdrawn, passive father to come out of his shell and be more open with his children.

I think that the mechanistic society we live in has led to mechanistic ways of child-rearing. In other words, there are certain "mechanics" of raising children. Scheduled feedings, for example, where there are certain hours that children have to be fed which has nothing to do with their natural rhythms and their own particular hunger—when and what they want to eat. In an age of technology we have the notion that we can fix up our children pretty much as we fix our cars. The child who becomes neurotic as a result then may go into a therapy that is mechanistic—whether it is biofeedback or behavioristic conditioning, and the parents get more "How-to" advice, more rules to bring up their child.

In my opinion 50 percent of the job is giving the baby a proper birth. An absolutely natural birth, as in the Leboyer method of delivery, provides the kind of strength to meet later trauma that can be gained in no other way. A traumatic birth leaves us vulnerable to even the slightest stress later on. A proper birth is something, though, that is partly within the parents' control and if there is any one thing you can try to give your child, it is that.

We must not forget the timetable of need. There are only certain critical times when certain needs can be fulfilled. Touch and caress in infancy is crucial and can only be fulfilled then, not later. The need goes on forever—but fulfillment too late is never adequate. The most obvious example of this is breast feeding—an absolute essential for a healthy child. If we don't get it when we need it, we can spend a lifetime looking for symbols of Mother's breasts in a vain attempt at—unconscious—fulfillment.

Thrusting a bottle into the mouth of a baby in a crib is traumatic. He must be held during feeding. Nobody likes to dine alone and this is true for babies who are and always will be human beings with the same needs and feelings as the rest of us. I believe one reason why some adults become depressed or anxious when they are faced with eating alone is because early in life it meant utter rejection.

From the time of birth until the first year, the infant needs to be in frequent physical contact with its parents. The closer to birth, the more continuous the contact needed; and the greater the trauma when it is missing. If the baby is left without physical contact with the mother for the first minutes or hours of life, there is a heavy penalty to pay in terms of stored Pain and lifelong tension. If there is no physical contact for the first few days—perhaps due to the illness of the mother or of the baby—one can be sure of lifelong tension.

There is no security to match a feeling of being next to the parent's body. The feeling of proximity, warmth, protection, emotional closeness, caring, full attention—all of that is implied.

The implication of what I'm saying is that very soon in life the baby should be sleeping with its parents—and not in a separate crib. Parents are anxious about the baby being crushed and so on, but all evidence controverts this notion. After several months of life, if the baby is carried in a papoose carrier when the parent goes out for a walk or to shop, those secure feelings are continued. The baby feels his parent physically and he sees what they see rather than lying passively in a baby buggy.

Just those two things—a good birth and plenty of relaxed physical contact—and the baby already has a healthy start in life. He will have a formidable strength to meet other traumas.

Of course, children need physical contact throughout their lives, but not nearly as much as when they are very young. Teenagers still need hugs and kisses but the results of not getting them at fifteen are nowhere near as crucial as not getting them at age one. Because an infant cannot understand words, there has to be some physical way to show that he is loved.

Early lack of touch affects both brain and personality development. Touch is one of the best tranquilizers in existence. When a child is hurt and cries, she needs to be picked up and held and comforted. Yet this elemental idea is difficult for many parents to grasp. If a child goes to the hospital, she should be held whenever possible, and that includes *during* surgery, if it can be arranged. It will ease the trauma of the surgery even though the child is unconscious. Both the surgery and the caress are fully processed by a lower level of consciousness.

EXPECTATIONS—THE BEGINNING OF THE END

Neurosis can begin in the womb. It may even begin before—in the heads and minds of the mother and father—in the very reasons for

having a child in the first place. If the reasons for having the baby are
neurotic, neurosis will follow inevitably in the child.

If the baby is an accident, which many are, then the parents, especially if they're young, are going to resent the intrusion because, instead of being the children they still are themselves, they are stuck in
the role of being parents.

Any number of women have a child to "lock" their husbands into
their marriage. This is one of the most destructive reasons for having a
baby because the baby is used as a ploy, a weapon, between the parents. The baby is used as a manipulation against the husband and is
never allowed to be a human being in her own right.

Many parents have a baby simply to have the family they never
had. They try to get out of that baby warmth, attention, love—things
they themselves may never have received. All of this, of course, is an
unconscious process. Still, the baby will be used to make the mother or
father feel that they belong—that they have a family—that there are
people who care about them—that there is someone who is going to
take care of them. It is quite amazing how early in life children are
pressed into service to take care of the parents, and especially to take
care of their needs.

Some parents have children because the father needs to be
"macho." He needs to prove that he is virile. The mother needs to
prove that she is a "real woman." So the child is used to prove something. The baby is always used for this or for that, instead of the parents' recognizing the *miracle of life*. They have lost the idea, somehow, that they have produced a new human being on this
earth—the most incredible, creative act in the world.

The baby is an intruder, an annoyance, someone to "shush," someone to get out of the way, someone to give orders to and make behave.
Rarely, someone to love and adore. Some parents have children whom
they hate from the time they are born. That is because the children
don't live up to their needs and expectations—expectations which
existed in the parents' minds long before the baby saw the light of day.

Having a baby, for many neurotic parents, especially young parents,
is like everything else in their life—a fantasy. When the reality hits
home, they flee to other avenues to keep the fantasy going. They will
party, work hard, stay away from the house whenever possible so as to
avoid the key reality of their life—the fact that there is a new human
being in the house who needs a lot of care.

What occurs in most households is a regime where repression of the
citizens of the household, especially the young citizens, is the order of
the day. Parents who need to feel respected and loved use their chil-

dren for that. The parent, who as a powerless child was himself abused and thrown around, will now have someone else to order about. He now has somebody else he can use to help him feel respected. What better object than a defenseless child? If you want to know if someone is going to abuse power they're given, watch how they act with their children. If they abuse that power, they will surely abuse any other power they have. If you watch the relationships between a parent and a child, you'll have a good idea how your friendships are going to turn out, because inevitably the way the parents treat a defenseless, vulnerable child is how they really are—a reflection, that is, of what their real needs are.

Perhaps some parents really don't want children—they want adults who can take care of themselves alone, by and large. They don't seem to want anyone hanging on them, needing various things from them—and yet, that is exactly what a child naturally does. Instead of a fearful little child, they want someone who can deny his fears, never complain, not even admit he's sick when he's sick. In other words, they don't want to take care of anybody, yet they have a child who needs a lot of care. Thus the child who is going to get "love" is the child who doesn't ask for anything and the one who never complains or demands at all. He is going to be the one to get approval simply because he doesn't want. In fact, the child who is really approved is the child who very soon in life can take care of his parents' needs—help clean the house, do the chores, or take care of the parents emotionally.

Parents can put their child into a neurotic struggle just by the way they are. If the parent is constantly sad, the child may spend a lifetime trying to cheer up his parent. Later, being very funny with others is a way of cheering up his parents symbolically. If he has to be the clown to be liked, then that's the kind of personality he's going to develop. If he has to be intellectual in order to be recognized, then that's the route he'll take. If the parents always have a despairing, unhappy, or angry look, that's going to put the child in a struggle, too, to try to please a parent who is suffering from God-knows-what. The child senses these moods to their deepest extent and reacts accordingly; he's in the struggle to make his parents into decent human beings—loving, happy, nondespairing persons.

A child has to stay in a struggle because to feel totally unimportant to the only people who could possibly love him is intolerable. He cannot feel disliked and go on living. He must struggle away from those feelings by struggling to get the parents' love, and later everybody else's. In schools, he becomes the "star," or becomes the behavior problem—he can't concentrate, he can't think, and he can't study.

The more he cannot do these things, the more the pressure is put on him—the more special attention, the special tutoring, all the things that he really can't take because his mind is in a whirlwind of impulses over which he has no control.

Parents direct the child's neurosis by fiat of what they are, not just what they say or do. A parent can tell a child he loves him all day long, but unless he fulfills the child's needs, there is no love being given. A child is confused by parents who tell him every once in a while that they love him so much. But his body cries out to be held—he needs someone to pay attention to him, to really look at him, talk to him, listen.

One of my patients who felt her own childhood became better able to understand her children:

"I feel closer to my children. I don't hurry through a maze of contingencies; I've abandoned household chores that are not essential. We share more. I am less angry and they often come to me for hugs, or to talk. There's a dual edge to this—because I also feel more intensely my need to *not* be with them and feel the impingement of the situation.

"Where once I'd been frantically worried about my future, the future of my children, the fate of this planet, the unscrupulousness of most of its inhabitants, the atrocious waste of human and earthly resource, I now consider how I might help implement change in a small but realistic way."

I have left out a host of considerations, such as the income level, the neighborhood the child grows up in, and so on because that is work for sociologists. But parents who do not have money and who have children without thinking often become irritable, complaining, edgy. The child again pays in the end.

Among the hidden reasons why parents have children, one of the most important is of trying to establish immortality—to live on beyond death in the form of another human being who has come out of you. For those who refuse to face death, this is another way of using the child in an unreal, fantasy manner. This child will generally have to achieve, or make a mark on the world, as it were; so that the parent can vicariously make his mark—so that the parent can endure through the works, fame, fortune of his child.

The kind of parent one becomes is determined back in childhood because lingering, unmet needs inevitably fall upon a helpless baby. Indeed, everything in this world is a foil in one way or another for the neurotic. Even babies can be turned into parent figures. Little children, when they are very aggressive and hostile, can make a parent give in to them because that parent is now behaving like a little child with his own hostile, aggressive parent from the past.

Everyone becomes a victim in neurosis because everyone is impelled by forces beyond their control. What child counseling tries to do, by and large, is control those forces; and, indeed, with enough "willpower" one can hold back one's neurosis for a few weeks or few months; but in the long run, neurosis always wins. Parents will always revert to their neurosis just as any of us do, whether it is in going on a diet, staying off alcohol, or trying not to be cranky and impatient with one's children.

We have all heard parents say to their children "now say thank you," "now say hello," "say bye-bye." Perhaps few of us are aware that this is a subtle process by which children are made neurotic. When they are forced to do things by rote or drill that are away from their feelings, this is the subtle, unconscious breeding ground for resentment and hostility. The child is not trusted to act in a considerate and grateful way, but is forced into certain conducts. This automatic diversion from one's feelings becomes a way of life—both for parents and for the child. The child, when grown, will insist on certain behaviors for his friends. He will say "you must stay the night," "you must go here with me," "you must do this," and in that way begins to force his friends, and later his own children, away from their feelings. People become uncomfortable around him because they cannot be themselves. All that chased them away was unmet need.

If anything is really destructive with children, it's constant criticism coupled with unrealistic goals from parents—such as high grades or excelling in sports. These make a child feel that he is never good enough and contribute to the total feeling of worthlessness. Eventually the driving parent, who wants the child to excel, produces exactly the opposite—the child who fails because he feels he can never "live up."

It is a perverse art form never to be able to say a good, praising word to someone else. The truth is that there are many parents who, in the total life of their children, have never been able to say anything decent and kind. There's an underlying hostility, disapproval, and total rejection that comes out in the form of criticism. It's like saying "you're not really what I want, you have to be something else" and the child soon learns unconsciously that he is not what they want; in fact, he is not wanted for the way he is, which is who he is. The final feeling is "I am not wanted."

A parent who is critical *as a way of being* is so because he needs his children to be something else, because he, the parent, needs. The criticism that he exhibits is based on his own past. Until that past is resolved he will continue to be critical.

What happens to this kind of child is that he becomes terribly afraid of everything. He's afraid to utter a single word without examining each thing that comes out of his mouth to see whether it's going to be approved or not. He grows up never realizing that he can act on his feelings and waits for orders because he knows that whatever he does will be criticized in any case. He just does what "they want" and no more. Therein lies safety.

THE REALITY OF CHILDREN

What is real for children? What are their real needs? Look at your children and you'll have the answer. They are not brimming with ambition, not climbing any social ladders. All they want to do is play and have fun, relax and be loved. That is all any of us wants. Yet we put so many obstacles in front of ourselves and our children. We make them competitive. We even make them kiss us in a dutiful way, and not of their own spontaneous feeling. Their natural impulses are the "real them." When you take away these natural impulses, what is left is the unnatural them.

Parents seldom can let children be what they are. If the child is lying around, a parent gets anxious and wants to know why the child is lying around—they've got to be doing something. The child has to be part of their projects and plans for the future instead of doing what he really wants. They sometimes consider the child a "bad child" because he doesn't want to do what the parents want to do but wants to lead his own life.

I think the general neurotic philosophy is that we do not raise children to be happy or to be loved or to have a good time. We raise children to produce and to achieve. Therein lies the problem. Children learn that they must work in order to be loved and yet they never seem to get that love. They don't even know after a time that the function of life is to relax and have a good time and enjoy the experiences that one has.

We seem to have built an unnatural environment for children so that everything that comes natural to them becomes prohibited. From the time they are born, an unnatural world is created. They are first of all drugged and handled harshly at birth. Then they are put in playpens or other kinds of cages. Their feelings are shut down and they are forced to sit in schools for unnaturally long times, at a very young age, when their concentration and attention spans are very low. Parents must leave children for many hours a day to go to work. We bring them up in polluted environments.

The ideal environment for a child would be modeled after the agrarian one where the child is with the parent during the day, either in the fields at work or in the home, so that somehow during the first years of his life he has a true family rather than parents who are rushing here and there, trying to make a living.

In a lifetime of deprivation there are a few experiences that stand out in the minds of most of us. Those experiences are absolutely crucial; and they are usually good ones. For example, I remember volunteering for the Navy during World War II, and I had to go down to the naval office to apply. I sat down with an older woman, who sat directly across from me and said in a very slow, measured, and kind way, "What is your name?" I told her my name and she looked at me and repeated it, very slowly, and then spelled it out. I felt an incredible feeling of warmth and some strange sensations I had never known before. That experience stuck in my mind for many years, until during Primal Therapy I suddenly realized that that was the first time that anyone had sat down and talked to me in a slow, measured, and kind way—even if it was only to ask me my name. That experience produced such warmth and relaxation that it remained lucid for decades afterward.

Many of our patients remember that a single experience—such as meeting a man who was fixing a boat or an engine and who talked to them nicely or offered to show them something about it—changed the direction of their lives in terms of the interests they took up. Many patients remember developing an interest in a subject only because a teacher was warm and kind. The values of these single experiences endure for a lifetime. This is particularly true if they lie against a total lifetime of barrenness, of a lack of interest and warmth.

EMOTIONAL ILLNESS IN CHILDREN

"Mental illness" in children is a bit different from what it is in adults. Children have less conceptual neurosis and psychosis because they have less ideational capacity. Their neurosis is, more or less, body-contained or body-oriented and is, in general, more on the emotional level. I think that delusions and schizophrenia develop later in life because the late teenager and the young adult finally have the brain capacity to become disturbed in a conceptual way.

Healthy children behave well and feel well simply because they have no reason not to. I think that all children are well behaved until they are made into neurotics. Children are basically intelligent until they have their intelligence dulled. They have a fluid, buoyant affect until they are shut down and repressed.

Being unreal is a fatal disease for children because for a lifetime the body must scream out its needs in various ways. Some children have to get sick, for example, in order to finally be cared for.

Children never grow out of the Pain beneath their symptoms, that much is clear. Bed-wetting, nail-biting, allergies, headaches, all stem from Primal Pain. The Pain doesn't evaporate under pills or other kinds of treatments; it must eventually be resolved. This is true whether the child stutters, has learning difficulties or physical symptoms. There is a long history to the final emergence of a symptom and it's that history that must be dealt with.

By and large, a child's neurosis is a very simple thing. Either he has symptoms such as a stomachache or he throws up frequently, or he's allergic and constantly getting colds, or he's throwing tantrums and being "emotional." It's probably hard to imagine as an adult how absolutely helpless and dependent a child is on the parents for their approval and their love. The slightest anger by both parents leaves the child without anything because he has nowhere to go with his feelings, no one to talk to, no one to help out. His parents are all the world to him. But a parent sometimes forgets that—especially a parent who himself feels worthless. He can't imagine that anything he does is going to have such a great impact on a child or that he could be so important to anyone, having never been important at all to his own parents.

Children's neurosis usually begins with simple fears or simple aggression. One of the more important fears is that of wanting, of showing what one needs. Children are rebuffed so often in their wants and needs that they come to fear asking parents for anything. Instead, they act out those wants in symbolic ways, such as stealing or lying. Then they lose touch with themselves. They finally do not know that they want at all.

There seems to be a great confusion between respect and fear. Parents feel that if they put enough fear in their children, they'll somehow gain respect. The truth is that respect is only another name for fear. Children are often afraid of the very people they shouldn't be afraid of—people who should love them totally, their parents. These fears that a child has to live with every day of his life become a part of the subterranean force that comes out at night in the form of animals in the room, or robbers, or in the form of nightmares, in a variety of ways.

What is important for parents to understand is that they must not say to their child, "There, there . . . that's a good boy or good girl, there's nothing to fear." The truth is that there is something to fear but neither the parent nor child knows what it is anymore. At least, one must allow the child to have his fears. If he wants the light on at night, permit him to have the light on. In other words, keep the fears on the surface so that they don't become repressed in themselves and become still another latent force.

What I have said about fears most assuredly applies to the giant traumas of life such as surgery, or other catastrophes. Here the child is truly in terror and what he needs most of all is his parent's comfort all the way throughout the hospital experience. He needs somebody there to hold him, touch him, caress him, reassure him. He must not be left alone because doctors are afraid that "hysterical parents" will upset the the child.

We do not "have" feelings, we *are* our feelings. Because that is true, when the feelings are unconscious, *we* are unconscious. What that means is that we remain unconscious of what we do to others. We can be pushing our children and never realize that we are doing it, even when it is pointed out to us. We can be rejecting our children or be sarcastic with them and still not be aware of the impact that it is having. No neurotic can see beyond his need. And that particularly applies to the way neurotic parents treat their chidren.

Neurotic parents don't see the horror of what they're doing to their children every day. This is a kind of symbiosis where the child fits into the parent's unconscious and the parent treats the child totally unconsciously; then they both begin to act out their roles thereafter.

It is never the one thing that the parent does that is destructive; it's the relationship day in, day out, hour by hour that matters.

Even if a parent, later on, should be contrite and want to make up for what he's done to his child, there is nothing really that he can do except be a loving parent at that point. He will never erase the Pain that has already occurred.

Children are never spoiled by parents giving in to their needs. After they've been deprived, however, they can be spoiled by parents giving in to their wants, since indulging neurotic wants is an endless job. But once a need is fulfilled, that is all there is to it. Children do not need and need and need, when they are fulfilled. The entire business of "growing up the hard way," so as to build character, is a myth—a myth that should be put to rest once and for all. There is only one way to really grow up and that is to have your needs fulfilled. If you "grow up the hard way," and you haven't had your needs fulfilled, you are not going to be grown up, no matter how old you are.

The answer lies in having a feeling parent. Whatever his child does will be natural and graceful and well timed. He won't demand things from his child that the child can't live up to. He won't have false ambitions out of his own unmet needs for his children or won't force the child to do what he doesn't want to. He won't have the mistaken assumption that the toughest school, in terms of driving children, is the best and highest academic one. He will understand that his child was not put on earth just to produce.

The best rule of thumb for child rearing is to do what makes sense. Children should be allowed to talk at the table—because they're human beings, not because they're children. They should be allowed to make their own choices when they go to restaurants. They should be allowed to play the hours they want and where they want—so long as it's safe.

It takes a great deal of faith to realize that children will want to make a very good life and even later on produce or study or do whatever they need to for themselves if they are left to their own devices and are not pushed. They may not come to it by the parent's timetable, but they'll come to it on their own, and that is the best way. It takes a great deal of patience and trust in children to do that. Most parents have the mistaken notion that you have to push, drive, cajole, exhort, or beat children into discipline when the best discipline of all is feelings.

Feelings are all-important in education. If children could be encouraged to understand feelings and learn that there are hidden forces within them from the very earliest age, they would have some control over their symptoms and behavior even though they had a very bad home or environment. If, for example, a child misbehaved in school, and acted up, and if the class and the child knew that he was acting up because of some unresolved Pain in the home situation, if there were rooms where children could go to talk and cry, at least that much pressure would be gone. The important thing is that children would have an understanding that it is feelings that drive them. That simple idea eludes nearly every child because his feelings have never been taken into consideration by the parents or the school. Feelings should not be excluded from the classroom—they should be brought in fully because they're a critical dimension of human existence, of "mind" and how fast one learns, how well one learns, and whether one learns at all. Generally, in most classrooms, feelings are considered a minor annoyance to be dispensed with as soon as possible rather than something that governs human life, memory, intellect, and curiosity —something that needs to be explored in full far more than a history or geography lesson.

After seeing the remarkable change in adults after they have been allowed to feel, we can understand what would happen to children if they were allowed to feel. Indeed, for those children who are Primalling—children of our staff, by and large—the changes are immediate and dramatic. Instead of teachers having meeting after meeting about how to control children, far better if they had meetings about understanding the feelings that drive the uncontrolled children.

It all boils down to the simple question as to whose needs are going to predominate. Is it the child's needs, or the parents' needs? Without doubt the parents and the school will win.

Feeling, the very thing that would lay bare and clarify so much of human behavior and motivation and would help children get along in the world, is the very thing that is ignored in the school system.

Children do not need all the things we used to think they do—discipline, lecture, punishment. What they need is to be listened to, talked to, guided, held, caressed, and appreciated for what they are. No parent can do this by rote, by drill, by exhortation. It all comes from one simple thing—having a good feeling about oneself and loving one's child. Once the love is there, everything comes after that. There's nothing anyone has to remember to do—there are no rules to follow. Feelings take care of it all. It is never what you do so much as who you are.

VI: THE PRESENT FROM THE PAST

HUMAN evolution is the encoded memory of Pain. The way we are built, the language we use, and our sophisticated toolmaking abilities evolved around a central core of Pain. The human system has been constructed out of adversity. We shared our beginnings with the great apes. Somewhere along the line in the phylogeny of apes, we branched off. We developed the larger cortex and the more sophisticated brain. Why? One answer is that we became the neurotic branch in evolution. Adversity enabled us to have a larger cortex with which to deal with that adversity, following what seems to be a biologic law whereby every intrusion or alien force creates in living organisms a biologic structure to deal with it. Necessity is not only the mother of invention of things, but may in itself be the mother of man, creating new human structures to meet that necessity. And of course these newly invented structures created new necessities, so invention is the mother of necessity. Civilization may turn out to be the branch of life which has the best defenses, which can best deal with Pain.

When I say that adversity accounted for the human branch, I mean there may have been a group of apes, isolated, whom providence did not shine upon, who could not find the ordinary means to survive. This group had to "figure out" new ways to maintain themselves. That "figuring out" became at once a means for survival and for defense. And here we are, millennia later, sitting in the analyst's office figuring out why we can't survive out there in the jungle called civilization.

Mankind is a species with a history, and this combined history is found in every man and woman. They *are* the history of mankind summed up. They are by their existence the recorded memory of mankind. What is true of the living patterns of men and women might also be true of mankind as an evolving species. Our personal development, our "ontogeny," is the recapitulation of our species. Through an understanding of a single individual we shall comprehend not only the human psyche but the psychic development of man in history.

Human consciousness is the result of mankind's history, which is ultimately summed up in the structure of the brain. Its capacities are determined by a genetic code which is the summation of our experience and memories. That code determines how and when the most recently acquired neocortex will become mature, and when certain nerve fibers will be ready to fire. In that way, the genetic code circumscribes the limits of consciousness. It holds all of our history in its hand, so to speak, dealing out maturation through a careful unfolding of each stage of our evolutionary development. All of our ancestral traumas and our ancient reactions and adaptations are reflected in that genetic material. Consciousness shapes the patterns of brain neurons and is in turn shaped by it; thus function and structure are in constant interaction. Life never ceases to create and in this creation continuously reforms its own consciousness.

Experiments at the National Institute of Mental Health have shown that even the most primitive of our ancestors, the fish, have tiny locks into which opiates fit like keys, and that possibly since time immemorial, since the first primitive forms appeared on earth, there was a biochemical function to deal with adversity by repressing Pain and reality. It has more recently been discovered that earthworms produce beta-endorphine, the same opiate-like chemical which in the human brain affects sensations of pleasure and pain and produces repression. In mankind, we produce these opiates, the endorphines, in the most primitive sections of the brain, the areas we have in common with fish that go back hundreds of millions of years. What becomes more sophisticated as we travel up the evolutionary scale toward man is the repression of aspects of reality. We have never lost touch with our primitive beginnings, not only because the human fetus has features such as gill slits early in its development, but because we have held on to the ability to repress in ever more sophisticated ways.

The ability to manufacture internal opiates—the endorphines—is the origin of the unconscious. Without them there would be no human civilization; *for human development itself depended on the ability to become unconscious.* If this were not true in evolution we would all be little more than writhing, thrashing concentrations of agony. And without repression and the ability to become unconscious we could not live; we would literally die of Pain—just as man as a species would likely have died out or never developed without repressive abilities. I don't think that the endorphine system would have existed in the first place, even in the most primitive of forms, if it were not needed—if the history of evolution were not also the history of pain. We may never have become *homo sapiens* without that system.

The infant who grows up into the "civilized" adult is the one who could become effectively unconscious. It is unconsciousness that is the survival mechanism. Paradoxically, neurosis is not only a perversion of mankind; it is also what produced us. To be unreal and self-deceptive, to lie and mislead oneself are in themselves adaptive mechanisms. If we could not do all this we would all be lying in dark pools of misery for most of our lives. Society, politics, and religion have simply developed ways to gather up all of our necessary unreality and put it into various systems. These systems are designed to maintain unreality, to keep ourselves deceived, repressed, and misled. It is how we go on.

The brain developed in order to direct an organism toward the fulfillment of need. It developed for survival reasons. It is a simple extension of the body and its needs. As need became frustrated, more brain was needed to find fulfillment. At that point at least two things happened. The organism, suffering from lack of fulfillment, eventually developed a structure, the cortex, to render itself unconscious of the need and Pain. At the same time the developing cortex was able either to find different ways to go about fulfillment or to divert need into symbolic channels and pursue those symbolic fulfillments instead of real ones. Along the way the cortex began to outdo itself. It became complex and could do more than deal with Pain. It could abstract, plan for the future, develop ideas and theories, integrate a multiplicity of inputs, separate out the extraneous, be logical, describe experience and communicate that description. A great many of these complex abilities may have originally been functions surrounding Pain. But they became viable, nevertheless, and allowed man to fulfill needs that never existed; he pursued fame, prestige, and honor. He wanted and sought out power. This complex cortex repressed and then twisted original simple need into substitute gratification. The agitation by Pain galvanized the growth of that cortex in the same way that Krech's rats grew heavier cortices under stimulation. We could now not only abstract, we could be abstracted from ourselves.

The fact that all of the intellectual functions I have described above can and do function as defenses gives us a clue about their origin. At some critical stage the child begins to have a more developed cortex. When that happens, he can disconnect from himself more easily. He is better defended and can use ideas as defense, something he did not have the luxury of doing just a few years before. He can abstract and twist his feelings into ideas. He can live in the future or in ideas instead of in his body, in the present. He can become totally involved in intellectual pursuits until he no longer can even recognize a need or a feeling when he has it. And finally he can deny with his mind that needs even exist. He has traveled the full route of civilization. He is now both "human" and "civilized." And he is now neither. For he has lost touch with his humanity. He has become "split" and in so doing fulfilled his legacy from that little fish with those tiny opiate receptors.

The highest level of nervous system organization is inhibition. That is truly what makes humans human. This faculty has become perverted until a mark of being civilized and sophisticated is to *be* inhibited. The church, schools, and government cultivate the virtues of inhibition. They reinforce the neurotic split. The cortex became split into two hemispheres, one dealing largely with feeling, the other with thinking and logic. The cortex became a dual system and mankind became split into consciousness and unconsciousness—one part dealing with internal reality, with need, the other part dealing with the outside world. This split parallels the development of infants. Indeed, children are only using their hereditary equipment from humanity's most ancient past and the past of all animal life to repress and thereby save their integrity. For example, the hypothalamus, a key structure in dealing with Pain, is as I have noted, largely the brain of the salamander. We never leave our past behind; we drag it along in evolution and build upon it. What we build depends on adversity, on what the environment has to offer or does not have to offer. But of course, it is not only adversity, it is how inner need meets that adversity.

Darwin's theory of adaptation as we have come to know it may not be true at all. The foundation of evolution resides in the way the organism utilizes its *own* inner resources for survival and changes internally in response to the external environment.

It isn't that the external environment "selects" those types most fit to survive but rather the environment actually produces different structures for survival. That is why the schizophrenic has a changed structural brain—to mediate a heavier "load" of Pain; and that is why under extreme stimulation the cortex of animals becomes heavier and thicker.

It would seem to me that Darwin's theory neglects how organisms and the environment interact and shape *each other*. Need determines a human being's structure. When the brain needs more dopamine receptors because of Pain, *it grows them*.

Need continues to make itself felt in the human system in a physiologic way—hence, chronic physical tension—and it is this physsiologic change that ultimately translates into structural alterations, such as dopamine receptors or heavier cortices under stimulation.

We required a neocortex as need became more and more difficult to fulfill. This is true of the child and of the childhood of mankind. In this sense, ontogeny does recapitulate phylogeny. Man's genetic unfolding throughout his life parallels the unfolding of his history since his very beginnings. The human fetus has gill slits, then a tail for a short time, and later, during gestation, he begins to develop a primitive nervous system, not much beyond what his ancient animal forebears had. And even after birth, he still doesn't have a fully functional cortex. That comes along years later. I always imagine that there must be some equation—so many years of individual life parallel so many millions of years of phylogenetic evolution.

One of the ways we see how ontogeny recapitulates phylogeny is in the representation of lower-level experience on the higher levels of consciousness. It is the way the brain brings the past into the present. The traumas of infancy are recorded in the neocortex, and it may well be that the traumas of the infancy of mankind are recorded by the *fact* of the cortex. Though early experience is recorded in the cortex, it is not directly linked to it. That is the split. That is why lifting the gates of repression causes a linkage of the two imprints; as though the different cells recognize each other and know what roads to take to function together.

We are not necessarily born split or neurotic but we are born with the *capacity* for it. As we evolve into adulthood that capacity becomes a reality; we grow up in time, personal and phylogenetic.

If we want to know more about what we used to be like, we should search out those animal forms which reflect the physiology and nervous system of the fetus, newborn, and infant. The more we know about them the more we shall discover what we are. And conversely, if we want to find out about our ancient ancestors, we have only to examine and analyze our own lower nervous system. The actions of the lower cells should not have changed that much over the history of life. Certainly, molecular biology has thrown light on the earliest cells in history and also at the same time our own primitive cells.

There is a biochemical way of finding which animal forms are closer to others and which of the animal forms are closest to humans. The method involves a test of the immunological system.[1] It shows how close mankind is to the African ape, closer than Old World monkeys are to New World monkeys. It is closer than the relationship of

[1] S. L. Washburn, "The Evolution of Man," in *Scientific American,* September 1978, p. 152.

dogs to foxes, as close as horses are to zebras. When we discuss our humanness we should keep that in mind. Our physiology and the needs reflected by it are not so different from lower forms. We are an "add-on." We are what we were and also what we have become. We are the summation of all of that history and more.

Primal Therapy reverses the evolutionary trend where the gap between thinking and feeling is widening. In healing the split we may well be restoring human being. *If evolution goes on as it has been, we shall die from our own survival mechanisms.* We are creating societies split off from mankind's needs, inventing structures that frustrate our needs and creating ideologies to deny that needs even exist or ought to be fulfilled.

Individuals have erected an entity called the State which is very much like a neocortical extension. It takes an independent form detached from the interests of individuals who comprise it, holding together society, its impulses and distortions, and ultimately predominating over the emotions and needs of its subjects. It discourages the expression of emotion, as the neocortex tends to do, and erects a superstructure over it, a superstructure of symbols. The more divorced a State is from its people the more intricate the superstructure. The institutions we erect are part of it. The schools, churches, government, and organizations come to reflect what we are as individuals. They want us to deny feelings, to abjure worldly pleasures, to suppress our needs, and to become more and more symbolic, philosophic, academic, religious, political, and all the other abstractions. They want us to become everything but ourselves. And into this mélange we must put the institution of psychotherapy, which again asks us to bury our needs, Pain, and feeling so that we can all assimilate the cultural values of drive, ambition, and productive work. We have enslaved each other with our shared values, values which arose to deal with Pain.

Psychotherapy grew out of a cultural milieu which believed that feelings were not as important as ideas and behavior, and that reflection and introspection were less valuable than work. It has mirrored that culture in its worship of ideas and insights, in its external orientation, in its desire for "adjustment" to the very culture that enhances the split and helps produce neurosis. The show of feelings, in the culture and psychotherapy in particular, is thought to be inimical, deleterious, wasteful, and a sign of pathology. Imagine! The very thing that can free us and make us human has been turned into pathology. And what will make us more split and neurotic has been apotheosized by the very people designated to heal us. What a bind we are in. Those who deify awareness as consciousness have not yet learned that there is no conscious way to the unconscious, no painless way to Pain, no self-transcending road to the self, and no behavioral way to profoundly change behavior.

We have erected the institution of psychotherapy to keep us neurotic. Consider what it involves: for the most part, drugs. Rather than getting at the self, they push it away. They enhance the split, keeping feelings away from thinking. *In the name of mental health we are getting mental disease.* As a matter of fact, next to mental illness the greatest affliction of mankind is the treatment for it. When the patient isn't being injected with drugs, he is being drugged in another way, by ideas. He is no longer experiencing himself; he is interpreting it. Indeed, the various psychotherapies have just found different ways to interpret the self, when the real task is to liberate it.

When an organism is traumatized by inattention to need, it changes its equilibrium, each subsystem compensating by overwork or underwork. This is precisely what happens to society when needs remain neglected. We develop neurotics who need psychotherapy, mental hospitals, prisons, and constant medical care. These are compensating institutions to handle the legacy of inattention to need. A child with all of his needs met does not become chronically ill, a criminal, or a mental case. The same is true of society. But we have a dual system of needs, the physical and the emotional. Fulfilling one set is not enough. The proper distribution of wealth, the elimination of poverty are essentials but they do not in and of themselves guarantee psychological health.

The more that need is suppressed or neglected the greater the proliferation of symbolic institutions. We can see it in simple ways. We have a real need to move about and to have a transportation system but that need is manipulated so that we buy cars, consume tremendous amounts of fuel, and seek out brand names like "Cougar" and "Panther," which certainly appeal to something other than the need for transportation. Our real need for transportation is never fulfilled in the sense of having an accommodating rapid transit system because each of us is running around pursuing his "individuality" via a car.

The lack of mass rapid transit then results in the continuing dominance of the motorcar. To accommodate the proliferation of the automobile we pave over more and more beautiful landscape, we pollute the air, then kill hundreds of thousands in auto accidents, and finally go to war or manipulate governments to protect the interests of those whose interest it is to frustrate our simple need, to get from one place to another. When need raises its head, as, for example, the proposal to go back to the electric trolley in Los Angeles, the petroleum companies buy up existing tracks to help make sure it doesn't happen. Are they mean and venal? Not necessarily. They are simply protecting their needs and interests—symbolic ones of money, profit margins, and power.

We have created a system that divides society and produces institutions whose purpose it is to frustrate individual need. At the same time, ideologies are created to justify this arrangement and to insure that it will continue. Those who are now out of touch with their need come to believe in the split of society and in the "system." As one major corporation puts it, "The system is the solution." And in their sense they are right. It solves *their* problems, and the people come to be suspicious of any change toward a system that deals with their need.

Any system, including a therapeutic one, that does not have human need at its core is ultimately led to reactionary solutions. More and more effort and money is then expended to deal with the *symptoms* of illness because everyone has lost sight of the cause. Our civilization has done its job and put us out of touch with real solutions, because modern civilization *means* being out of touch with need. Fulfillment of all needs of our ape ancestors would have obviated any need to change. The solution that politicians and even therapists discuss is not attention to need but to more repression. Drug the sick and anxious, shock the psychotics, punish the criminals.

Just as individuals collapse after experiencing a certain level of Pain, so do social structures disintegrate. The symptoms get out of hand, there is no longer any order; crime and corruption rule. Nature is abused. Life support systems are threatened and we live in areas where we can no longer breathe the air. Our survival is threatened and yet we accommodate to what is happening because of the very survival mechanism—repression. We don't see reality or what we do not wish to face. No one, neither the politicians nor the psychotherapists, deals with the central contradiction, the key dynamic that elaborates into a sickness, the contradiction between the forces of expression—of need and feeling—and the forces of repression. A psychotherapy which understood that simple paradigm would have to reorient its whole approach. Once it did, the symptoms would begin to fall away; not overnight, because it took a long time to arrive at that point. The same is true for a society. Once the key contradiction between those who need and those opposed to expression and fulfillment is solved, the sickness of society will diminish—and not until. All of the rest one does is patchwork.

The resolution of our problems, personal and social, involves consciousness of real need. It must begin with the individual because consciousness of self evolves into a social consciousness. Once someone can feel, he can feel for others. Until then it is all pretense. If we are in touch with our own needs we know what others need. We know what our children require to grow up healthy—a decent birth, plenty of hugging, kissing, attention, and concern. Having relived the agonies of our own birth, we know instinctively that having a decent birth is terribly important to the job of child rearing. Giving a child a good birth is one of the most important things a parent will ever do for his child. Having felt the horrors of school life, we know that very young children should not have to sit still for eight hours a day in a classroom. We have relived our love for a teacher and know with a certainty that children learn best through warm relationships and not through rigid, military-like drill. And we know what is important to learn and what isn't.

A Primal patient who has learned through his body and his experience can live without sophisticated theories about learning and psychology. He knows the human psyche as few do. He knows what makes people sick with high blood pressure, migraine and heart disease; because, in many cases, he has suffered them and knows exactly what feelings caused them. He knows the value of feeling.

Too many people dream about the life others are leading. They may believe that life is "out there." They are perpetually searching for an answer to the mystery of life without ever realizing that they have the key to unlocking that mystery—the key that will liberate their bodies and minds and bring them into the only life that matters—their own. That key is feeling. Everything that happens in life is meaningless without that.

A person who feels is conscious. He is conscious because he has access to his depths, something we have lost perhaps for thousands of years.

Fulfillment of need, permitting feelings, freedom of expression, freedom of movement, that is the way to prevent a sick society. Unfortunately, we have grown up in Pain; we have had repressive parents and we have become adults expecting the State to take over from our parents. It isn't "big brother" we have to worry about. It is "big mommy and daddy." We accept all that State control only because we have been preconditioned by parents who "bought the program." We are enslaved by ideology because we cannot feel.

Perhaps we shall continue until there are no feelings left, until they aren't acknowledged to exist. "1984" will then have arrived because frontal lobe repression will predominate and we shall become little more than robots parroting appropriate phrases and doing what we are told. To some extent this has already happened. Those bereft of their feelings live like robots, saying what is appropriate, approved, and socially sanctioned. They obey the State and whatever it does and says just the way they obeyed their parents. They remain enslaved by their childhood—prisoners of Pain, responding to a reality that no longer exists; or, more accurately, re-creating an old reality again and again.

Fulfilling social need is very important but it does not in itself guarantee that emotional needs will be attended to. In this respect, it doesn't matter if the economic system is capitalist, socialist, or feudal. The only meaningful revolution is that of the psyche; it is the way toward permanent revolution, which means toward continual change and adaptation to changing conditions.

The true contribution of Primal Therapy lies not in research but in an instinctive recognition of some central reality, a long-lost, perhaps inexplicable something that we dimly remember we had in our childhood. It is a truth in excess of the scientific facts, an emotional truth that cannot be proved by tables and graphs but only by experience.

Those who feel their Pain, change in many important ways. They do not become different beings, yet the differences which develop are profound. The question is, how did they get that way? In fact, the great and eternal debate in psychotherapy is, "What makes for profound change?" The answer is not far away, for we have only to ask about how someone changed into a neurotic. We observe someone's childhood, note the drunken father, the neglectful mother, the orphanages, the beatings, and the lack of care, and it all is logical. The dynamics for change from neurosis to health involve *those very traumas that made for the original change*. The task is that of undoing the effects of those traumas.

Each of us is in reality a time capsule. Sometimes the contents are deeply buried. Primal Therapy is a journey back through time to those dark and hidden caverns of the unconscious which are filled with the artifacts of our lives. The exploration of all of those artifacts surrenders up the patterns of our lives and the bonds which hold those patterns in place.

The neurotic patient has within him the seeds of his own cure. He doesn't get well because of different theories and different approaches. He gets well because he has been given the tools and a lever into himself. He doesn't have an "image problem," or an "identity crisis," for example, because images reflect feelings; and feelings provide us with ourselves. There is no "identity" needed. No therapeutic patient is going to express his feelings honestly until he knows what they are. When he does, he can finally be honest—and not until.

Carl Sagan makes the point in his *Dragons of Eden* that to achieve a lasting peace you must first find harmony among the various components of the brain. This is a perceptive insight; for whatever we create outside of ourselves depends on how we function internally. If our brain is not acting harmoniously, if one section dominates another or is detached and removed, then what is done externally will reflect that disharmony, whether it is in television violence, war, architecture, or psychotherapy.

We have it in our grasp to eliminate the unconscious as we have known it, or at least to eliminate the bifurcation between consciousness and unconsciousness. And certainly, the more conscious the population, the more liberated the society they will create.

Primal Therapy eventually will negate itself. The more feelings are expressed, the less need there will be for the therapy. The more Pain felt, the less there is to feel. The more a person feels of his agony, the less Pain and more joy he has. The neurotic's chief danger is the consciousness of Pain. He avoids it in every way he can, but it is also his key liberation. A curious paradox: to be liberated by what is most dangerous.

There is no present until you're done with your past, and there is no future until you can live in the present. For the neurotic, the present *is* his past. To have relived the past is to have received the gift of the present. And the deeper you delve into the past, the further you are wholly brought into the present.

Understanding the Primal approach is more than a matter of being "open-minded." I don't think anyone can be open until he has become open to himself. Those who have come close, who suffer from chronic anxiety or who have had frequent nightmares, have an idea of what lies below. Those who are well defended live in a universe apart from it. It is simply not in their experience.

Pain is not just an *idea*. It is an experience. I have tried to convey what that experience is, but words are a poor substitute to describe emotional states organized on levels where there are no words. One experience of Primal Pain says more than this entire volume.

Appendix A

SURVEY RESULTS FOR SUBJECTS OF GOODMAN-SOBEL BIOCHEMICAL STUDY

SYMPTOM	EARLY PRIMALLERS' IMPROVEMENT PERCENTAGE		LATE PRIMALLERS' IMPROVEMENT PERCENTAGE
Depression	100%	vs.	33%
Insomnia	50%	vs.	33.3%
Tics	100%	vs.	0%
Obesity	0%	vs.	0%
Diarrhea	100%	vs.	0%
Phobias	100%	vs.	0%
Suicidal Impulses	50%	vs.	25%
Social Withdrawal	100%	vs.	25%
Agitated Depression	50%	vs.	25%
Nightmares	67%	vs.	33%
Poor Concentration	67%	vs.	0%
Daydreaming	75%	vs.	67%
Melancholic Depression	100%	vs.	33%
Difficult to be Relaxed	75%	vs.	0%

The 1979 questionnaire was distributed randomly to more than 200 former and current Primal patients who had been in therapy for at least one year. The 200 respondents represent approximately an 8 percent sample of *all patients* treated at the Primal Institute in a ten-year period. In addition, the questionnaire was distributed to a randomly selected control group of 50 applicants for Primal Therapy.

The 62-page, 250-item questionnaire was designed and written by David J. Carlini and Barry M. Bernfeld, doctoral candidates at the California Graduate Institute. (Bernfeld is also a member of the staff of the Primal Institute.) The survey data was compiled and organized by Dr. Charles Swigert, member of the technical staff of Hughes Research Laboratories, exploratory studies department, and an authority in both computer design and the nature of the holographic brain.

From the 250 completed questionnaires there were approximately 100,000 computer entries of data which generated more than 700 tables. Dr. Swigert tested the questionnaire for statistical significance and determined that it has a "confidence level" of 95 percent; that is, there is a 5 percent likelihood that any particular response or reported change is due to chance factors and therefore not significant.

Appendix B

SOME IMPLICATIONS

Although the 1979 survey is a pilot for further study, and the survey instrument is to be refined and the study population enlarged, some interesting trends are suggested by the data gathered thus far. The researchers have made some instructive comparisons between results from subjects who said they had gained first-line access and those who said their Primals were second-line only. The findings indicate that resolution of first-line trauma is important—but not always necessary —for the disappearance of several symptoms. They also indicate that, with deep access, one can reverse serious problems, such as suicidal impulses.

TOTAL STUDY POPULATION (200 respondents)

SYMPTOM	NUMBER OF PEOPLE WITH SYMPTOM	CATEGORY OF RESPONSES						
		% NO RESPONSE	% MORE SEVERE & MORE FREQUENT	% UNCHANGED	% LESS SEVERE & MORE FREQUENT	% MORE SEVERE & LESS FREQUENT	% LESS SEVERE & LESS FREQUENT	% DISAPPEARED
•TENSION HEADACHES	107	0.9	4.7	7.5	4.7	12.1	52.3	17.8
•MIGRAINES	31	3.2	12.9	6.5	6.5	12.9	48.4	9.7
•RAPID HEARTBEAT	51	0.0	2.0	17.6	0.0	7.8	51.0	21.6
•MUSCLE TENSION	162	0.0	8.0	16.0	3.7	4.9	60.5	6.8
•TEETH GRINDING	87	0.0	3.4	16.1	0.0	4.6	47.1	28.7
•NAIL BITING	66	0.0	1.5	28.8	0.0	4.5	43.9	21.2
•STOMACH DISORDERS	81	1.2	4.9	11.1	0.0	3.7	65.4	13.6
•FREQUENT URINATION	63	0.0	7.9	46.0	---	---	34.9	11.1
•SKIN DISORDERS	57	0.0	3.5	26.3	0.0	1.8	52.6	15.8
•HEMORRHOIDS	46	0.0	4.3	21.7	0.0	4.3	47.8	21.7
•HYPERSENSITIVITY TO HEAT/COLD	83	0.0	6.0	45.8	0.0	4.8	30.1	13.3
•STARTLE REACTIONS	72	1.4	5.6	18.1	1.4	1.4	58.3	13.9
•ALLERGIES	60	1.7	3.3	41.7	0.0	1.7	41.7	10.0
•ASTHMA	10	0.0	10.0	20.0	0.0	10.0	40.0	20.0
•FREQUENT COLDS	79	0.0	1.3	10.1	2.5	3.8	51.9	30.4
•THROAT DISORDERS	55	1.8	3.6	20.0	0.0	3.6	47.3	23.6
•HEARTBURN	66	0.0	1.5	6.1	1.5	4.5	48.5	37.9
•INSOMNIA	95	0.0	6.3	14.7	2.1	6.3	46.3	24.2
•NIGHTMARES	99	1.0	8.1	12.1	3.0	7.1	55.6	13.1
•RECURRING DREAMS	83	0.0	8.4	15.7	---	---	37.3	38.6
•CHRONIC OVERSLEEPING	90	0.0	4.4	17.8	0.0	0.0	51.1	26.7
•ALCOHOLISM	32	0.0	3.1	3.1	3.1	3.1	46.9	40.6
•SMOKING	67	0.0	1.5	9.0	---	---	31.3	58.2
•PRESCRIBED MEDS. USE	50	0.0	4.0	6.0	---	---	40.0	50.0
•OBESITY	73	1.4	4.1	12.3	2.7	0.0	63.0	16.4
•MENSTRUAL DIFFICULTIES	36	0.0	16.7	25.0	2.8	5.6	38.9	11.1
•FRIGIDITY	49	0.0	4.1	26.5	0.0	0.0	44.9	24.5
•IMPOTENCE	35	0.0	11.4	14.3	2.9	2.9	51.4	17.1
•PREMATURE EJACULATION	37	5.4	0.0	13.5	2.7	2.7	48.6	27.0
•EXCESSIVE MASTURBAT'N	91	1.1	5.5	15.4	1.1	0.0	59.3	17.6
•PORNOGRAPHY	57	1.8	1.8	15.8	0.0	5.3	59.6	15.8
•HOMOSEXUAL DESIRES	65	0.0	10.8	13.8	4.6	4.6	47.7	18.5
•HOMOSEXUAL ACTIVITIES	19	0.0	15.8	15.8	5.3	0.0	26.3	36.8
•SUICIDAL IMPULSES	100	2.0	7.0	8.0	3.0	8.0	34.0	38.0
•SUICIDE ATTEMPTS	15	0.0	0.0	0.0	0.0	0.0	13.3	86.7
•AGITATED DEPRESSION	104	0.0	7.7	7.7	1.0	6.7	51.0	26.9
•MELANCHOLIC DEPRESSION	159	0.0	6.9	8.2	1.9	11.3	56.0	15.7
•COMPULSIONS	98	0.0	1.0	11.2	2.0	6.1	60.2	19.4
•OBSESSIONS	115	0.0	4.3	11.3	0.9	4.3	68.7	10.4
•PHOBIAS	95	1.1	1.1	17.9	0.0	8.4	61.1	10.5
HALLUCINATIONS:								
•VISUAL	26	0.0	7.7	7.7	0.0	11.5	15.4	57.7
•AUDITORY	26	0.0	0.0	23.1	0.0	3.8	30.8	42.3
•PARANOID IDEATION	86	0.0	3.5	10.5	2.3	7.0	57.0	19.8
•INAPPROPRIATE ANGER	133	0.8	7.5	5.3	3.8	9.8	60.2	12.8
•INTROVERSION	153	0.0	1.3	9.2	1.3	5.9	71.9	10.5
•EXTROVERSION	34	0.0	2.9	0.0	0.0	2.9	82.4	11.8
•WITHDRAWAL	147	0.7	2.7	11.6	1.4	2.7	66.0	15.0
•WORKAHOLISM	80	1.3	3.8	5.0	1.3	1.3	43.8	43.8
DIFFICULTY IN:								
•SPEAKING IN PUBLIC	145	0.0	2.1	27.6	---	---	70.3	---
•ASKING FOR NEEDS	185	0.0	0.5	9.2	---	---	90.3	---
•CRYING	120	0.8	0.0	11.7	---	---	87.5	---
•EXPRESSING PROBLEMS	150	0.0	2.0	15.3	---	---	82.7	---
•MEETING NEW PEOPLE	146	0.7	2.1	20.5	---	---	76.0	---
•MEETING OPP. SEX	129	0.8	5.4	25.6	---	---	68.2	---
•FUNCTIONING	115	0.0	1.7	14.8	---	---	83.5	---

VETERAN POPULATION: PRE-1976 (62 respondents)

NUMBER OF PEOPLE WITH SYMPTOM	% NO RESPONSE	% MORE SEVERE & MORE FREQUENT	% UN-CHANGED	% LESS SEVERE & MORE FREQUENT	% MORE SEVERE & LESS FREQUENT	% LESS SEVERE & LESS FREQUENT	% DIS-APPEARED
33	0.0	3.0	6.1	6.1	9.1	51.5	24.2
9	0.0	22.2	0.0	0.0	11.1	44.4	22.2
15	0.0	6.7	0.0	0.0	6.7	53.3	33.3
51	0.0	2.0	7.8	2.0	0.0	80.4	7.8
28	0.0	3.6	7.1	0.0	3.6	42.9	42.9
18	0.0	0.0	22.2	0.0	0.0	55.6	22.2
20	0.0	0.0	5.0	0.0	0.0	60.0	35.0
13	0.0	7.7	30.8	---	---	53.8	7.7
11	0.0	0.0	9.1	0.0	0.0	72.7	18.2
15	0.0	13.3	13.3	0.0	0.0	40.0	33.3
26	0.0	0.0	30.8	0.0	0.0	42.3	26.9
19	0.0	0.0	15.8	0.0	0.0	57.9	26.3
17	0.0	0.0	47.1	0.0	0.0	41.2	11.8
3	0.0	33.3	0.0	0.0	0.0	33.3	33.3
24	0.0	0.0	12.5	0.0	4.2	54.2	29.2
11	0.0	9.1	9.1	0.0	9.1	54.5	18.2
22	0.0	4.5	9.1	0.0	4.5	36.4	45.5
26	0.0	0.0	11.5	0.0	0.0	46.2	42.3
26	0.0	0.0	3.8	0.0	0.0	76.9	19.2
30	0.0	3.3	10.0	---	---	40.0	46.7
27	0.0	7.4	11.1	0.0	0.0	48.1	33.3
13	0.0	7.7	7.7	0.0	0.0	61.5	23.1
26	0.0	0.0	3.8	---	---	34.6	61.5
18	0.0	5.6	11.1	---	---	50.0	33.3
19	5.3	0.0	5.3	0.0	0.0	68.4	21.1
10	0.0	10.0	20.0	0.0	10.0	30.0	30.0
17	0.0	11.8	17.6	0.0	0.0	29.4	41.2
8	0.0	37.5	0.0	12.5	0.0	50.0	0.0
9	0.0	0.0	0.0	0.0	11.1	55.6	33.3
21	4.8	0.0	23.8	0.0	0.0	57.1	14.3
16	0.0	0.0	31.3	0.0	0.0	62.5	6.3
16	0.0	18.8	31.3	0.0	0.0	25.0	25.0
7	0.0	0.0	28.6	0.0	0.0	28.6	42.9
30	0.0	3.3	3.3	3.3	6.7	26.7	56.7
6	0.0	0.0	0.0	0.0	0.0	0.0	100
32	0.0	3.1	0.0	0.0	3.1	59.4	34.4
46	0.0	4.3	0.0	2.2	8.7	67.4	17.4
23	0.0	0.0	8.7	0.0	0.0	52.2	39.1
30	0.0	6.7	3.3	0.0	3.3	73.3	13.3
27	0.0	0.0	7.4	0.0	7.4	66.7	18.5
6	0.0	0.0	0.0	0.0	0.0	16.7	83.3
6	0.0	0.0	16.7	0.0	0.0	50.0	33.3
20	0.0	0.0	0.0	0.0	0.0	80.0	20.0
42	2.4	7.1	4.8	2.4	2.4	64.3	16.7
42	0.0	2.4	2.4	0.0	0.0	83.3	11.9
9	0.0	0.0	0.0	0.0	0.0	66.7	33.3
36	0.0	0.0	11.1	0.0	2.8	69.4	16.7
25	0.0	0.0	4.0	4.0	0.0	56.0	36.0
43	0.0	0.0	30.2	---	---	69.8	---
55	0.0	1.8	3.6	---	---	94.5	---
36	2.8	0.0	5.6	---	---	91.7	---
47	0.0	2.1	6.4	---	---	91.5	---
40	0.0	0.0	15.0	---	---	82.5	---
35	0.0	2.9	14.3	---	---	82.9	---
33	0.0	0.0	3.0	---	---	97.0	---

NAIL BITING

As indicated in the chart for the symptom of nail-biting, there appears to be a correlation between total disappearance of the symptom and the resolution of first-line Pains. As innocuous as it seems, nail-biting is not a simple symptom. The underlying causes appear to be deep. This apparent association provides food for thought and suggests that the psychoanalytic explanation of the symptom as anger turned against itself is insufficient. We can also see the possible dangers in meddling with even as "mild" a symptom as nail-biting without regard for the underlying Pain.

COMPULSIONS

TOTAL POPULATION ——— 1ST LINE PRIMALLERS ——— VETERAN GROUP ·······

TOTAL GROUP

1ST LINE PRIMALLERS

2ND LINE PRIMALLERS

CATEGORY OF RESPONSE

PERCENT OF RESPONSES

0 NO RESPONSE
1 MORE SEVERE & MORE FREQUENT
2 UNCHANGED
3 LESS SEVERE & MORE FREQUENT
4 MORE SEVERE & LESS FREQUENT
5 LESS SEVERE & LESS FREQUENT
6 DISAPPEARED

We had considered compulsions to be strictly a first-line symptom. But the plot for the results in this category suggests that this is not precisely the case. Apparently, certain symptoms may begin to disappear with the easing of second-line Pains, even when those symptoms may have their origins in first-line Pain.

PHOBIAS

The evidence (see table) for early-trauma origins of phobias contradicts the notion that phobias are simple learned habits—that is, socially conditioned responses that one must unlearn through various conditioning methods. There is no way to uncondition a birth trauma without addressing oneself to the trauma itself by reexperiencing it. The phobia symptom has an attachment deep in the system and it is not unthinkable that driving away a phobic symptom will only assure the later occurrence of more severe symptoms, perhaps even paranoia.

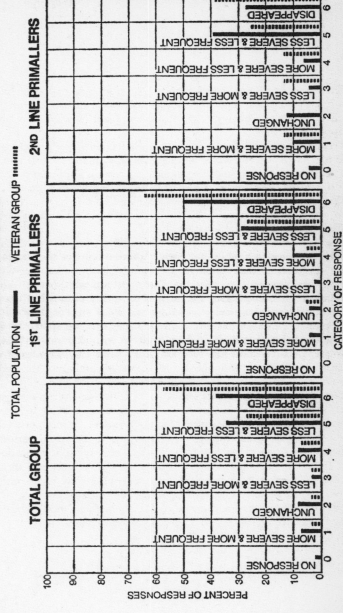

SUICIDAL IMPULSES

Fifty percent of those with suicidal impulses who reported having first-line Primals also reported complete disappearance of the impulse; 27 percent of those having only second-line feelings reported a similar disappearance.

Feeling second-line Pain usually reduces the level of Pain enough to take the "edge" off suicidal impulses; that is, to make them less impulsive. Nevertheless, the impulses appear to remain until there is first-line resolution. This trend of the data offers important hints to those dealing with suicidal persons. It is clear how vain it is, over the long term, to try to talk someone out of a recurring suicidal impulse. It is dealing on the third level with first-line Pain.

Suicide is an important public health problem in our well-defended society. In 1964, in the United States, suicide was the fourth leading cause of death of those between fifteen and twenty-four, and it has been the twelfth leading cause of death for the total population for the past ten years. Gregory Zilboorg, the psychoanalyst, said that the problem of suicide was unsolved from a scientific point of view.

The survey data indicate, in a preliminary way, considerable progress in the treatment of suicidal impulses in Primal patients. The improvement rate is particularly noteworthy since the entering Primal patient population is undoubtedly far more suicidal than the general population.

The plot of results for this symptom indicates that the less access or resolution the suicidal person has, the more danger he is to himself. Access to feelings is the crucial factor. An amateur or unsupervised attempt to do Primal Therapy is very dangerous to a suicidal person because it may drive the person into first-line Pain without resolution of that Pain. The Freudians, then, are correct when they say that removal of defenses is dangerous—but only dangerous when one removes defenses *without permitting access to feelings.* So long as defenses are removed and access is achieved, there is no inherent danger. Then there is only a return to a previous natural state.

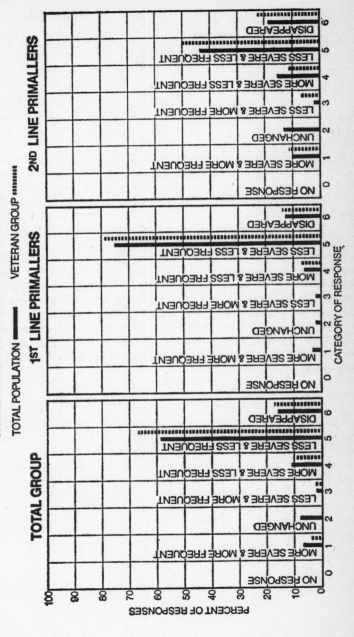

MELANCHOLIC DEPRESSION

TOTAL POPULATION ▬▬▬   VETERAN GROUP ┄┄┄┄┄

TOTAL GROUP   **1ST LINE PRIMALLERS**   **2ND LINE PRIMALLERS**

PERCENT OF RESPONSES

CATEGORY OF RESPONSE

NO RESPONSE — 0
MORE SEVERE & MORE FREQUENT — 1
UNCHANGED — 2
LESS SEVERE & MORE FREQUENT — 3
MORE SEVERE & LESS FREQUENT — 4
LESS SEVERE & LESS FREQUENT — 5
DISAPPEARED — 6

As indicated in the table, the improvement rate for melancholic depression was markedly higher for those Primalling on the first line. Clearly, the resolution of first-line trauma has important implications for the resolution of deep depression. It is difficult to believe that any amount of "positive thinking" can overturn that state.

The preliminary data indicate that the longer one continues to feel and gain Primal access, the less likely one is to be depressed. This trend supports the observation that deep depression is in fact deep repression.

Appendix C

PROTOTYPIC PAINS & PHYSIOTYPES

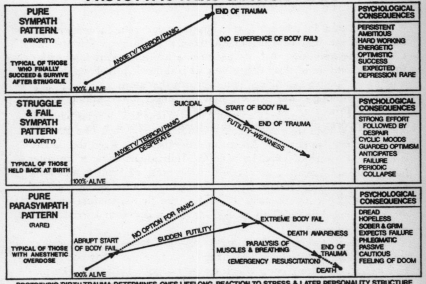

PROTOTYPIC BIRTH TRAUMA DETERMINES ONES LIFELONG REACTION TO STRESS & LATER PERSONALITY STRUCTURE

Appendix D

ABREACTION

We know very well that Primals have been faked, often unknowingly. Indeed, the hallmark of mock Primal Therapy[1] seems to be inducing abreaction instead of Primals. Abreaction is a defense which is far easier to abide than real Pain. Abreactions may look like Primals, which can deceive both the patient and the therapist. Even the patient is often not aware of what he is doing. Individuals come to us after having one solid year of abreaction in the guise of Primals and have never known the difference. One reason is that abreaction offers relief of tension, albeit, temporarily. It is also true that hysterical episodes often resemble Primals. This has led some to imagine that Primals are really hysterical fits.

Abreaction, the discharge of the energy of a feeling without proper connection, cannot provide deep insights because there has not been a true experience of a feeling which drives symbolic behavior. The person is not feeling the need which lies below his behavior, he is discharging its energy. He may scream, thrash, pound walls, and even cry but there is a shallow quality to it. He is making deliberate, controlled efforts. A person who wants very much to feel but actually has little or no access may try to produce feeling by effort. He has some *idea* as to what feeling and expressing Pain is and therefore tries to galvanize himself into showing it. He can put on a very dramatic show

[1] "Primal Therapy" performed by unlicensed and untrained persons.

but unfortunately a show is all it is. The topmost level of consciousness tries to force its will, its pace upon a lower level, which ultimately widens the division and strengthens the inhibition against the very feelings aimed at.

The processes of abreaction are generally confined to a single level —constant crying, for example—without really connecting to the reason for it. It is the random discharge of nonspecific Pains: the release of the tension generated by a host of Pains, none of which are specifically linked to consciousness.

Abreaction involves different neural pathways from a Primal.[2] It is the difference between specific Pain pathways which delineate the nature and origin of a Primal Pain, and the pathways dealing with suffering which offer only general information of unspecified agony. It is easy to be misled by abreaction because there can be that element of suffering where the person imagines he truly has reexperienced a real, old Pain. But suffering is not feeling Primal Pain. Pain involves both kinds of pathways as it gathers up all levels of consciousness on its way to be felt. Abreaction, on the contrary, is confined to the suffering system.

When a feeling is activated, it energizes a dual system—the limbic system and the neocortex simultaneously. With feeling, there is a proper balance between these two systems, and one is specifically aware of what one feels. But in abreaction, only a single aspect of this system is activated.

Abreaction occurs when Primal Therapy is done in haphazard fashion, where Pains are dealt with out of sequence. If the patient is pushed too hard or too fast, he will be plunged into feelings whose charge value is too high to be integrated. We have seen patients who had been in mock Primal therapy where abreaction went on for years, draining off Primal energy in a single characteristic way—such as baby wails—for all of that time, and no one knew any better.

Just as with any method that fails to address the Pain, one is forced to repeat the ritual of abreaction over and over again to obtain relief. Fortunately, we can differentiate abreaction from true feeling by observation and biological measurement.

A key biologic sign of abreaction is that the vital signs do not move upward or downward together as in Primals. They move in a haphazard, sporadic way as if the body functions are not working together but are going off in different directions. This, I suggest, is another indication that abreaction deepens internal divisions and perpetuates disharmony in the biologic system and, therefore, the psyche.

[2] See the discussion of Luria's work in *Primal Man*.

Index

THE DROWNED AND THE SAVED
PRIMO LEVI

Shortly after completing *The Drowned and the Saved*, Primo Levi committed suicide. The manner of his death was sudden, violent and unpremeditated, and there are some who argue that he killed himself because he was tormented by guilt – guilt that he had survived the horrors of Auschwitz while others, better than he, had gone to the wall.

'*The Drowned and the Saved* dispels the myth that Primo Levi forgave the Germans for what they did to his people. He didn't, and couldn't forgive. He refused, however, to indulge in what he called 'the bestial vice of hatred', which is an entirely different matter. The voice that sounds in his writing is that of a reasonable man . . . it warns and reminds us that the unimaginable can happen again. A would-be tyrant is waiting in the wings, with 'beautiful words' on his lips. The book is constantly impressing on us the need to learn from the past, to make sense of the senseless'
PAUL BAILEY

'One of the most devastating masterworks of our era'
OBSERVER

0 349 10047 0   NON-FICTION   £3.99

Abacus now offers an exciting range of quality fiction and non-fiction by both established and new authors. All of the books in this series are available from good bookshops, or can be ordered from the following address:

Sphere Books
Cash Sales Department
P.O. Box 11
Falmouth
Cornwall TR10 9EN.

Please send cheque or postal order (no currency), and allow 60p for postage and packing for the first book plus 25p for the second book and 15p for each additional book ordered up to a maximum charge of £1.50 in U.K.

B.F.P.O. customers please allow 60p for the first book, 25p for the second book plus 15p per copy for the next 7 books, thereafter 9p per book.

Overseas customers, including Eire, please allow £1.25 for postage and packing for the first book, 75p for the second book and 28p for each subsequent title ordered.